Medicine, Malpractice and Misapprehensions

There is now incontrovertible evidence that medical mistakes and mishaps occur in significant numbers every year. What are the causes of the upsurge in claims over the past twenty years? How can patients be assured that their treatment will be safe? How can doctors practise medicine in the best interests of patients without the fear of complaints and litigation? This book examines the uncertainty and some of the myths surrounding errors and claims in healthcare, and aims to place the arguments surrounding the so-called compensation culture on a stronger statistical, and hence epistemological basis. It argues that far from living in a compensation culture, we are almost certainly experiencing a culture of under-compensation. It is possible to see, by means of the time-line and illustrative graphs in this book, that there are certain trends that are likely to continue. Yet never in the course of history has medical practice in the UK been subject to such stringent regulation and so much political interference. Never have healthcare professionals been subject to such an unrelenting barrage of external investigation and demands. Many of these pressures are identified in the course of the journey taken in the book from the founding of the NHS to the opening years of the twenty-first century, and the role of legal and other mechanisms is examined in the search for solutions to the growing litigation crisis faced by healthcare professionals and the patients they treat. Among the topics covered are:

- The quest for truth in the maze of contradictory data about error and litigation in healthcare
- Trends in the level of errors and claims for clinical negligence
- The underlying causes of the rise in claims as the twentieth century drew to a close
- The role of the media
- The changing relationships between doctors and patients over the course of the past fifty or more years
- The complex relationship between defensive medicine, clinical governance, and risk management
- The role of Government, managers, the courts, the regulators, and advertisers
- The impact of political change, constant restructuring, devolution, fragmentation and the increasing pressures on healthcare professionals

This book is an essential resource for healthcare professionals and those interested in medical law.

Vivienne Harpwood is Director of the Centre for Medico-Legal Studies, at Cardiff University Law School, and is also a barrister with experience in practice.

Biomedical Law and Ethics Library

Series Editor: Sheila A.M. McLean

Scientific and clinical advances, social and political developments and the impact of healthcare on our lives raise profound ethical and legal questions. Medical law and ethics have become central to our understanding of these problems, and are important tools for the analysis and resolution of problems – real or imagined.

In this series, scholars at the forefront of biomedical law and ethics contribute to the debates in this area, with accessible, thought-provoking, and sometimes controversial ideas. Each book in the series develops an independent hypothesis and argues cogently for a particular position. One of the major contributions of this series is the extent to which both law and ethics are utilised in the content of the books, and the shape of the series itself.

The books in this series are analytical, with a key target audience of lawyers, doctors, nurses, and the intelligent lay public.

Available titles:

Human Fertilisation and Embryology (2007)
Reproducing Regulation
Kirsty Horsey and Hazel Biggs

Intention and Causation in Medical Non-Killing (2006)
The Impact of Criminal Law Concepts on Euthanasia and Assisted Suicide
Glenys Williams

Impairment and Disability (2007)
Law and Ethics at the Beginning and End of Life
Sheila McLean and Laura Williamson

Bioethics and the Humanities (2007)
Attitudes and Perceptions
Robin Downie and Jane Macnaughton

Defending the Genetic Supermarket (2007)
The Law and Ethics of Selecting the Next Generation
Colin Gavaghan

The Harm Paradox (2007)
Tort Law and the Unwanted Child in an Era of Choice
Nicolette Priaulx

Forthcoming titles include:

Assisted Dying
Reflections on the Need for Law Reform
Sheila McLean

Medicine, Malpractice and Misapprehensions
Vivienne Harpwood

Euthanasia, Ethics and the Law
From Conflict to Compromise?
Richard Huxtable

Best Interests of the Child in Healthcare
Sarah Elliston

Values in Medicine
The Realities of Clinical Practice
Donald Evans

Medicine, Law and the Public Interest
Communitarian Perspectives on Medical Law
J. Kenyon Mason and Graeme Laurie

Healthcare Research Ethics and Law
Regulation, Review and Responsibility
Hazel Biggs

The Body in Bioethics
Alastair Campbell

About the Series Editor

Professor Sheila McLean is International Bar Association Professor of Law and Ethics in Medicine and Director of the Institute of Law and Ethics in Medicine at the University of Glasgow.

Medicine, Malpractice and Misapprehensions

Vivienne Harpwood

Routledge·Cavendish
Taylor & Francis Group

Learning Resources
Centre

13735039

First published 2007
by Routledge-Cavendish
2 Park Square, Milton Park, Abingdon, Oxon, OX14 4RN

Simultaneously published in the USA and Canada
by Routledge-Cavendish
270 Madison Avenue, New York, NY 10016

Routledge-Cavendish is an imprint of the Taylor & Francis Group, an informa business

© 2007 Vivienne Harpwood

Typeset in Times New Roman and Gill Sans by
Florence Production Ltd, Stoodleigh, Devon
Printed and bound in Great Britain by
TJ International, Padstow, Cornwall

British Library Cataloguing in Publication Data
A catalogue record for this book is available from the British Library

Library of Congress Cataloging in Publication Data
Harpwood, Vivienne.
    Medicine, malpractice and misapprehensions/Vivienne Harpwood.
        p. cm.
    1. Physicians – Malpractice – Great Britain. 2. Medical personnel – Malpractice
    – Great Britain. 3. Liability insurance claims – Great Britain. I. Title.
    KD2960.M55H37 2007
    344.4104'11 – dc22   2007017235

ISBN10: 0–415–42809–2 (pbk)
ISBN10: 0–415–42807–6 (hbk)
ISBN10: 0–203–94045–8 (ebk)

ISBN13: 978–0–415–42809–5 (pbk)
ISBN13: 978–0–415–42807–1 (hbk)
ISBN13: 978–0–203–94045–7 (ebk)

This book is dedicated to the memory of my father, Stanford Robinson.

Contents

List of illustrations	ix
List of abbreviations	x
Acknowledgments	xii
Introduction	xiii

1 Data, accuracy, compensation and error: what should we believe? — 1

The increasing volume of claims in the twentieth century 1
The injuries giving rise to claims 29
How common are errors in healthcare? 29
The balance of claims against errors 41
The balance of claims against complaints 42
The culture of under-compensation 43
The litigation process 44
Conclusion: reflections on the figures 46

2 Reasons for the increase in claims: who is to blame? — 48

Introduction 48
Reflections on the causes of the rise in claims 49
Charting the causes by time-line 75
Conclusion 78

3 The compensation culture in healthcare: myth or reality? — 79

Is there a compensation culture in the UK? 80
The quality of the evidence 85
*Who asserts that there is a compensation culture: who denies
    its existence? 87*
Why disapprove of a compensation culture? 103
Conclusion 103

4   Perpetuating the myth: should we blame the media?   **106**

Introduction 106
Fact or melodrama? 106
Responsible media practices, freedom of information and
    public concerns 111
Criticisms of media coverage in the healthcare context 116
The power of media-based advertising 119
The value of media analysis 121
What do people believe anyway? 124
Counting the media involvement 126
Conclusion 128

5   Doctors: over-paid, out of control and under-regulated?   **130**

Are doctors overpaid? 130
Are doctors out of control and under-regulated? 146
The consequences of over-regulation: demoralisation and
    defensive practice? 153
Conclusion 162

6   Treating the affliction: are there any remedies?   **163**

Diagnosis and treatment 163
The role of the courts 164
Government intervention 167
Legal procedural reforms 192
Making amends and statutory intervention 194
Concluding recommendations 208

Index   219

Illustrations

Figures

1 Number of clinical negligence claims by year of incident as at
  31/03/06   17
2 Projected figures over next 20 years   21
3 Total value of CNST claims by specialty at 31/03/06   27
4 Time line showing key events   76
5 Projected number of claims by year of incident   77
6 Number of written complaints by regulatory 2005–6   148

Tables

 1 Types of claim against Welsh Ambulance Service NHS Trust   9
 2 Trend in number of claims   10
 3 Number of formal clinical negligence claims against
   NHS Trusts 2002–2006   10
 4 Number of claims under Existing Liabilities Scheme   11
 5 Number of claims under Ex-Regional Health Authorities Scheme   11
 6 Welsh Risk Pool statistics for clinical negligence claims over
   £25,000   14
 7 CRU data for clinical negligence claims   14
 8 Claims and payments under Vaccine Damage Payments Act 1979
   since April 2000   16
 9 Number of claims by date of incident   18
10 Recent payments by the NHS for clinical negligence in England   24
11 2006 categories of claim in highest awards   25
12 International patient safety incidents   36
13 Number of written complaints in England 1999–2005   169

Abbreviations

ADR	Alternative Dispute Resolution
AHCJ	Association of Health Care Journalists
AvMA	Action Against Medical Accidents
BMA	British Medical Association
BMJ	*British Medical Journal*
BRTF	Better Regulation Task Force
CAB	Citizens Advice Bureau
CFA	Conditional Fee Arrangement
CHI	Commission for Health Improvement
CHRE	Council for Healthcare Regulatory Excellence
CNST	Clinical Negligence Scheme for Trusts
COSHH	Control of Substances Hazardous to Health
CPR	Civil Procedure Rules 1998
CPS	Crown Prosecution Service
CRU	Compensation Recovery Unit
DoH	Department of Health
DWP	Department for Work and Pensions
ECJ	European Court of Justice
GAO	US General Accounting Office
GMC	General Medical Council
GP	General Practitioner
HFEA	Human Fertilization and Embryology Authority
HIW	Health Inspectorate Wales
HPA	Health Protection Agency
IBNR	incurred but not reported
ICAS	Independent Complaints Advisory Service
IOM	Insitute of Medicine
LHB	Local Health Board
LINks	Local Involvement Networks
MDU	Medical Defence Union
MHAC	Mental Health Act Commission
MHRA	Medicines and Healthcare Products Regulatory Agency

MJA	Medical Journalists' Association
MoD	Ministry of Defence
MPS	Medical Protection Society
NCAS	National Clinical Assessment Service
NCSC	National Care Standards Commission
NHLSA	National Health Service Litigation Authority
NHS	National Health Service
NICE	National Institute for Health and Clinical Excellence
NMC	Nursing and Midwifery Council
NPSA	National Patient Safety Agency
OFT	Office of Fair Trading
ONS	Office for National Statistics
ONS	Office of National Statistics
PCT	Primary Care Trust
PPI	patient and public involvement
PSLA	Pain, suffering and loss of amenity
RCM	Royal College of Midwives
RCN	Royal College of Nursing
RHA	Regional Health Authority
ROC	Retained Organs Commission
RoSPA	Royal Society for the Prevention of Accidents
WHO	World Health Organisation
WRP	Welsh Risk Pool

Acknowledgments

This book was written during a time of family upheaval, when the NHS provided valuable care and support, for which I am very grateful. I would also like to thank numerous colleagues, particularly David Burnet, who read early drafts of the text, and Peter Gooderham who updated me on some of the many developments in the healthcare context while the book was being written. Thanks are also due to staff at the National Health Service Litigation Authority, Welsh Health Legal Services, The Welsh Risk Pool, the National Patient Safety Agency, the Council for Healthcare Regulatory Excellence, and Velindre NHS Trust, and to Andy Tomlin, all of whom were extremely helpful and supportive in supplying information and reading some sections of the book in draft.

Finally, I would like to thank my younger children, Robert and Olivia, for their patience.

Introduction

Apart from its alliterative appeal, the title of this book expresses a serious topical purpose. In the midst of statistical uncertainty, and even obfuscation, how is it possible to assess the extent of errors and clinical negligence claims in the UK? We are constantly told that we do or do not live in a 'compensation culture', which is usually carefully not defined, but what are the facts about the number of errors made in our health service in the course of a year? What is the truth about trends in clinical negligence litigation over recent years? Do doctors practise defensive medicine? Who or what is to blame for the upsurge in claims towards the end of the twentieth century? How can patients seek reassurance that the treatment they receive will be safe? How can doctors practise medicine in the best interests of patients without the fear of being sued? One ambition of this book is to put the debate about the so-called compensation culture on a sounder statistical, and hence epistemological basis, and it will be argued that the current Governmental pronouncements, sceptical of the very existence of such a culture are sadly, possibly deliberately, short of the mark in the healthcare context.

This book takes a snapshot of the state of error and litigation in the NHS. Obviously, it is very difficult in the climate of 'initiativitis,' fragmentation, devolution, and hyper-regulation that afflicts the NHS today, to be categorical about the underlying causes of any significant trends in the discovery of, and responses to, medical malpractice, but it is equally possible to see, by virtue of the time-lines and illustrative graphs in this book, that there are certain trends that are likely to continue. There is now incontrovertible evidence in the UK and abroad that medical mistakes or mishaps occur at a significant level on a daily basis, and it is therefore important to assess the effectiveness of any legal or other mechanisms for controlling error and handling complaints and litigation in the aftermath of such events.

The book takes a journey through the richly diverse landscape of the NHS, in which patients may travel overseas for treatment; GPs seldom visit patients in their homes; nurses and pharmacists can diagnose and prescribe; surgery is frequently performed during a brief morning visit; telephone consultations are common place; young doctors are unable to find work in the vocation for which they are trained; the relationship between health and social care, and in some instances between the NHS and private care, is confused; and healthcare has become a 'marketplace'. The complexities of the system that cares for us 'from cradle to grave' are such that it is impossible to unearth precise statistical information on a number of important matters, but in the course of the journey there is an attempt to explore what have come to be regarded as 'urban myths' about the state of our healthcare system.

Chapter 1 examines such information as is available about the number of claims and errors occurring in healthcare and what this costs the public purse, concluding from the maze of contradictory data that there is almost certainly a culture of under-compensation. Chapter 2 speculates as to the possible causes of the increase in clinical negligence claims, drawing a time-line against which rising levels of claims and compensation can be plotted. There is an account of the changing relationships between doctors and patients over the course of the past fifty or more years; the role of Government, lawyers, advertisers, and the media. Chapter 3 considers assertions about the existence of a compensation culture in the UK generally, and healthcare in particular, and Chapter 4 endeavours to analyse the role and influence of the media in informing the nation of developments in healthcare litigation. In Chapter 5 there is an attempt to draw some conclusions concerning popular notions about those who work in healthcare, with particular focus on the role of doctors, who, we are told, are over-regulated, out of control, practise under pressure, and act defensively in order to avoid complaints and claims. Chapter 6 reflects upon some of the many Government interventions that have sought to diagnose and remedy the perceived afflictions in the NHS, and the role of the law in dealing with them. The book concludes with some tentative recommendations, which may result in progress toward a better understanding of the many misapprehensions about error and litigation in healthcare.

Vivienne Harpwood
April 2007

Chapter 1

Data, accuracy, compensation and error

What should we believe?

There is an indisputable need to inform the public about medical errors, and consequently there is no shortage of media coverage of mistakes and scandals in healthcare. The high profile given by the media to this matter has raised the political temperature, and medical malpractice has become a political issue. The history of the rise in the volume of claims will be outlined in this chapter, and in the chapter that follows the statistical information will be considered against the background of a growing consumer rights culture, multifaceted changes in society and medical practice, developments in the litigation process and case law, and the developing National Health Service (NHS). However, despite a general public understanding, and indeed a belief among healthcare professionals, that the number of claims involving medical error is rising, some assertions have been made that perceptions of a litigation crisis in the UK healthcare system are unfounded. An inquiry into the truth or otherwise of such matters will form the central theme in Chapter 3.

The increasing volume of claims in the twentieth century

In the three decades immediately following the Second World War there was a gradual but steady increase in claims against medical practitioners, and by the mid-1970s there was a rapid acceleration in that trend. By 1978 when the Pearson Report[1] on personal injury compensation was published, there were an estimated 500 claims against the NHS annually. There is considerable evidence following that finding that the volume of claims and the cost of defending them increased greatly during the last decades of the twentieth

---

1   Royal Commission on Civil Liability and Compensation for Personal Injury, *Report of the Royal Commission on Civil Liability and Compensation for Personal Injury*, Cmnd 7054, 1978, London, HMSO.

century[2] and into the new millennium. Peter Cane roughly estimated the rise in the number of clinical negligence claims between 1977 and 2005 as a 125-fold increase since 1977, allowing for inflation,[3] commenting:

> No other area of tort litigation has grown anything like this extent in the past 30 years.

In fact, as will be seen, the level of claims had risen significantly higher than that rough estimate – by as much as 1,200 per cent between 1978 and 2006.

By the late 1980s, litigation had become a luxury that only the richest members of society could afford, and was well beyond the financial means of the majority of people who might have wished to bring claims for medical negligence, though legal aid was available to the poorest. Yet despite many practical difficulties faced by claimants, and although many were doomed to fail in their attempts to achieve redress[4], the number of clinical negligence claims against the NHS rose steadily throughout the last two decades of the twentieth century,[5] reaching an estimated figure of between 5,419 and 6,979 by 1990–91.[6]

In 1989, the last year of the old system of funding the defence of claims for clinical negligence, the Medical Defence Union (MDU) paid almost £30 million in damages and costs, more than twice what was paid in 1985.[7] The Medical Protection Society (MPS) recorded similar trends and noted that costs of claims alone had quadrupled between 1976 and 1985, with the number of claims against doctors increasing from around 1,000 in 1983 to more than 2,000 in 1987.[8] A single case[9] was settled by the MDU for just over £1 million, a sum that was 97 per cent greater than the amount paid in the whole of 1975 in damages and settlements. These increases were accompanied by corresponding rises in subscription rates for members of the defence organisations and led to the introduction of NHS indemnity when

2   Ham, C., Dingwall, R., Fenn, P. and Harris D., 'Medical Negligence: Compensation and Accountability', 1988 cited in Kennedy, I. and Grubb, A., *Medical Law* (3rd edn, Butterworths, London, 2000), p 541. See also Medical Protection Society and Medical Defence Union Reports issued between 1974 and 1986.
3   Cane, P., *Atiyah's Accidents, Compensation and the Law* (7th edn, Cambridge University Press, 2006), p 221.
4   38.01 per cent of claims are abandoned by claimants, according to the NHSLA Report 2005.
5   See McHale, J., 'Medical Malpractice in England – Current Trends' (2003) *European Journal Health Law* 1: 135–51.
6   Fenn, P., Hermans, D. and Dingwall, R., 'Estimating the Cost of Compensating Victims of Medical Negligence' (1994) 309 *BMJ* 389.
7   See Annual Reports of the MDU.
8   See Kennedy and Grubb, *Medical Law* (3rd edn, Butterworths, 2000), p 537.
9   The name of this unreported case has been withheld.

the healthcare system was restructured in the early 1990s.[10] The defence organisations continued to handle claims against general practitioners (GPs) after that time, and the MPS reported that negligence claims against GPs had increased 13-fold between 1989 and 1998.[11] In the years between 1993 and 1998, the MPS has spent nearly £7 million dealing with cases that were subsequently abandoned, though that money could not be recovered from the claimants. It is not surprising that from 1999, all GPs and dentists were required to have defence cover.

By the beginning of the 1990s it had become apparent that there was an urgent need for reform of the way in which patient dissatisfaction was handled within the NHS. Complaints and claims are closely related and are usually managed in the same managerial departments within NHS organisations. At the same time, the main stimulus for the reform of complaints systems lay in large-scale structural changes in the delivery of healthcare introduced by the Conservative Government at the beginning of the 1990s, and in the realisation that the current complaints systems were so complex and outmoded as to be of little practical value. The demand for change was also driven by a variety of other related factors, including a shift of emphasis in the centuries-old relationship between doctors and patients, generated by the new climate of consumerism in healthcare, and what was seen as a developing compensation culture that had led to a significant rise in the number of claims against the NHS.[12] It was thought, rather naively, that by encouraging complaints, many potential claims would be defused.[13] Paradoxically, this does not appear to have happened, as claims continued to escalate after the new NHS Complaints System was established in 1996.

Sources of data

There has been, for a variety of reasons, some considerable complexity in the process of reporting and analysing the number of claims for negligence in healthcare in the UK. Information was gathered on the number of claims for medical negligence for the Pearson Commission,[14] which reported in 1978, though its main remit concerned road traffic accidents. Thereafter, the most reliable sources of data were the doctors' defence organisations, the MDU and MPS, though these organisations were concerned only with claims against

10   HC(89)34 relieved hospital medical practitioners from their obligation to join a defence organisation, and district health authorities were instructed to assume responsibility for new and existing claims for negligence.

11   Dyer, C., (1999) 318 *BMJ* 830 (27 March).

12   Ham *et al.*, fn 1 supra.

13   'Being Heard', Report of the NHS Complaints Review Committee, 1994.

14   Royal Commission on Civil Liability and Compensation for Personal Injury, *Report of the Royal Commission on Civil Liability and Compensation for Personal Injury*, Cmnd 7054, 1978, London, HMSO.

doctors (and in their related branches, dentists), and did not record data relating to other healthcare professionals except in so far as it affected claims against doctors. Research studies, most of excellent quality, though limited in scope, also provide information about the picture in the 1980s and 1990s.[15]

After the introduction of NHS Indemnity in 1990, it was no longer a relatively simple exercise to obtain precise information on the current level of claims in the NHS (let alone those brought against practitioners in the private sector), because of the devolved nature of healthcare in the UK and because for some time no single organisation was responsible for collating the final figures for all claims against GPs and other healthcare professionals. There is only limited information concerning clinical negligence claims between 1990 and 1996, but some figures can be found in official reports subsequently produced, relating back to the earlier claims period, and in circumscribed research studies.[16]

It is, however, possible to find detailed records of the cost of clinical negligence claims against NHS Trusts since 1996. The National Audit Office,[17] which reviews public spending in the UK on an annual basis, has obtained data since that date that give an indication of the level of claims against NHS organisations, and separate figures are collected for Northern Ireland, Wales, and Scotland. Figures produced by the National Health Service Litigation Authority (NHSLA) in England since 2002 relate only to its own expenditure and estimated future liabilities. In 2003, the Government produced a consultation document entitled 'Making Amends'. Figures quoted in that report relate to the entire NHS, but only cover the years before 2003.

Answers to parliamentary questions are also useful sources of information, as they are the product of research undertaken with the co-operation of the NHSLA[18] (although that organisation deals only with claims in England).[19] The NHSLA records claims in respect of which a pre-action protocol letter has been received, and of course the figures quoted by the NHSLA tend to vary as they are updated, with the result that it is extremely difficult to establish definitive data. For example, sums quoted as having been paid to claimants as damages are also unreliable indicators of the actual sums eventually paid, as it is not always clear whether the figures stated include structured settlements. If there is a structured settlement and the claimant dies within a few years,

---

15   Ham, C., Dingwall, R., Fenn, P. and Harris, D., *Medical Negligence: Compensation and Accountability* (King's Fund, London, 1988).
16   Fenn, P., Hermans, D. and Dingwall, R., 'Estimating the Cost of Compensating Victims of Medical Negligence' (1994) 309 *BMJ* 389; Fenn, P., Diacon, S., Gray, A., Hodges, R. and Rickman, N., 'Current Cost of Medical Negligence Claims in NHS Hospitals: Analysis of Claims Database' (2000) 320 *BMJ* 1567; also 'Making Amends', CMO's Consultation Report 2003.
17   www.nao.org.uk
18   See for example, Kennedy, J., Hansard, HC vol 435 Col 1342W, 28 June 2005.
19   Welsh Health Legal Services undertakes a similar role in Wales.

the amount actually paid would be greatly reduced. In any event, at least as far as claims on behalf of brain-damaged infants are concerned, it is likely that whatever figures are quoted, in many cases the real costs are much higher because special education, nursing care, continuing health problems and social services are not necessarily included.[20] In *Crofton v NHSLA* [2007] ENCA Civ 71, the Court of Appeal held that damages paid by insurers should be reduced by the amount being paid by local authorities to support claimants.

Data produced by the Compensation Recovery Unit (CRU) presents a rather different picture from that supplied the NHSLA, as its information does not relate solely to England. The CRU is charged with the task of administering the scheme for recovering any social security benefits that have been paid to claimants from compensation payable to them in the course of a claim.[21] Although not every claimant has been in receipt of benefit,[22] all compensators are required to inform the CRU promptly of claims made against them for personal injuries. It should therefore be able to provide accurate and up-to-date information about the number of claims for clinical negligence as well as those relating to other accidents and injuries. It has been suggested[23] that the CRU is the most reliable source of data on clinical negligence claims, and to some extent this is true, but the data held by the CRU can only be of assistance to researchers in relation to claims made since the year 2000,[24] as the figures relating to claims made before that date have not been made public. As far as claims made before 1997 are concerned, the CRU data will inevitably be unreliable because benefit could not be recovered if an award of less than £2,500 was made. Lewis *et al.*, in their breakdown of the data supplied by the CRU relating to claims since 2000, offer the best available analysis of the number of clinical negligence claims.[25]

The NHSLA handles negligence claims on behalf of the NHS in England under several different schemes. The schemes most relevant to this discussion are first, The Clinical Negligence Scheme for Trusts (CNST), which is a voluntary risk-pooling scheme for clinical negligence claims that arise as a result of events occurring after 1 April 1995. This is funded out of members' contributions, and all NHS Trusts and Primary Care Trusts (PCTs) in England choose to belong to the scheme. The second scheme is The Existing Liabilities

---

20   Rogers, L., *Sunday Times*, 27 August 2006 and *Crofton v NHSLA* [2007] ENCA Civ 71.
21   Social Security (Recovery of Benefits) Act 1997, which amended the Social Security Act 1989.
22   Indeed, a surprising number of claimants do not apply for benefit, particularly if they are being cared for by family members – personal communication Ann-Louise Ferguson, lead solicitor NHSLA.
23   Lewis, R., Morris, A. and Oliphant, K., 'Tort Personal Injury Claims Statistics: Is There a Compensation Culture in the United Kingdom?' (2006) *Torts Law Journal* 14(2): 158; republished (2006) *Insurance Research and Practice* 21(2): 5–14.
24   Ibid., 160.
25   Lewis, R., Morris, A. and Oliphant, K., op. cit.

Scheme, which covers clinical negligence claims arising out of events occurring before April 1995. This is not a contributory scheme, and the costs of funding settlements that are made under it are covered centrally by the Department of Health. The third relevant scheme is The Ex-RHAs Scheme, which covers liabilities incurred by the Regional Health Authorities before they were abolished in April 1996, for which the NHSLA acts as defendant. Wales, Scotland, and Northern Ireland have bodies of their own, which operate schemes that are roughly similar to those of the NHSLA.

In Wales, for example, Welsh Health Legal Services performs a similar function to that of the NHSLA in England (though it does not operate in the precisely the same way) and this organisation, together with the Welsh Risk Pool (WRP) and the National Audit Office for Wales, supplies some data about the number and value of claims against NHS Trusts in Wales. At the time of writing, Welsh Health Legal Services did not have a detailed website containing data about clinical negligence claims, and consequently there were no statistics on clinical negligence in Wales were not as clear as those available from the NHSLA. All potential claims are registered with the WRP, which is a mutual organisation funded by all Trusts and Local Health Boards (LHBs – roughly the equivalent of PCTs) in Wales. This organisation does produce data relating to claims, but only in respect of those settled for more than the £25,000 excess figure below which Trusts and LHBs manage their own claims. The difficulty that arises in this respect is that not all Trusts necessarily report claims with a value below the £25,000 excess. All claims settled over the value of £1,000 but below £25,000 should be notified to the WRP as required by the Welsh Assembly Government. If there was certainty that this reporting was being done, it would allow for reasonably accurate collection of data relating to negligence in the course of hospital treatment. For many of the same reasons as apply in England, however, there are limits to the accuracy of the information supplied about all claims for clinical negligence in the devolved region.

The private healthcare sector does not undergo systematic assessment of the number and value of claims for clinical negligence, and the result is a deepening mystery as to the precise figures for clinical negligence claims and medical errors outside the NHS. Independent healthcare organisations include all private, voluntary, not-for-profit or independent healthcare establishments under the regulatory remit of the Healthcare Commission. They are required to register with the Commission under the Care Standards Act 2000, as amended by the Health and Social Care Act 2003, and must comply with Private and Voluntary Health Care (England) Regulations 2001. In April 2004, the Healthcare Commission took over responsibility for the regulation and inspection of the independent healthcare sector, which had previously been under the auspices of the National Care Standards Commission (NCSC). The Healthcare Commission is responsible for monitoring standards in the independent healthcare sector, and in its 2006 report it indicated that 6 per cent of acute hospitals in the independent healthcare sector were substandard in at least five of the 32 minimum standards, including those relating to quality of care, safety, hygiene and decontamination. Inspectors found that over the previous year 10 per cent of independent acute hospitals had failed to maintain adequate health records, and 8 per cent had failed to ensure that temporary staff were adequately trained. However, there do not appear to be any reliable statistics available concerning the rate of errors or claims in this sector.[26] This is especially worrying, as there is an increasing role for private healthcare establishment in the care of the elderly.

General practitioners and dentists working in the NHS are covered by the MDU and the MPS. These organisations are not strictly insurance companies, but they pay compensation to patients injured by the negligence of their members out of funds generated from subscriptions. The MDU calculates subscriptions on the basis that they will ensure that there are adequate funds to cover claims against its members, and like the MPS, it offers indemnity on an incident occurrence basis.

Other information produced in 2004 by the Office of Fair Trading[27] (OFT) compares the number of clinical negligence claims with those relating to other types of injury, as does evidence provided by a report for Citizens Advice Bureaux (CAB) on personal injury statistics.[28] However, the figures produced by these organisations are not sufficiently comprehensive to provide a reliable indication of the true picture. The UK Office for National Statistics holds certain information relating to health, but does not provide information about claims and errors in healthcare. The same is true of data held by the Government statistical service, though a Bill is now before Parliament which might remedy this situation.[29] The Statistics and Registration Service Bill was introduced in the House of Commons on 21 November 2006, and received the Royal Assent in July 2007.

There is no suggestion that there has been deliberate obfuscation of the true figures, although the Government would no doubt be content for the picture to remain blurred in the light of its attempts to discourage the notion that we live in a compensation culture.[30] The confusion is probably a product of the complexity of the system for bringing and defending claims against healthcare organisations in a devolved 'United' Kingdom within which patients are treated privately and by the NHS, in hospitals and in the community, or by a combination of care systems. The continuing outsourcing of information services will not assist those in search of reliable data,[31] and in some respects

---

26   As reported in the *Guardian*, 20 December 2006.

27   An Analysis of Current Problems in the UK Liability Insurance Market June 2003, OFT.

28   Sandbach, J., 'No Win, No Fee, No Chance'. See Appendix 2 CAB Evidence on the Challenges Facing Access to Injury Compensation, December 2004.

29   The Statistics and Registration Service Bill, introduced in the House of Commons on 21 November 2006.

30   See Chapter 4, and speech by Tony Blair reported in the *Guardian*, 16 May 2005.

31   See Pollock, A., *NHS plc* (Verso, London, 2004) Chapter 3, p 50.

it is convenient for the Government that complete sets of statistics are unavailable. Despite the fact that data collected by the CRU provide the most reliable source of information currently available, the total CRU figures are not consistent with those provided by other organisations.

The number of claims

It is widely recognised that claims for clinical negligence increased dramatically between 1975 and 1996. It is important to distinguish between the number of claims made annually in the UK, and their financial cost. The Pearson Commission Report[32] in 1978 stated that the number of claims for medical negligence was around 500 a year, and that only between 40 per cent and 60 per cent of these were successful. Drawing on all the available sources, in particular the annual reports of the doctors' defence organisations[33] before 1990, it is possible to produce information which indicates that claims continued to rise until the introduction of NHS Indemnity, and that the upward trend continued afterwards, reaching a peak in the early years of the present millennium.

The most recently published figures[34] suggest that although more money is paid in total to claimants, it was in the year 2002–03 that the number of claims reached a peak, then they began to fall[35] slightly in number, but rose to reach a plateau by the year 2004–05. However, claims started to rise again in the year 2005–06. The Scottish Executive, which issues information concerning the number of claims in Scotland, has revealed that the number of claims alleging clinical negligence had begun to rise and was at its highest level in four years, with 465 actions initiated in 2006, and 400 in 2005. A similar pattern has been revealed in Wales.

The NHSLA in its Fact Sheet for 2005–06 describes what it calls its 'Headline Figures':[36]

In 2005–06, the NHSLA received 5,697 claims (including potential claims) under its clinical negligence schemes and 3,497 claims (including potential claims) in respect of its non-clinical schemes. The figures for 2004–05 were

---

32   Royal Commission on Civil Liability and Compensation for Personal Injury, *Report of the Royal Commission on Civil Liability and Compensation for Personal Injury*, Cmnd 7054, 1978, London, HMSO.
33   The MDU and MPS.
34   Charles Lewis suggests that 'Governments will produce statistics to prove whatever they want to prove; but usually their statistics are biased, often demonstrably so', Lewis, C., *Clinical Negligence: A Practical Guide* (Tottel Publishing, West Sussex, 2006).
35   The same is true in Wales, where the Auditor General for Wales reported that at 31 March 2004, liabilities for clinical negligence claims on the balance sheets of NHS bodies were £134.5 million, against £155.7 million in the year ending 31 March 2003.
36   Totals rather than more detailed figures – the sort of figures that might be found in a headline, rather than in the body of an article.

5,609 for clinical claims and 3,766 for non-clinical; in 2003–04 the figures were 6,251 and 3,819 respectively. The Authority had 18,748 'live' claims as at 31 March 2006, and CNST claims are now settled in an average of 1.46 years, counting from the date of notification to the NHSLA to the date when compensation is agreed or the claimant discontinues their claim.

As will be seen, peaks and troughs in the number of claims may not indicate a realistic account of incidents of actionable errors (errors which satisfy the legal criteria which need to be met for a claim to be initiated), but are rather an indication that for some reason fewer claims are being pursued – perhaps because the rules of the Legal Services Commission on the provision of financial assistance to claimants have recently changed, and because Conditional Fee Arrangements (CFAs) (the no-win, no-fee system) have proved less helpful that had originally been anticipated to many potential claimants.[37]

The nature and proportion of claims brought by patients and others depends upon the functions of each individual NHS Trust. For example, the Welsh Ambulance Trust reported that 'the number and cost of Road Traffic related claims continues to be the predominant cause of claim'.[38] The figures quoted for that particular Trust are as follows:

Table 1 Types of claim against Welsh Ambulance Service NHS Trust

Category	Dec 2002	Dec 2003	Dec 2004	Dec 2005	Change Dec 2002
Slip/trip	18	15	17	16	−2
Manual handling	41	33	24	18	−23
Equipment	17	19	18	18	+1
RTA	76	73	70	55	−21
Medical negligence	8	4	6	7	−1
Other	19	19	22	17	−2
Total	**179**	**163**	**157**	**131**	**−48**

This is one of several NHS Trusts which report a larger number of claims brought by their employees in respect of work accidents than claims by patients for clinical negligence.

37 Sandbach, J., 'No Win, No Fee, No Chance', CAB Report on the challenges facing access to injury compensation, December 2004.
38 Welsh Ambulance Service NHS Trust. 'Claims Position and Lessons Learned', January 2006.

Statistics quoted in Hansard (see Figure 3) on the basis of information supplied by the NHSLA confirm that the slight downward trend in clinical negligence claims continued until 2004.[39] As can be seen from the tables below, and figures quoted on the NHSLA website, the figures do tend to vary, presumably because they are updated regularly and are presented according to different criteria. The most definitive figures must presumably be those that the NHSLA supplies to Parliament in its Annual Report.[40]

Table 2 Trend in number of claims

Year	Claims
1996–97	4,136
1997–98	6,932
1998–99	6,916
1999–00	7,036
2000–01	6,915
2001–02	7,125
2002–03	6,257
2003–04	4,844

Table 3 Number of formal clinical negligence claims against NHS Trusts 2002–2006

Year	Formal letter of claim received
2002–03	5,614
2003–04	4,168
2004–05	4,316
2005–06	5,427

Despite the information published in these tables, in February 2007 the NHSLA reported that for the year 2005–06, it received 5,697 claims under its clinical negligence schemes, and that for 2004–05 the figures were 5,609 for clinical claims. A statement on the NHSLA website read:

In 2005–06, 5,697 claims of clinical negligence and 3,497 claims of non-clinical negligence against NHS bodies were received by the NHSLA. This compares with 5,609 claims of clinical negligence and 3,766 claims of non-clinical negligence in 2004–05.

39   Hansard, HC 159, The Stationery Office, 2005.
40   See Annual Report and Accounts for 2006, HC 1179.

In their Annual Report for 2006, the figures are broken down according to each of the three schemes currently operated by the NHSLA as follows:

Table 4 Number of claims under Existing Liabilities Scheme

Year	Under investigation	Formal letter received	Total
2003–04	140	334	474
2004–05			
2005–06			

Table 5 Number of claims under Ex-Regional Health Authorities Scheme

Year	Under investigation	Formal letter received	Total
2003–04	0	2	2
2004–05	0	7	7
2005–06	0	0	0

As can be seen, the 2005–06 NHSLA figures reveal an increase in the number of claims in England, and the CRU figures show a total of 9,321 for the UK as a whole. However, the NHSLA data suggests a large increase in England in the cost of defending claims and compensating injured patients.[41] This is because there continue to be some extremely high awards, though these are made in only a small proportion of claims; the most frequent being for negligence in obstetrics, which inevitably attracts very high compensation and receives considerable publicity, so creating the impression that awards are generally very high.

The NHSLA produces estimates of its total liabilities, which include the cost of paying claims already in the pipe-line and others that are likely to be made but have not been reported. These figures relate to a long period of time, rather than to a single year. In fact the payments that are actually made usually fall well below the sums that are estimated, so this practice can be extremely misleading.[42] In the year 2001, the National Audit Office high-lighted several issues of concern in this context and estimated that a total of £3.9 billion would be paid in England on potential claims that were pending in the years immediately ahead. The estimate in 2001 was that under the existing

41   Source NHSLA.
42   See Marshall, D., 'Dressing Up the Figures' (2002) *NLJ* 1632.

liabilities scheme, legal costs amounted to more than the damages paid to claimants in 44 per cent of cases on average,[43] 8 per cent of the entire NHS budget.[44]

All too frequently the estimates of future NHS liabilities are seized upon by the media, and even by academics,[45] to produce sensational headlines; and as the figures quoted are very high indeed, this reaction is predictable. For example, the NHSLA estimated that as at 31 March 2005, it had potential liabilities of £7 billion, of which £6.89 billion related to clinical negligence claims. That figure represented the estimated value of all known claims to that date, together with an actuarial estimate of those incurred which had not yet been reported (IBNR), which might settle or be withdrawn over future years. The figure estimated by the NHSLA for 2006 was more than £8 billion:

> The NHSLA estimates that its total liabilities (the theoretical cost of paying all outstanding claims immediately, including those relating to incidents which have occurred but have not yet been reported to us) are £8.22 billion for clinical claims and £0.13 billion for non-clinical claims.[46]

An area of medical practice giving rise to great concern is obstetrics. The NHSLA released information following a Freedom of Information Act 2000 inquiry by *The Sunday Times*, showing the number of babies in England who are damaged by errors in the course of their delivery.[47] Between April 2005 and 12 months to April 2006 more than 300 claims were initiated for negligence resulting in severe injuries suffered by babies. During the same period healthcare staff reported a further 174 incidents, suggesting that too few eligible children have been compensated for the negligence that caused their injuries. In the five years covered by data held by the NHSLA there were 2,763 claims in England, most of which were made on behalf of children who sustained brain damage as a result of delayed delivery.

Claims under the terms of the Consumer Protection Act 1987 (where harm is caused, for example, by a defect in the manufacture of a drug or piece of equipment, or in a pharmaceutical or blood product) are subject to only limited defences even if the producer can demonstrate that he exercised reasonable care. In other words, according to the NHSLA, as liability is strict,

43   National Audit Office Report, 'Handling Clinical Negligence Claims', May 2001.
44   These figures were supplied by Rosie Winterton, for the Government, in response to a parliamentary question, and were a summary of the National Audit Office findings, Hansard, col WA143, 19 July 2001.
45   Ferudi, F., 'Courting Mistrust – The Hidden Growth of a Culture of Litigation in Britain', Centre for Policy Studies, April 1999.
46   NHSLA website, February 2007.
47   Rogers, L., 'Hospitals botch 300 births a year', *Sunday Times*, 27 August 2006.

the claim would not be for negligence, so under normal circumstances NHS indemnity would not apply 'unless there was a question whether the health care professional either knew or should reasonably have known that the drug/equipment was faulty but continued to use it.'[48] It is not clear whether the NHSLA includes the figures relating to this category of claims in its statistics. It is assumed, however, that claims which do not involve negligence, for example trespass to the person (e.g. treatment against a patient's wishes), against doctors or other healthcare professionals working in the NHS, are included in the figures released by the NHSLA.

The figures relating to the progress of claims are an interesting indicator of success rates for claimants. It is not insignificant that the NHSLA indicates that, on its own analysis of the data collected between 1996 and 2006, 38 per cent of claims were abandoned by the claimant and 43 per cent were settled without ever reaching court. Only 4 per cent were finalised by a court judgment in favour of the claimant, and even these included those claims which required the formality of approval by the High Court because they concerned settlements already reached in respect of children. Of the cases reaching trial (87 in total), 26 per cent were decided in favour of claimants, and 68 per cent in favour of an NHS body.[49] Other research indicates that 60 per cent to 70 per cent of claims that are contemplated do not proceed beyond the stage of initial contact with a solicitor or disclosure of the claimant's medical records.[50]

Information gathered by the CRU since 2000 shows that throughout the UK the number of clinical negligence claims fell between the years 2000 and 2005.[51] The CRU reported an overall rise in *general* personal injury claims of 3 per cent in those years. However, between 2004–05 and 2005–06, the CRU data revealed a jump from 7,196 to 9,321 – a significant rise of 29.35 per cent, bringing the number of claims closer to their peak of 10,890 reached in 2001. It is too soon to conclude that this indicates the start of another dramatic increase in claims, but in the light of the wide publicity given to the prevalence of hospital infections, it is certainly possible that claims will continue to climb over the next few years, as the empirical research suggests that people are more likely to claim once they become aware that they might be able to obtain compensation for their injuries.[52] Certainly the increase in the number of letters of claim reported by the NHSLA suggests that the number of claims

---

48   NHS Indemnity: Arrangements for Clinical Negligence Claims in the NHS, NHSLA.
49   NHSLA Annual Report and Accounts 2006, op. cit., p 10.
50   Making Amends, op. cit., p 5.
51   Lewis, R., Morris, A. and Oliphant, K., 'Tort Personal Injury Claims Statistics: Is There a Compensation Culture in the United Kingdom? (2006) *Torts Law Journal* 14(2): 158; republished (2006) *Insurance Research and Practice* 21(2): 5–14.
52   Lloyd Bostock, S., 'Fault and Liability for Accidents: The Accident Victim's Perspective', in Harris, D., *et al.*, *Compensation and Support for Illness and Injury* (OUP, Oxford, 1984).

are set to increase. The total number of letters of claim received in 2005–06 was 4,516, an increase of 4.6 per cent on the previous year and of 8.3 per cent over the two previous years.

Similarly, data produced in Wales does not provide a clear picture of the number of claims in any given year, nor whether claims are rising in number, as the sums paid out will almost certainly relate to incidents that occurred in preceding years. However, there is an indication that the value of awards being paid to claimants is continuing to rise.[53]

Table 6 Welsh Risk Pool statistics for clinical negligence claims over £25,000

Year	Number of claims	Cost
2004–05	226	£30,186,490
2005–06	206	£20,264,893
2006–07	155	£37,924,506

Even if an increase in the volume of claims does occur, there is still likely to be a wide gap between the number of claims and the much higher number of recognised errors in healthcare. On the basis that the Government estimates that the average time that it takes for a claim to be processed is 1.36 years, the rise in the number of claims will not be reflected in actual payments of compensation until 2007–08.

Table 7 CRU data for clinical negligence claims

Year	Clinical negligence claims
2000–01	10,980
2001–02	9,773
2002–03	7,973
2003–04	7,109
2004–05	7,196
2005–06	9,321

Group actions

One area of legal activity which has seen a rise in successful claims is the class action. Mass tort claims arising from asbestosis,[54] and alleged injury caused

53   The author is grateful to the WRP for providing the figures.
54   *Lubbe and Ors v Cape plc* [2000] UKHL 41.

by silicone gel breast implants,[55] to take two examples, have been relatively successful, though as Haltom and McCann[56] point out in relation to the US picture, it is interesting that those cases are almost never mentioned by those who are anxious to criticise the tort system and are demanding reform. In the UK[57] the progress of group actions has been described as 'dismal' by one of the leading writers on clinical negligence and product liability in healthcare. However, there is still the potential for developing this arena, for example, in relation to defective smear tests and blood products.[58]

Ministry of defence clinical negligence claims

The clinical negligence claims brought by service personnel against the Ministry of Defence (MoD) are not included in the overall calculations for the UK. Details obtained under the Freedom of Information Act and published in *The Times* indicate that clinical negligence claims account for a significant percentage of the money paid in compensation and legal fees by the MoD. For the year 2005–06, clinical negligence claims against the MoD accounted for £4.5 million.[59] There were 28 cases settled during that year, with the sums involved ranging from the payment of £1 million for the negligent treatment of a soldier's head injury after he fell from a military vehicle, and sustained brain damage, to a £500 settlement for the negligent treatment of a wart. The MoD is still attempting to deal with a number of group actions, which include one from 'volunteers' for biological and chemical research tests at Porton Down laboratories in Wiltshire in the 1950s and 60s.

Vaccine damage payments

There are very few claims for compensation under the Vaccine Damage Payments Scheme, and still fewer are successful. As the scheme is administered by the Department for Work and Pensions (DWP), they would not be included in the statistics issued by the Department of Health or the NHSLA.

---

55 Successful claims in these cases and in other group actions are frequently made in the courts of the jurisdiction most likely to make the highest awards. For an excellent discussion of the issues surrounding the silicone gel breast implant cases, see Angells, M., *Science on Trial* (Norton, New York, 1996).

56 Haltom, W. and McCann, M., *Dis-torting the Law: Politics, Media and the Litigation Crisis* (University of Chicago Press, Chicago and London, 2004).

57 Lewis, C., *Clinical Negligence: A Practice Guide* (6th edn, 2006, Tottel, West Sussex), p 469.

58 *A v National Blood Authority* [2001] Lloyds Rep Med 187, in which the judge ruled that consumers are 'entitled to expect' blood to be 100 per cent pure, although there was no known way of purifying it.

59 Tendler, S., *The Times*, 10 April 2007.

Table 8* Claims and payments under Vaccine Damage Payments Act 1979 since April 2000

I April to 31 March	Number of claims received	Number of claims successful
2000–01	205	0
2001–02	146	2
2002–03	417	5
2003–04	165	4
2004–05	111	4
2005–06	106	4
2006–07 (to 7 June 2006)	14	2
Total	**1,164**	**21**

Source: Vaccine Damage Payments Unit Database.
* Taken from House of Commons Hansard Written Answer 7 June 2006.

The true picture

There is little point in attempting to grapple with the statistical problems by looking across different sets of figures in order to access a complete picture of what is happening in the claims arena. Even the various sets of statistics issued by the NHSLA relate to different matters and are produced for different purposes, so they differ considerably. The information analysed (see Figure 1) is derived from Fact Sheet 3 issued by the NHSLA in July 2006. As this information is only relevant to clinical negligence claims for which the NHSLA is responsible, it should only be viewed as representative of what is happening in that sector – although all NHS Trusts and PCTs in England are members of the CNST, so it covers the vast majority of clinical negligence claims in England (obviously excluding those against GPs, dentists and practitioners in the independent sector). 'Making Amends', the consultation document on reform of clinical negligence litigation, contains a range of information about the levels of claims recorded by the defence organisations, but as that information was produced in 2003 it does not provide assistance with more recent levels of claims in that arena.

The information set out in Fact Sheet 3 (see Figure 1), is used as the basis of the discussion that follows. It should be noted that the figures shown in this graph are the most useful yet produced by the NHSLA, as they indicate the number of claims allocated to the year in which the incident which gave rise to the claims occurred. This begins to allow for analysis which is 'date of cause' sensitive and therefore reflects more accurately when the alleged negligence occurred, as opposed to simply charting how many claims are received year on year in total.

In fact, however, this graph and the figures that it represents are not particularly helpful, in view of the fact that of the 5,697 claims received in

2005–06 'headline' figures given in the same Fact Sheet,[60] only 472 appear to be related to incidents that occurred in the same year. The remaining 5,225 claims then must be spread over preceding years. It is impossible for the NHSLA to produce more precise figures because many more claims relating to earlier years will be made in future years. It follows that when the figures for next year (2008) are released, because they also relate mainly to previous incident years, the 2005–06 figure will inevitably rise from the 472 shown.

The question is – what will the final figure be for 2005–06 when all the claims that will be received in future years have been taken into account? The NHSLA was very helpful in providing the author with a breakdown of the 5,967 claims received in 2005–06 relative to their year of incident to assist the attempt to answer that question. This is set out in the table below. The information in the table highlights the difficulties which the NHSLA must experience in processing claims, given that almost 2 per cent of all claims received relate to incidents that occurred at least 20 years ago. Indeed, the prospect of having to account for claims arriving some 44 years after they occurred, as happened in one case this year, must be daunting.

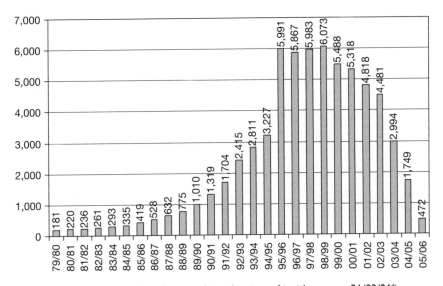

Figure 1 Number of clinical negligence claims by year of incident as at 31/03/06*
* Taken directly from NHSLA Fact Sheet 3, July 2006.

60   Presumably the term 'headline' simply means no more than 'significant'.

Table 9 Number of claims by date of incident

Incident year	CNST			ELS			Total
	Claim	Incident	Total	Claim	Incident	Total	
61/62				1		1	1
67/68				1		1	1
68/69				1		1	1
69/70				1	1	2	2
70/71					2	2	2
71/72				2		2	2
72/73				1	1	2	2
73/74				5		5	5
74/75					1	1	1
75/76				3	2	5	5
76/77				2	1	3	3
77/78				3		3	3
78/79				6	3	9	9
79/80				3	1	4	4
80/81				3	2	5	5
81/82				4	4	8	8
82/83				2	3	5	5
83/84				9	7	16	16
84/85				7	7	14	14
85/86				11	6	17	17
86/87				9	3	12	12
87/88				6	10	16	16
88/89				8	6	14	14
89/90				5	8	13	13
90/91				9	6	15	15
91/92				13	6	19	19
92/93				11	13	24	24
93/94				15	7	22	22
94/95				20	9	29	29
95/96	44	12	56				56
96/97	40	16	56				56
97/98	49	21	70				70
98/99	64	16	80				80
99/00	80	24	104				104
00/01	113	30	143				143
01/02	355	48	403				403
02/03	1,103	157	1,260				1,260
03/04	944	229	1,173				1,173
04/05	1,252	276	1,528				1,528
05/06	472	82	554				554
Total	**4,516**	**911**	**5,427**	**161**	**109**	**270**	**5,697**

As would be expected, the number of claims that relate to incidents occurring in the same year as the claims relating to them are received is comparatively small – less than 10 per cent. Clearly, it takes some time for a potential claimant to recover sufficiently to seek legal advice, for the solicitor who is consulted to obtain the relevant medical records and related information, and for a decision to be made to initiate proceedings. Not surprisingly, in view of the standard three-year limitation period in personal injury cases, some 80 per cent of all claims received in any one year relate to incidents which occurred within the preceding three years. This means, of course, that the remaining 20 per cent of claims received must relate to incidents which occurred outside the usual three-year limitation period. Many of these can be explained by the date of knowledge on the part of the claimant falling beyond three years from the date of the alleged negligence. Others may be brought in the hope that the exercise of judicial discretion will permit a claim to be brought by disapplying the usual limitation period, or because time does not start to run for some years because the patient was a minor – or even because time never starts to run because the patient lacks mental capacity.

The complexity of the law concerning the time limits within which claims should be brought adds considerably to the problems of those attempting to calculate the rate of future claims. The Limitation Act 1980 requires a claim for personal injuries or death to be brought within three years[61] from the date when it is first realised that a person has suffered a significant injury that may be attributable to the negligence of a third party. For a minor, the limitation period starts to run from the date that he or she attains the age of 18 years and may be extended where material facts are not known. A person of 'unsound mind', as long as he or she remains under the disability in question, can bring a claim without limit of time through a 'next friend'. After the death of such a person, the limitation period will run against his personal representative(s).

The three-year personal injury limitation period starts to run from the date of personal injury or death, or date of knowledge that a claim might be available. The date of knowledge is the first date on which the claimant has knowledge that the injury in question was significant; that the injury was attributable to negligence; the identity of the defendant. Judges have a discretion, under certain circumstances, to extend the limitation period for personal injuries under s 33 of the 1980 Act. This does not apply, however, in the case of claims for torts other than negligence, for example claims arising from trespass to the person,[62] where the limitation period prescribed by s 2(1) of the 1980 Act is six years. If the claim is brought under the Consumer Protection Act 1987,[63] for example for injuries arising from defective equipment such as

---

61   s 11.
62   *Stubbings v Webb* [1993] AC 498, under reconsideration by the House of Lords having been referred there in *A v Iorworth Hoare* [2006] EWCA (Civ) 395 at the time of writing.
63   Limitation Act 1980, s 11A (4).

prostheses, or products, such as blood,[64] the usual three-year limit applies for personal injuries, though the action accrues when the damage was sustained, regardless of the claimant's awareness of it, and the judicial discretion cannot be exercised after the 'long-stop' limit of ten years from the date at which the product was last supplied by the producer.[65]

The table provided by the NHSLA (Table 9), indicating years of incident, is of the greatest assistance in calculating how many claims will eventually be brought relating to incidents that occurred in 2005–06. In order to make this calculation, a number of conservative assumptions were made, based on the experience of previous years.

First, it was assumed that the same time pattern of incident to claim will apply in future years as occurred in 2005–06. Second, it was assumed that the rate at which claims will be received will remain stable for all future years, at the 2005–06 rate, in line with the suggestion in the NHSLA Report and Accounts for that year that the claim rate has now 'stabilised'. The third major assumption in the calculation is based on the way in which the NHSLA includes what they refer to as 'incidents' in the total claim figures shown for the year. The total number of claims received this year is given as 5,697. However, as can be seen from the table above, some 1,020 of those are in fact not claims but reported incidents, which may or may not turn into claims in due course. As no information is available which might help determine the actual conversion rate, the author's analysis assumes that 50 per cent will convert to claims.

The graph below (Figure 2) has been drafted by taking the NHSLA figures and projecting what may happen to them in the next 20 years, by which time 98 per cent of the claims that relate to incidents in these years will have been received.

Since the projection is deliberately conservative, and is based on only one set of figures, and as the calculations necessarily involve making certain assumptions, these figures suggest that the level at which the 'compensation culture' is running remains incredibly high, standing 1,200 per cent higher than it was 20 years ago. However, it must be recognised that the NHSLA did not come into being until 1995, so the data it holds on an occurrence basis for earlier years is obviously incomplete. If one takes this into account, the graph shows a remarkably level number of claims from the date when the NHSLA was created. A large percentage of the claims made between 1990 and 1995 would have been handled in-house by NHS Trusts themselves, so the NHSLA's figures alone are insufficient indicators of the true picture over the entire time. However, there is indisputable evidence of a dramatic increase in the number of claims made between 1980 and 2006. Since the number of claims per year, whether analysed by year of incident or year of claim, has been consistent over a ten-year period, there is a clear indication that there has been a compensation culture for the past ten years in the UK.

---

64   *A v National Blood Authority* [2001] Lloyds Rep Med 187.
65   Limitation Act 1980, s 33(1A)(a).

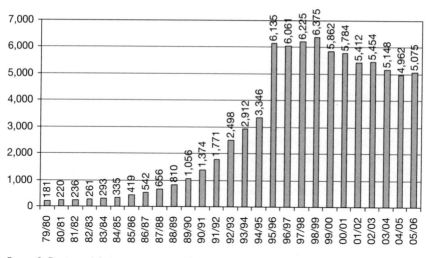

Figure 2 Projected figures over next 20 years

Even small changes to the rate that claims are received in future years, perhaps as a result of population growth or an increase in claims arising from hospital-acquired infections, will make significant differences to the way in which the figures will appear in 20 years' time. The rate of such changes for the next 20 years needs to be monitored very carefully and it is to be hoped that the NHSLA will continue in its present spirit of openness to release annual figures which enable accurate comparisons to be made.

Prognosis

There is evidence that the population of the UK is increasing. The population increased by 375,000 in the year from mid-2004 to mid-2005. This is the largest annual rise in numbers since 1962. The difference between births and deaths contributed one-third of the annual population increase, and migration and other changes contributed the other two-thirds. The net international migration into the UK from other countries was the main reason for the steep rise in population growth. There were an estimated 588,000 people during that period migrating to the UK for a year or more, which was 59,000 higher than the previous mid-year period, and this was mainly attributable to a rise in the number of citizens coming to the UK from the ten countries that joined the European Union in May 2004.[66] The European Court of Justice (ECJ) appears

66   Office of National Statistics, March 2005.

to be engaged in strengthening the rights of EU citizens to healthcare in any of the Member States[67] and as one commentator[68] put it:

> EU citizens should be delighted with their new rights and appreciative of the clever attention devoted by the Court of Justice to their health and well-being.

As the population increases, so more people will be treated by the NHS, increasing the potential for a rise in the number of claims. In addition, there are forecasts in a research report issued by the Institute of Psychiatry at the London School of Economics, that by 2051 there will be 1.7 million people suffering from dementia as the population ages.[69] This, according to the estimates in the report, would mean that the total number of people in the UK suffering from dementia in the UK will increase to 940,110 by 2021, and to 1,735,087 by 2051. This factor, coupled with other diseases of ageing, is also likely to increase the number of people receiving treatment, and consequently the possibility of further clinical negligence claims year on year, although compensation payments to elderly people are unlikely to be as high as those payable to young claimants requiring a lifetime of care. It is also likely that there will be more claims arising from hospital-acquired infections, given the high level of publicity that this topic receives and the new ways in which victims are beginning to claim.

Counting the legal cost

The NHSLA has expressed concern about the relatively high legal costs incurred in clinical negligence claims, and in particular the high level of fees paid to lawyers acting for claimants. In the year 2005–06, under the CNST, defence costs amounted to 16.2 per cent of damages paid out, and claimant costs were significantly higher at 28.37 per cent of damages.[70] The total costs involved in all three NHSLA schemes amounted to £290,494,614, a significant rise over the previous financial year. Although the majority of claims are settled out of court, and in spite of the levelling in the number of claims and the fact that fewer than 50 cases per annum actually reach trial,[71] the legal

---

67   See Newdick, C., 'Citizenship, Free Movement and Healthcare: Cementing Individual Rights by Corroding Social Solidarity' (2006) *Common Market Law Review* 43: 1645–68.

68   Kaczorawska, A., 'A Review of the Creation of the European Court of Justice of the Right to Effective and Speedy Medical Treatment and its Outcomes' (2006) 12 *European Law Review* 345, 370 cited by Newdick, supra, p 1645.

69   Albanese, E., Fernandez, J., Ferri, C., Knapp, M. and McCrone, P., London School of Economics, Institute of Psychiatry Research, research report published March 2007.

70   NHSLA Report and Accounts 2006, HC 1179 (HMSO, London, 2006) 14.

71   NHSLA Report and Accounts 2006, HC 1179 (HMSO, London, 2006) 10–11.

costs involved are startlingly high and still increasing, reaching £560 million in 2005–06.[72] Some success was achieved by the NHSLA in obtaining a costs capping order on a single claim as opposed to a group action.

In evidence presented for 'Making Amends', in the majority of claims resulting in the payment of damages under £45,000, the legal and administrative costs exceed the value of the claim, and the smaller the payment, the larger the proportion of legal costs to damages.[73]

As long ago as 1998, Frank Dobson, then Secretary of State for Health, said on the BBC's news and current affairs programme 'News Night':

> The best place for a lawyer is on the operating table … Lawyers are milking the NHS of millions of pounds every year – money that would be better spent on patient care.

In a similar vein, Dr David Pickersgill, chair of the British Medical Association's Medico Legal Committee, speaking at the BMA Conference in 1999,[74] claimed that recent research indicated that 800 medical mistakes are committed in hospitals in the UK every day, but still chose to blame the lawyers, as his estimate at that time was that claims took six years on average to settle and only 10 per cent were decided in favour of claimants:

> Personal injury claims and suing doctors has become an exponential growth industry amongst the legal profession.

While there may be some truth in the notion that the use of lawyers is a substantial drain on NHS resources, clearly lawyers cannot be blamed for the negligence of healthcare professionals. The 2005 report of the National Audit Office estimates, following research that included retrospective studies of patients' records and surveys of NHS Trusts in England, suggest that around 10.8 per cent of patients suffer adverse events and that there is significant under-reporting of deaths as a result of patient safety incidents. The number of such deaths for 2004–05 is estimated at somewhere between 840 and 34,000, though in reality the report acknowledges that 'we simply do not know'.[75] This suggests that there are many more patients injured or killed as a result of clinical errors than there are claims for compensation. The conclusion was reached by a commentator on the US position:[76]

> The problem is not that there are too many claims; the problem is that there are too few. And, because our healthcare system does such a poor

72   Ibid.
73   Figures indicated by the NHSLA and cited in 'Making Amends', op. cit., p 8.
74   Reported in the BBC coverage of the BMA Conference in Belfast, 6 July 1999.
75   Ibid., fn 18.
76   Baker, T., *The Medical Malpractice Myth* (University of Chicago Press, 2005).

job of giving injured patients the information they need to tell whether their injuries were due to malpractice, too many patients have to file lawsuits to find out.

There are several reasons, beside financial considerations, why people decide not to pursue claims – not least the acrimony in which litigation is frequently conducted, which causes stress at a time when people are least able to cope with it, following serious illness, suffering, or bereavement. The complexities involved in proving what the law requires for a claimant to succeed in a negligence action are probably also a major factor in the relatively low proportion of claims to incidents.

The level of awards

It is not only the number of claims that was giving rise to concerns but also the level of damages awarded, and the cost of claims has risen more than the rate of inflation for a variety of reasons, outlined below. In 1996–07 £235 million was spent on clinical negligence claims; in 1997–08 the figure dipped to £144 million, but after that the amount paid rose steadily to reach £446 million for 2001–02 covering some 7,000 claims, representing a rise of 50 per cent in three years. In 2002–03, the figure remained stable at £446 million, but in 2003–04 it fell slightly to £422.5 million. In 2004–05, the cost of clinical negligence claims amounted to £502.9 million, of which £150 million represented legal costs.[77] The 2005–06 data suggest that perhaps the level of awards has started to rise again.

Table 10 Recent payments by the NHS for clinical negligence in England

Year	Payments to nearest £ million
1996–97	235
1997–98	144
1998–99	221
1999–00	373
2000–01	415
2001–02	446
2002–03	446
2003–04	423
2004–05	503
2005–06	560

77   National Audit Office Report (HC 456; 2005–06).

By October 2002, the highest award to date was £7 million plus a structured settlement of £250,000 per annum to a woman who suffered brain damage during childbirth. This was an approved settlement arrived at as a result of earlier mediation between the parties. A glance at Lawtel's database of quantum reports reveals many other large awards in 2006, to take just one recent year, the highest being made to claimants who have suffered brain damage during birth or surgery. In Wales, some recent very high awards of damages for clinical negligence have been made against NHS Trusts – in the order of £4 million and £5 million, which, unlike many of the awards recently recorded in England, were outright lump sum payments and did not contain an element of grossed-up structured settlement. The Scottish NHS has paid almost £40million compensation to claimants in the course of the past five years, according to official figures obtained by the SNP. Compensation payments peaked in 2004–05 at £8.3 million, slipping to £7.8million in 2005–06.

Figures produced by the CNST for the ten highest awards in England as at 31 December 2006 are as follows:[78]

Table 11 2006 categories of claim in highest awards

Cause of complaint	Damages paid (£)
Failure/delay in responding to an abnormal foetal heart rate	5,555,000
Delay in diagnosis of foetal distress	5,620,290
Informed consent not correctly obtained	5,624,976
Failure/delay in diagnosis	5,749,111
Failure to respond to birth complications	5,793,782
Failure/delay in responding to an abnormal foetal heart rate	5,800,000
Failure/delay in diagnosis	6,248,845
Failure to monitor second stage labour	6,635,000
Failure to perform tests	8,300,000
Failure to diagnose pre-eclampsia	12,400,000

Other awards during the first four months of 2006 include the payment to a 19-year-old man of a lump sum of £1,900,000 plus periodic payments for brain injuries he suffered during the neonatal period in October 1986, leaving him with severe and uncontrollable epilepsy and profound learning disabilities;[79] £2,350,638 to a 26-year-old man for the brain injuries sustained as a result of a delay in repairing a congenital heart defect following his birth in 1979;[80]

78   Rosie Winterton, in answer to a House of Commons written question, Hansard, 29 January 2006.
79   *Raphael v Norfolk, Suffolk & Cambridgeshire Strategic Health Authority* QBD (2006) unreported, 27 February.
80   *Crofton v NHS Litigation Authority* QBD (2006) unreported, 19 January.

£2 million to a five-year-old girl for brain damage sustained during her birth in May 2000, resulting in quadriplegic cerebral palsy, microcephaly, visual impairment and epilepsy with a much reduced life expectancy;[81] £1,100,000 lump sum plus periodical payments to a 13-year-old boy for the brain injuries sustained during his birth in June 1992;[82] £4 million to an eight-year-old girl who suffered brain damage during her birth;[83] £3,375,000 to a 19-year-old man for brain damage sustained during a heart operation in February 1997;[84] £4,200,000 to a 14-year-old boy for brain injuries sustained during his birth in June 1991.[85]

While the majority of claims are brought against doctors, it is interesting that the same database includes a series of awards to people who had suffered as a result of negligence in the course of dental treatment, one of which amounted to £24,000 for the dental pain and suffering as a result of a dentist's failure to diagnose, treat and monitor periodontal disease between 1974 and 2002.[86]

The graph below, issued by the NHSLA,[87] demonstrates clearly that the highest sums are awarded as a result of obstetric negligence. This would be expected, given the costly long-term care required for patients who were brain-damaged at birth.

Stratospheric figures of the kind awarded to brain-damaged patients who require constant care over many years are partly the result of recent changes in the law relating to the calculation of damages for personal injuries, including the assessment of general damages, which include a sum for pain and suffering, and particularly the assessment of awards for future losses where lump sum payments are made. There have been recent significant changes in the way that damages are calculated. Levels of awards for non-pecuniary losses of more than £10,000 increased after the Court of Appeal decision in *Heil v Rankin*[88] in which it accepted in part the Law Commission's views on the need to increase the level of awards.[89] In that case, involving conjoined appeals, the Court of Appeal established guidelines for courts to follow for the calculation of damages for non-pecuniary losses. The result is that there are tapered increases for non-pecuniary awards between that sum and the highest sums, and it has been estimated that the very highest awards of damages for pain and

81   *D v Burton Hospitals NHS Trust* QBD (2006) unreported, 10 January.
82   *Flynn v Thames Valley Strategic Health Authority* QBD (2005) unreported, 2 December.
83   *Popat v Leicester Royal Infirmary NHS Trust* (2005) unreported, 16 November.
84   *Revett v South East London Strategic Health Authority* QBD (2005) unreported, 25 October.
85   *Amass v Barts And The London NHS Trust* (2005) unreported, 17 October.
86   *Dey v Sanders* (2005) unreported, 18 August.
87   NHSLA Fact Sheet 3 2006.
88   [2001] QB 272.
89   See Law Commission, *Damages for Personal Injury: Non-pecuniary Loss*, Report No. 257, 1999.

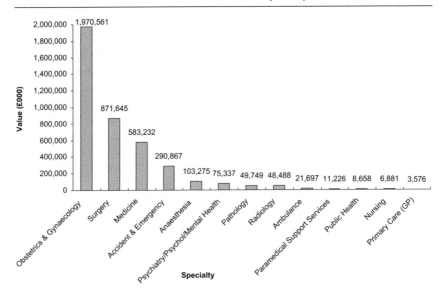

Figure 3 Total value of CNST claims by specialty at 31/03/06

suffering and loss of amenity[90] (PSLA) have increased by around one-third to £200,000. The rise in value of claims for general damages has been less dramatic than had originally been anticipated,[91] but it inevitably had an impact on higher value claims, which are those that most impress the media, and in accordance with the Court of Appeal guidelines the sums awarded for non-pecuniary loss should be increased on a regular basis in line with the retail price index. Many of the high sums awarded for PSLA are in claims against the NHS.

There have also been important changes in the calculation of future pecuniary losses as a result of the House of Lords decision in *Wells v Wells*,[92] which resulted in the payment of very much higher awards to those who have suffered injury and illness as a result of clinical negligence, as well as negligence in other spheres. The use of the Ogden Tables was approved by the House of Lords in that case, and this means that estimates of survival are more realistic than in the past, leading higher awards based on the need to provide care for claimants over a longer period of time than in the past. The estimates

---

90   A head of damages that was much criticised by Professor Atiyah, see Cane, P., *Accidents, Compensation and the Law* (Butterworths, London, 2006) p 164.

91   See Lewis, R., 'Increasing the Price of Pain. Damages, the Law Commission and *Heil v Rankin*', www.law.cf.ac.uk/research/pubs/repository/401.pdf

92   *Wells v Wells* [1998] 3 All ER 481; *Page v Sheerness Steel* [1999] 1 AC 345.

of future liabilities made by the NHSLA are strongly affected by the 'discount rate' set by Government. Current estimates of damages payable are very high because the discount rate was changed on 1 April 2003 from 6 per cent to 3.5 per cent as a result of the decision in *Wells v Wells*, and it was again reduced, on 1 April 2005 to 2.2 per cent. The NHSLA's estimated liabilities of £7 billion at 31 March 2005 were based on the discount rate of 3.5 per cent, but if they had used the new 2.2 per cent discount rate the estimated liabilities would have been £7.638 billion.[93] The MDU has estimated that the change in the discount rate from 3 per cent to 2.5 per cent could add £1.5 million per annum to their liabilities in future, and £8 million to their existing liabilities. The MPS estimates that the cost of the change will be £6.7 million in respect of incidents which have already happened, and an increase of £1.25 million per annum could be assumed for future liabilities using the ratio implied by the MDU. Lewis *et al.* also suggest that the increased awards in recent years are a reflection of increased earnings, which are one of the main factors on which awards are calculated.[94]

Another factor in the rising cost of negligence to the NHS could well be the increased life expectancies of claimants because of improvements in medical and nursing technologies and treatments,[95] added to which is the greater readiness of the courts to take into account a wider range of care needs than previously (schedules of damages are now extremely detailed and extensive in that respect). Theoretically, the cost of progress through new technologies and treatments means that mistakes will inevitably be made.[96] The stark reality of this is illustrated by the dramatic effects on human volunteers of a drug successfully tried previously on animals.[97]

Although the cost of compensating claimants is high, there is ample evidence before the courts that the recipients of compensation deserve recompense for their suffering and financial support to meet their needs, and research carried out in the 1980s indicated that many of the personal injury claimants surveyed did not receive adequate financial support to meet their needs.[98] The Courts Act 2003, which came into force on 1 April 2005, requires the claimant's needs, rather than his wishes, to be paramount, and courts now have the power to order periodical payments rather than a lump sum to compensate for future losses. In many instances regular payments are more suited to the needs of the claimant than a single lump sum award, and there are potential advantages both to claimants and defendants in such a system. However, for a

93   NHSLA Report July 2005.
94   Op. cit., fn 19 at p 173.
95   In *Heil v Rankin* (supra) the Court of Appeal was clearly influenced by this factor.
96   See Merry, A. and McCall Smith, A., *Errors, Medicine and the Law* (Cambridge University Press, Cambridge, 2001), p 42.
97   See the Report of The Northwick Park Inquiry (DoH, December 2006).
98   Harris, D., MacLean, J., Genn, M., Lloyd-Bostock, H., Fenn, S., Corfield, P. and Brittan, Y., *Compensation and Support for Illness and Injury* (Oxford University Press, Oxford, 1984).

variety of market-driven reasons, the way in which that system is operating is not without problems.[99] The figures produced by the NHSLA relating to some compensation payments could well fall following the decision in *Crofton v NHSLA* [2007] ENCA Civ 71 (see p 5).

The injuries giving rise to claims

People bringing claims against the NHS seek compensation for a variety of injuries. According to the data[100] compiled for the Government by the NHSLA for use in 'Making Amends', the consultation document on clinical negligence litigation reform, the most common complaints were of unnecessary pain (11 per cent), followed by fatality (10.5 per cent), cerebral palsy (7.2 per cent), poor outcome (6.5 per cent), additional surgery (5.9 per cent), and psychiatric injury (5.5 per cent). However, these figures were derived from the claims that would potentially result in the highest awards of damages, and are not representative of the smaller claims. Of all incidents occurring in hospitals up to 30 April 2003, most concerned alleged negligence in the course of surgery (36 per cent), followed by obstetrics and gynaecology (26 per cent), medicine (16 per cent), and accident and emergency (10 per cent). In claims for negligence in the course of general practice, the chief causes were alleged failed or delayed diagnosis (57 per cent) and medication error (22 per cent). For those who do not seek financial recompense, but want explanations and apologies, the NHS complaints system is the best avenue to follow.

How common are errors in healthcare?

It has been estimated that around 2.5 million people in the UK sustain some kind of accident resulting in personal injuries every year.[101] The Pearson Commission concluded that between 1973 and 1975 there were an average of 2,819 deaths in England and Wales as a result of adverse effects of drugs, and 77 deaths resulting from complications of medical care. In terms of injuries in medical care, the figures for the UK as a whole were put at 24,000 caused by adverse effects of drugs, and 13,000 caused by medical complications, though the reliability of the data is probably questionable because in those days still fewer error reporting systems existed than today.[102] In 1988, a group

99   See Lewis, R., 'Clinical Negligence and the NHS Refusal to Structure Settlements with Profits' (2003) www.law.of.ac.uk/research/pubs
100   In claims above the excess limit for NHS Trusts, between 1995 and 2001.
101   This is a rough estimate produced by the Royal Society for the Prevention of Accidents (RoSPA) and is drawn from public statistics relating to a range of accidents occurring in the home, in education, healthcare, on the roads, and in the course of other activities.
102   Royal Commission on Civil Liability and Compensation for Personal Injury, *Report of the Royal Commission on Civil Liability and Compensation for Personal Injury*, Cmnd 7054, 1978, London: HMSO, vol 2, paras 233–35.

of renowned researchers expressed the view that it was 'really quite impossible to determine' whether rates of medical error in the UK had increased over the previous ten years.[103] The reason for this uncertainty lies in the fact that there was some ambiguity about what should be classified as 'medical error', and in the lack of available evidence, as figures had not been systematically collected and analysed during the years in question.

It is difficult to identify the precise meaning of 'error' in the context of healthcare. The words 'adverse event', 'untoward event', 'accident', 'error', 'mistake', 'malpractice', 'negligence', 'disaster', 'patient safety incident', and 'iatrogenic harm' are frequently used interchangeably.[104] Some words, such as 'accident' have neutral connotations,[105] while others, for example, 'malpractice,' imply deficiency on the part of a healthcare professional.

It is important to recognise that not all errors amount to what the law would define as negligence. Many mistakes are made by professional people in the course of their careers, but relatively few form the basis of legal claims. While it is difficult to define 'error' for the purposes of this discussion,[106] it may be possible to identify different varieties of error. Merry and McCall Smith define error in the medical context as:[107]

> Unintentional failure in the formulation of a plan by which it is intended to achieve a goal, or an unintentional departure of a sequence of mental or physical activities from the sequence planned, except when such departure is due to chance intervention.

This definition presupposes that something goes wrong with a plan of treatment, but that the error is unintentional, though it does not appear to take account of recklessness, which can be actionable as a civil claim or even result in a prosecution in the event of a death, for gross negligence manslaughter[108] – which amounts to criminalisation of medical errors.[109]

Action Against Medical Accidents (AvMA), the registered charity which states that it is committed to promoting better patient safety and justice for people who have been affected by a medical accident defines a 'medical accident' as:[110]

---

103   Fenn *et al.* op. cit., fn 1 supra.
104   See Quick, O., 'Outing Medical Errors. Questions of Trust and Responsibility' (2006) *Medical Law Review* 14(1): 22–43.
105   See Green J., 'Risk and Misfortune: The Social Construction of Accidents' (1997, UCL Press) at 2, cited in fn 17, Quick, supra.
106   For a generic definition of error, see Reason, J., *Human Error* (Cambridge University Press, 1990).
107   Merry, A. and McCall Smith, A., *Errors, Medicine and the Law* (Cambridge University Press, 2001).
108   *R v Adomako* [1995] 1 AC 171.
109   For a clear account of what is involved in this crime in the medical context, see *Student BMJ* 2004; 12: 1–44, February, ISSN 0966–6494.
110   AvMA brochure and website 2007.

where unintended harm has been caused as a result of treatment or failure to treat appropriately. This includes where the care has been negligent, but does not necessarily mean that it was.

Other definitions suggest that perceptions of what is an error are subjective, and Espin *et al.* emphasise, in their analysis on an empirical basis, of different perceptions of what amounts to an error, and therefore reportable as such, that:

> both healthcare professionals and patients agreed that errors occur where rules are broken. Where there were no rules, standards, or procedures in place to prevent the event occurring, errors were more ambiguous and were identified by assessing the resulting harm experienced by the patient.[111]

The National Patient Safety Agency (NPSA) defines error in two ways, first as a 'patient safety incident':

> any unintended or unexpected event that leads to death, disability, injury, disease or suffering for one or more patients.

Second as 'near miss':

> any situation that could have resulted in an accident, injury or illness for a patient, but did not, due to chance or timely intervention by another.[112]

Of course, not all the litigation initiated by patients against NHS and other healthcare organisations concerns negligence. Some of the cases that find their way into the statistics involve decisions about resource allocation, end of life decision-making, and other matters, which involve measured thought processes, and it is not always clear from the figures produced by the NHS whether they exclude such claims. However, as far as this analysis is concerned, the focus is on clinical negligence, and the NHSLA is one organisation at least which indicates that its published figures do separate negligence claims from others brought against the NHS.

In terms of a taxonomy of error, Reason, whose work has been highly influential in defining and classifying medical error,[113] describes skill-based error, rule-based error and knowledge error, distinguishing between errors of

---

111   Espin, S., Levinson, W., Regehr, G., Baker, G.R. and Lingard, L., 'Error or "Act of God"? A Study of Patients' and Operating Room Team Members' Perceptions of Error Definition, Reporting, and Disclosure', (2006) *Surgery* 139: 6–14.

112   'A Safer Place for Patients: Learning to Improve Standards', NPSA 2006.

113   Op. cit., fn 41, at p 74.

skill and errors of judgment – a distinction rejected at least for the purposes of negligence claims in the UK by the House of Lords in *Whitehouse v Jordan*,[114] a case that confirmed the Bolam defence. The comment of Lord Bridge in that case is instructive:

> Counsel for Mr Jordan persisted in submitting that his client should be completely exculpated ... at worst he was guilty of an error of clinical judgement. ... It is high time that the unacceptability of such an answer be finally exposed. To say that a surgeon committed an error of clinical judgement is wholly ambiguous, for while such errors may be completely consistent with the due exercise of professional skill, other acts or omissions in the course of exercising 'clinical judgement' may be so glaringly below proper standards as to make a finding of negligence inevitable.

Reasons' classification[115] of medical errors distinguishes between mistakes and slips or lapses. Whereas a slip will occur when the action is not what was intended, a mistake follows a pattern that was intended but does not achieve the expected outcome because the original plan was wrong. He also drew a distinction between latent errors, which are beyond the control of the actor, such as machine failure, and active errors, which are within the sphere of control of the actor. All errors, he acknowledges, can be serious and may have the potential to lead to death. In its analysis of medical error, the Institute of Medicine in the US defined patient safety as 'freedom from accidental injury', and medical error as 'the failure of planned action to be completed as intended or the use of a wrong plan to achieve an aim'. Adverse events are regarded as injuries that are due to medical intervention rather than the condition from which a patient was suffering.[116]

According to the NPSA, over 1 million people are successfully treated each day by NHS acute trusts, ambulance trusts, and mental health trusts, and this factor alone makes it difficult to estimate the number and type of errors that occur in healthcare. Obviously, those which result in claims are recorded, but in the case of unsuccessful claims, should errors falling short of negligence be counted as errors at all? The NPSA believes that such incidents should be recorded and the Government is encouraging an environment of openness in which mistakes are admitted and form part of a learning process by which the delivery of care can be improved. Errors which remain undiscovered by patients may never come to light unless those who make them are prepared to acknowledge their mistakes, or their colleagues are prepared to disclose them.

114   [1981] 1 WLR 246 (HL).
115   Reason, J.T., *Human Error* (Cambridge University Press, Cambridge, 1990).
116   IOM, 'To Err is Human', op. cit., supra, 'Errors in Healthcare: A Leading Cause of Death and Injury', 26–48.

As long as the blame culture that generates claims continues to exist, there will inevitably be reluctance on the part of the healthcare professionals to own up to mistakes. Mistakes that cause injury are more likely to come to light than the 'near misses', even if they never result in claims. Not all errors are actionable, as for example, where the error does not result in injury because the outcome for the patient was inevitable whether or not the error occurred. This makes it even more difficult to calculate the relationship between errors and claims. For the purposes of the discussion in this book, errors which a lawyer would consider worth challenging because they meet the criteria for bringing a negligence claim with some chance of success are described as 'actionable errors'.

The methodology of error identification

A variety of different methods may be used to identify errors in healthcare, each carrying different advantages and disadvantages.[117] These rely on a range of different data for analysis – such as patients' records, observations, data taken from closed claims, and so on – and on differing methodologies, which have included error reporting systems analysis, claims analysis, administrative data analysis, reviews of paper and electronic records, observations of patient care, root cause analysis, clinical surveillance, autopsies and internal inquires into deaths, and so on. Each has its own relative merits, but none is completely reliable.[118] Since 1990 there have been serious attempts in the UK, through a variety of mechanisms, including audit and the Confidential Inquiries, and more recently clinical governance, to identify errors in healthcare organisations, and more recent research has produced estimated figures of the number of adverse incidents occurring in healthcare in the UK, though there are widely disparate conclusions. Exercises carried out for 'An Organisation with a Memory'[119] and for the consultation on clinical negligence litigation reform, reported in 'Making Amends', have provided some useful information, though it is impossible to be completely certain of its accuracy. The methodology used to collect information leaves room for considerable doubt, as it depends on the honesty of healthcare staff in reporting their own experiences. The results also depend on the proper understanding of what amounts to an 'adverse event' – whether that term presupposes a preventable injury, or simply an injury caused by medical treatment. Similar problems have been experienced in

---

117   See Thomas, E. and Petersen, L., 'Measuring Errors and Adverse Events in Healthcare', *Journal of Internal Medicine* 18: 61–67, cited in *Studies of Errors and Adverse Events in Healthcare: The Scale of the Problem*, New Zealand, based on Vincent, C.A., Ennis, M. and Andley, R.J. (Oxford University Press, Oxford, 1993).

118   'Studies of Errors and Adverse Events in Healthcare: the Nature and Scale of the Problem' New Zealand Study, op. cit., p 33.

119   DOH 2001.

research carried out in the US and Australia, as Tom Baker observed in his analysis of the research conducted there,[120] mostly in hospitals, into the alleged malpractice epidemic,[121] commenting that although few hospitals today are willing to open themselves up to intense public scrutiny, observational studies conducted by anonymous observers in hospitals are likely to provide a fuller and more accurate picture than retrospective studies. Almost all the studies that have been conducted in the UK and elsewhere are retrospective.

The experience outside the UK

A research study conducted by means of a review of patients' records was undertaken as far back as the 1970s in California, with a view to considering whether a system of no-fault compensation would be feasible.[122] Contrary to expectations, the study concluded that there was considerably more malpractice in hospitals than had previously been thought, and that 140,000 of the patients in the study had been injured as a result of negligence, with almost 10 per cent of those dying of their injuries. Its findings were largely suppressed[123] once it was discovered that a no-fault scheme would be far too expensive to fund.

The Harvard Medical Practice Study[124] produced findings that were publicised more widely than the California conclusions, and which shocked the medical world. It took the form of 30,121 structured reviews of randomly selected patients' case records selected from 51 randomly selected acute care hospitals in New York State in 1984. It found that adverse events occurred in 3.7 per cent of admissions, of which 27.6 per cent could be attributed to negligence, with 2.6 per cent causing serious injuries, and 13.6 per cent resulting in death. A later study conducted in Utah and Colorado[125] by the New York team produced findings closer to the Australian experience outlined below, as did 'Making Amends' in the UK, and it is thought that the Harvard approach, which was designed and conducted by doctors, with trained nurses carrying out an initial review of the patients' records, was by its nature very conservative in

120   Baker, T., *The Medical Malpractice Myth* (University of Chicago Press, Chicago, 2005).
121   Ibid., p 24 et seq.
122   Mills, Study sponsored by the California Hospital and Medical Associations, 1978, cited in Baker, T., op. cit., at p 2.
123   Ibid., see Studdert, D.M., Brennan, T.A. *et al.*, 2000, 1647–48.
124   Brennan, T.A., Leape, L.L., Laird, N.M, Hebert, L. Localio, A.R., Lawthers, A.G., Newhouse, J.P., Weiler, P.C., and Hiatt, H.H., 'Incidence of Adverse Events and Negligence in Hospitalized Patients: Results of the Harvard Medical Practice Study' (1991) 324 *New England Journal of Medicine* 370–76; also Leape, L.L., Brennan, T.A., Laird, N.M., Lawthers, A.G., Localio, A.R., Barnes, B.A., Hebert, J.P., Newhouse, P.C., Weiler, P.C. and Hiatt, H.H., 'The Nature of Adverse Events in Hospitalized Patients: Results of the Harvard Medical Practice Study 11' (1991) *New England Journal of Medicine* 377–84.
125   Thomas, E.J., Studdert, D.M., Burstin, H.R., Orav, E.J., Zeena, T., Williams, E.J., Howard, K.M., Weiler, P.C. and Brennan, T.A., 'Incidence and Types of Adverse Events and Negligent Care in Utah and Colorado' (2000) 38 *Medical Care* 261–71.

its method of identifying negligent medical management.[126] Like the California study, this found that the more serious the injury, the more likely it was to have been caused by negligence. The conclusion was that there were over seven malpractice injuries for every negligence claim that was made.

A new controversy has raged in the US since the publication of findings in a report entitled 'To Err is Human: Building a Safer Health System'[127] by the US Institute of Medicine (IOM), which claims that between 44,000 and 98,000 unnecessary deaths occur every year as a result of medical mistakes. In reaching this conclusion the IOM extrapolated from the findings of the Harvard study and from another study conducted in Colorado and Utah in the 1990s. Although the findings of the IOM Report were challenged[128] as being unreliable, another estimate suggested that the true incident of medical errors could exceed twice the IOM figures.[129] In 2002, a different group of researchers reported that medication errors occurred on a daily basis in one out of every five properly prescribed doses in a typical hospital with 300 beds.[130]

Australian research[131] has revealed still more startling figures, which can be explained by the more clearly defined definition of 'adverse event' that was used, and by its more flexible methodology. For the purposes of this study, an adverse event was defined as 'an unintended injury or complication which results in disability, death or prolonged hospital stay, and is caused by healthcare management'. Unlike the US studies, the Australian researchers included injuries that were discovered after the study period, but had occurred within it. Other aspects of the research design were very similar to the Harvard Medical Study, and 14,179 patient records were reviewed from a total of 28 acute care hospitals in 1992 in New South Wales and South Australia. Researchers found adverse events occurring in 16.6 per cent of admissions, of which 51 per cent were thought to have been 'highly preventable'. Permanent disability was sustained in 13.7 per cent of the adverse events and 4.9 per cent of patients died. An early study[132] based on observational methods had been conducted in the 1960s, and had found that there was a 20 per cent rate of injury from adverse events. This was followed by a similar study in

---

126   See Baker, T., op. cit., at p 29.

127   Institute of Medicine, Committee on Quality of Healthcare in America, 'To Err is Human: Building a Safer Health System' (National Academy Press, Washington, DC, 2000).

128   See Clement, J., McDonald, M.D., Weiner, M., Sui, L. and Hui, A., 'Deaths Due to Medical Errors are Exaggerated in Institute of Medicine Report', (2000) JAMA 93–95.

129   Health Grades Quality Study, 'Patient Safety in American Hospitals', Colorado, Health Grades Inc, 2004.

130   Barker, K.N., Flynn, E.A., Pepper, G.A., Bates, D.W. and Mikeal, R.L., 'Medication Errors Observed in 36 Healthcare Facilities', *Archives of Internal Medicine* (2002) 162:16: 1897–1903.

131   Wilson, R. McL., Runicman, W.B., Gibberd, R.W., Harrison, B.T., Newby, L. and Hamilton, J.D., 'Australian Quality in Healthcare Study' (1995) *Medical Journal of Australia* 458–71.

132   Schimmel, 1964, cited Baker, op. cit., at p 34.

the 1980s,[133] which revealed a 36 per cent rate of errors, many of which were described as 'very serious'.

Observational studies were carried out by a research team in Chicago at a large teaching hospital in 1989–90 over nine months.[134] This was an extremely thorough and intensive exercise conducted by four specially-trained researchers, who noted what staff said to one another in discussion of adverse events, including whether there was someone to blame and whether the patient suffered injury as a result. Records and incident report forms, patients' charts and complaints were analysed, and the researchers discovered that mistakes were made on almost 50 per cent of patients, with 20 per cent seriously injured or dying as a result.

Table 12 International patient safety incidents*

Country	Year	Number of case records	% adverse incidents	% prevented
California	1975	20,864	4.6	0.78
NY State	1984	30,121	3.8	0.95
Utah–Colorado	1992	14,700	2.9	0.93
Australia	1993	14,179	16.6	8.4
England	1999	1,014	10.8	5.2
Denmark	2000	1,097	9.0	3.6
New Zealand	2000	1,326	10.7	4.3
Canada	2002	3,745	7.5	2.8
France	2002	778	14.5	4.0
Average		9,758	8.9	3.4

* Figure produced by Graham Neale, cited in *International Best Practice Guide*, Ambicentres, 3 November 2005.

Continued investigations in the UK

It must be accepted that research findings drawn from other jurisdictions may not be helpful in the UK context, although they are interesting in their own right.[135] Within the UK, strenuous efforts are now being made to identify the number and causes of errors in healthcare. These efforts take a number of forms, and studies have been, and are still being, undertaken for a range of different purposes. One such is the NHS Staff Survey (excluding GPs who are independent contractors) in England, conducted by the Healthcare Commission in 2005, which recorded that the number of staff in the survey who said

133 Steel *et al.*, 1981, cited Baker, T, op. cit., at p 34.
134 Danzon *et al.*, 1981, cited Baker, T., op. cit., at p 34.
135 Walshe, K., 'International Comparisons of the Quality of Healthcare: What Do They Tell Us?', *Quality and Safety in Healthcare* 2003, 12: 4–5.

they had witnessed at least one error, near miss or incident in the previous month had dropped from 44 per cent in 2004 to 40 per cent in 2005.[136]

The NHS is anxious to learn from industry how mistakes can be avoided, and it is believed that it is only possible to ensure safety in a climate of honesty, which cannot exist unless a blame-free environment is created. For that reason, the Government established the NPSA, some of whose work is described above. This organisation encourages reporting and investigation of incidents, collects information about the number and frequency of errors in the NHS, and seeks to create a safer system for patients. Part of this exercise has involved changing the terminology used to describe errors, so that adverse events and clinical errors are now called 'patient safety incidents'. The UK Government has acknowledged that in the healthcare setting there is a large potential for error:

> Modern healthcare is delivered in a complex, pressured environment, often involving the care of vulnerable, seriously ill patients. More than any other industry in which risks occur, healthcare is reliant on people, more often than machines, to make the decisions, exercise the judgement and execute the techniques which will determine the outcome for a patient.[137]

Since large-scale studies have been undertaken on the subject of patient safety, the average figure that has consistently been quoted for medical error by most Western countries in which research has been undertaken is around 10 per cent. This figure has been arrived at by using similar, but not identical, methodologies, so it is not safe to draw comparisons. Research in the UK, undertaken for 'An Organisation with a Memory', indicated that 10 per cent of hospital in-patient episodes led to harmful adverse events, 50 per cent of which were preventable, which resulted in a direct cost to the NHS of £250,000 for 1,011 admissions in additional days in hospital.[138] In the retrospective study it was estimated that adverse incidents cause permanent impairment in 6 per cent of cases and contributed to death in 8 per cent of cases.

The NPSA states,[139] on an analysis of 96 per cent of acute, ambulance and mental health trusts, that in 2003–04, there were 885,832 recorded patient safety incidents and near misses, and the results of a survey conducted by the National Audit Office show that in 2004–05 there were 974,000 reported events, though the figures for both years could have been higher because few of the trusts included hospital-acquired infections in their statistics.[140] The number of avoidable deaths reported by the 169 NHS Trusts able to do so for the year 2004–05 was 2,181, but the NPSA and National Audit Office

---

136 Healthcare Commission Staff Survey Report 2005.
137 'Making Amends', op. cit., p 7.
138 'An Organisation with a Memory', DOH 2000.
139 National Audit Office Report HC 456, 2005–06.
140 It has been estimated that if hospital acquired infections had been included the figure would have been closer to 300,000 incidents of which 30 per cent could have been prevented.

acknowledge that there is serious under-reporting of deaths and serious incidents. For the half year to June 2006, the number of reported incidents collected by the NPSA was 788,188.

Although the methodology employed to investigate the perceptions of a sample of the population about their own experiences of medical care must be questionable, a survey undertaken by MORI in 2002 revealed that of the sample of the public interviewed, almost 5 per cent reported that they had suffered illness, injury or impairment which they thought had been caused by medical care, and of that group 30 per cent believed that the incident had resulted in permanent damage to their health. Fifty-five per cent of the reported events had occurred in NHS hospitals, and 25 per cent in the primary care setting.[141]

Of the incidents that were recorded, the most commonly occurring were injuries to patients due to falls, medication errors, problems with equipment and records, and communication failure.[142] It is believed that there is still considerable under-reporting of incidents, but more accurate figures should be obtained if and when the culture is changed, as the Government hopes, to allow for 'blame-free' incident reporting. The NPSA recommends that Trusts target those groups of staff who are less likely to report incidents and that they should develop strategies to encourage reporting of near misses. Trusts are required to report accurately all relevant incidents to the NPSA, but other bodies also demand reporting,[143] and this can cause confusion as to the accuracy of data. The NPSA therefore requests all Trusts, which have not already done so, to move to electronic reporting systems as soon as possible, and it is hoped that the Department of Health will consider a single entry point for all reporting, while still allowing data to be captured by several different organisations.[144]

The National Audit Office collects and publicises data on accidents in hospitals in the UK, but the information it gathers is still not sufficiently reliable to offer meaningful statistical evidence on patient safety.[145]

Reporting systems are still fairly rudimentary, and not all Trusts yet use electronic reporting methods. It is likely that, through the frailty of human nature, there will always be the potential for under-reporting. However, Sir Liam Donaldson, Chief Medical Officer for England, warned publicly in 2006 that the risk of dying in hospital as a result of medical error is one in 300, citing clinical misjudgements or errors as the cause. He estimated that the odds of dying as a result of being treated in hospital are 33,000 times higher than those of dying in an air crash:

---

141   Research carried out by MORI commissioned for the DOH and reported in 'Making Amends', op. cit., p 33.
142   'An Organisation with a Memory', op. cit., fn 100.
143   E.g. the MHRA, the Healthcare Commission, the GMC, the Coroner, to name but a few.
144   'A Safer Place for Patients', op. cit., 8.
145   NHSLA Report and Accounts 2006, HC 1179, HMSO, London, 2006, 10–11.

In an airline industry, the evidence … from scheduled airlines is the risk of death is one in 10m. If you go into a hospital in the developed world, the risk of death from a medical error is one in 300.[146]

Attempts at understanding the causes of accidents are also still at an early stage of development, with healthcare falling well behind industry in this respect[147] both nationally and internationally.

However, since data on this has been collected, the estimated number of incidents in the UK has remained roughly stable, so it may be possible to assume that a similar pattern of incidents existed in the earlier decades of the NHS and exists in the private healthcare setting. The NPSA is continuing to collect and analyse information from a wide range of sources and from several reporting systems about medical error in the NHS, and this will provide invaluable information on which to base safety measures in the future. Some of the UK research has included general practice, but most of the studies which have been undertaken to date into adverse events focus on acute hospitals, and if mental health hospitals and care homes were to be included it is possible that a higher percentage of adverse events would be found.

Only recently has there been comprehensive monitoring of hospital acquired infections, and if these are to be classified as adverse events, the figures are likely to rise still more dramatically. In a speech to publicise the next stage of a campaign by the World Health Organisation (WHO) to improve patient safety by reducing the number of hospital-acquired infections, Sir Liam Donaldson stated that between 5 per cent and 10 per cent of patients admitted to modern hospitals in the developed world acquire one or more infections, and at least 5,000 deaths can be directly attributed to healthcare-acquired infections in England every year. Figures for 2004 show that 1,300 people died after contracting *Clostridium difficile* in hospital, and 360 of died as a result of infection by MRSA acquired in hospitals in England alone.[148] For the year 2005–06, the figures indicate that MRSA and *Clostridium difficile* are thought to have been responsible for more than 5,400 deaths in 2005, a rise since the previous year, according to figures published by the Office for National Statistics (ONS) in 2007. Once this additional information is added to the overall picture of medical error, a fuller appreciation can be developed of the true extent of medical mistakes in the UK. Further confusion about errors in healthcare was generated by the general panic on the release of data relating to hospital infections published in February and March 2007. Figures published by the Office for National Statistics in 2007 displayed an apparent

---

146 Speech to publicise the World Health Organisation's campaign to improve cleanliness in hospitals, reporter in the *Guardian*, December 2006.

147 The airline industry was referred to in 'An Organisation with a Memory' by the Department of Health as model for reporting and analysing adverse events.

148 Op. cit., fn 60.

disparity with those published by the Health Protection Agency (HPA) in March 2007, and only on closer examination was it to be revealed that one set of figures related to the general incidence of infections and the other to deaths caused by them.

In Scotland, there is evidence that almost one-fifth of patients who died soon after undergoing surgery in 2005 had developed an infection in hospital, though figures issued by the Scottish Audit of Surgical Mortality showed an improvement on the number of similar deaths in 2004. Of those who died after surgery, 7.6 per cent had MRSA, a total of 126 patients. The report acknowledged that almost half of patients in whom MRSA was identified already had the infection when they were admitted to hospital, suggesting that this is a problem which will be difficult to overcome. Although it was thought that many of these claims would not be actionable, a new approach by claimants' lawyers based on breach of statutory duty has altered the position significantly and many more claims can be expected.[149] There were 301,894 surgical admissions to Scottish hospitals in 2005, and of those 240,302 patients underwent surgery. Of the patients who died after surgery, 17.8 per cent had developed a hospital-acquired infection compared with 23.5 per cent of people who died after surgery in 2004. The number of patients in hospital who died after surgical care amounted to 4,147, and 3,698 deaths were audited. The vast majority of deaths, 3,132, occurred in cases where the patient had been admitted as an emergency.[150] MRSA is giving rise to a large number of out-of-court settlements as lawyers are becoming aware of novel approaches to claiming which are more likely to succeed than traditional negligence claims.[151]

Despite the fact that more claims are made for negligent medical treatment than in the early years of the NHS, it is only possible to speculate as to whether there is more negligence in the course of treatment and care than there was in the past. Perhaps this is the case, in view of the fact that doctors are now trained differently – and some would argue, less rigorously. It is possible, however, that the introduction of new technologies has created the potential for more incidents of equipment failure and related problems, and it is not insignificant that this has been identified as one of the main causes of patient safety incidents.[152] Nevertheless, although the introduction of new equipment might be blamed for adverse incidents, human error, coupled with complex related stresses,[153] is still likely to be the most frequent cause. Allyson Pollock[154] suggests convincingly that as a result of money currently being spent on defending claims which could have been used to care for patients:

---

149   See Chapter 3.
150   Scottish Audit of Surgical Mortality 2006. See Harpwood, V., *Medical Law Monitor*, December 2006, p 7.
151   See Harpwood, V., ibid.
152   Ibid., p 1.
153   See 'Understanding Performance Difficulties in Doctors', NCCA Report 2004.
154   Pollock, A., *NHS plc: The Privatisation of our Healthcare* (Verso, London, 2004) p 52.

Failures of care are caused by faster throughput, overstretched staff, smaller ratios of highly trained to less-trained to less-trained staff, etc. And it is a cost the NHS budget will have to continue to cover, even though the increasing fragmentation of the NHS, and the inclusion of for-profit surgical service providers of unknown quality, has the potential to drive it up further still.

The National Clinical Assessment Authority[155] investigated the factors prevalent among NHS staff, other than clinical incompetence, that might be responsible for patient safety incidents. Among the causes identified are physical ill-health and disability, mental ill-health, including alcoholism and drug addiction, cognitive impairment, such as memory loss, tiredness, personal characteristics, weaknesses in education and training, and organisational and cultural failings.[156] As Paul Fenn pointed out in a *BMJ* editorial in 2004:[157]

> Much more work remains to be carried out on the causes of patient safety incidents in order to progress cultural and organisational changes and assessment and monitoring of individuals before measures can be fully implemented to bring about a safer environment for patients. Whatever system of patient compensation is in place, it will inevitably generate information of potential benefit for risk management purposes. The way this information is fed back to those best placed to take remedial action at the organisational level is crucial. Counting the cost of clinical negligence is important: making it count is even more so.

The balance of claims against errors

It is extremely likely that there are many more errors in healthcare than there are claims for negligence. It is difficult to make a precise calculation of the percentage of claims in relation to the number of errors because of the complexity of the available data,[158] but this should become possible once the NPSA begins to provide reliable data about errors which can be compared with such information as is available on the number of claims. Many errors are trivial and claimants might not consider it worthwhile to claim. Many do not give rise to injury, and would not be the subject of litigation (i.e. are not actionable), since under the law of negligence damage must be suffered

---

155 Now subsumed into the National Patient Safety Agency.
156 NCAA, 'Understanding Performance Difficulties in Doctors' (DOH, November 2004).
157 Paul Fenn, *Professor of Insurance Studies*, Centre for Risk and Insurance Studies, Nottingham University Business School, Nottingham NG8 1BB.
158 See above 'Sources of Data'.

before a claimant will succeed.[159] Although some incidents might be regarded as very serious near misses, potential claimants are best advised to make a complaint if they have suffered no damage. Taking what should be the best available source of information on the number of medical errors in England, the National Audit Office, it can be seen that the estimated number of medical errors in the year 2004–05 was 97,000.[160] In the same year, the CRU figures reveal that there were only 7,196 claims – though it is impossible to know how many of the errors were actionable, and many of those claims would have arisen from errors that occurred in previous years. Thus, the rate of claiming was only 7.4 per cent. The situation is exacerbated by the fact that one single error might have the potential to lead to a large number of claims; for example, if one technician makes an error processing blood products with the result that many patients become ill.

The balance of claims against complaints

NHS organisations have an obligation to record and report all complaints made by patients and their representatives. The number of complaints made in the NHS is recorded quarterly and on an annual basis, and the Healthcare Commission has reported that in England the number of complaints referred to it for Independent Review has trebled since it was given the role of dealing with that stage in the complaints in 2004. It reported that it is called up to resolve around 8 per cent of complaints (8,500 a year), and that 54 per cent of complaints relate to the way NHS staff treat death, with around a quarter of complaints concerning patient safety. Other common complaints concern lost notes, mixed wards, and hospital-acquired infections.[161]

At the time of writing it has only been possible to obtain figures up to the year 2003–04. Many complaints are made about matters that would not be actionable. A large number are made orally, and are usually resolved at an early stage at a local level. These concern matters such as poor quality food, dirty lavatories, rudeness, staffing problems and so on, for which patients would not qualify for compensation even if they were to claim. However, there are some complaints that could theoretically give rise to claims and it may be of interest, though not particularly useful, to consider the number of written claims against the picture presented by the number of complaints. Taking the position in England, then, the level of written complaints remains remarkably stable. In 2002–03 there were 133,867 written complaints; in

---

159 That is not necessarily the case in trespass to the person, and it is at least arguable in the light of *Chester v Afshar* [2004] UKHL 41 that there is no need to prove damage to succeed in a claim for negligent failure to communicate adequate details of risks and side-effects of proposed treatment.

160 It has been estimated that if hospital-acquired infections had been included, the figure would have been closer to 300,000 incidents of which 30 per cent could have been prevented.

161 See *Guardian*, 1 February 2007.

2003–04, there were 133,469 written complaints; and in 2004–05, the number of written complaints was 133,820. It can be seen that there were many more written complaints than there were claims in England in the relevant years.

The culture of under-compensation

The reasons for the disparity between errors and claims are difficult to identify. It is not clear why so few people who have been injured as a result of errors in healthcare decide to make claims. Hazel Genn conducted some excellent empirical research into the motivation of accident victims generally, and found that many people were reluctant to use lawyers because they had no faith in the legal process.[162] In 2003, a Department of Health research study[163] concluded that only around one-third of people who brought claims against the NHS said they wanted financial support, and that most wanted an explanation and an apology. A study conducted by Mulcahy et al., which reported in 2000,[164] also found that the majority of people who claim are not as interested in receiving financial compensation as they are in an acknowledgment of errors, an apology, and an assurance that a similar fate will not befall others. Similar findings were made at the time of the Wilson Inquiry, and these led to the establishing of the present complaints system in the NHS. However, the research results are counter-intuitive and some cynicism must be brought to bear on those who could as easily receive explanations, assurances, and apologies through the NHS Complaints System but prefer to bring claims.

In the case of road traffic accidents, the percentage of people who claimed damages in 2004–05[165] was considerably higher than for medical accidents, though the data for medical claims, as has been seen, is very difficult to analyse. According to the CRU, the number of claims arising out of traffic accidents was 40,892 for 2003–04 when there were 313,309 people killed or injured in traffic accidents. This discrepancy can possibly be explained by the likelihood that those injured in road accidents are well aware that they could have a claim and that an insurance company will pay their compensation. In the healthcare context it is possible that many patients never discover that their injuries are attributable to medical error; sick and dispirited patients may lack the will and energy to pursue claims; many potential claimants fall outside the scope of financial support offered by the Legal Services Commission; some may not be accepted for no-win, no-fee legal support; some (often older) patients

162   Genn, H., *Paths to Justice: What Do People Think About Going to Law* (Hart Publishing, Oxford, 1999).
163   CMO 2003:75.
164   Mulcahy, L., Selwood, M., Summerfield, M. and Nettern, A., 'Mediating Medical Negligence Claims' (University of London, London, 1999).
165   United Nations Economic Commission for Europe Road Transport Division.

may be too deferential to doctors to question their treatment; some families are prepared to support sick and injured people, preferring not to undergo the long and uncertain process of litigation. All of this is speculation and requires careful research before any of the suggestions can be verified. Nor are there any definitive answers as to why people decide to bring claims. It has been suggested that the reason for some may be financial necessity, and for others the need to receive an explanation.[166]

Although the figures are heartening for the NHS, they do suggest that there is a strong culture of under-compensation in the UK, which is counter-intuitive in the light of media claims. This matter is discussed in Chapter 3. Consideration of the complexity of the litigation process may be helpful at this point.

The litigation process

The procedure for claiming compensation for damage caused by clinical negligence is complex, long and tortuous. In order to succeed, the claimant must satisfy three hurdles: by establishing the existence of a duty of care owed to him or her by the defendant; breach of that duty; and damage flowing from the breach. If the claimant is able to overcome these first three hurdles, the amount of compensation payable must then be quantified. At any stage in the three levels of this process there may be a dispute between the parties, but the most common disputes involve breach of duty and/or proof of causation. It is necessary for the claimant to find evidence as to the facts of what errors may have been made and their effect on his health.

Proof of breach of duty involves establishing that a healthcare professional was at fault. Although this implies moral culpability of some kind, the reality of the fault principle is that the standard of care is objectively assessed. The term 'negligence' suggests unintentional or inadvertent error, and what the claimant is required to prove in a clinical negligence claim against a healthcare professional is professional behaviour or decision-making which does not match the standard required by law. A large body of substantive law has developed covering the many points that arise in the course of a claim, and some of this is discussed at various points in this book. However, it is also instructive to examine the procedures that must be followed when a claim is made. A highly simplified version of that process is outlined here,[167] and for a detailed explanation it is necessary to examine the Civil Procedure Rules and the Protocol for the Resolution of Clinical Negligence Disputes.

The claimant may or may not first use the complaints procedure (though this might have resulted in refusal to investigate the complaint if the complaints

---

166   Symon, A., 'Causation: A Medico-Legal Problem', *British Journal of Midwifery* (4 June 1998) 6(6): 395–97.
167   For an in-depth description and analysis see Lewis, C., *Clinical Negligence: A Practical Guide* (6th edn, Tottel Publishing, 2006).

handler discovered that there is an intention to bring a claim), after which he or she instructs a solicitor. The complexities of clinical negligence claims make it virtually impossible for a litigant to proceed in person. Solicitors and counsel follow strict procedural rules and adhere to protocols established for the purpose of streamlining litigation for clinical negligence and keeping the costs as low as possible.[168] The question of how the claim is to be funded will be considered and the claimant will be advised on this matter. The defence will also instruct a solicitor as soon as the defendant Trust or the NHSLA have notice of the fact that the claimant has done likewise. The claimant's solicitor makes a request for the claimant's medical records, and at this point the defence usually commissions independent expert advice. If, on examining the records, the claimant's solicitor takes the view that there may be a valid reason for claiming damages, an independent expert will be found for the claimant. However, many claims are withdrawn at this stage, as the patient's medical records frequently reveal that the patient's perception of what has happened does not accord with the legal concept of negligence, and the claim is doomed to failure.

If the claim is to continue, the expert will advise on the standard of healthcare given to the claimant, and whether the claimant suffered a preventable injury as a result of sub-standard treatment or care. The claimant's solicitor then writes a Letter of Claim setting out the alleged facts, any criticisms of the patient's management, details of the injury sustained by the patient, and an approximate valuation of the claim. The defendants' solicitor will answer with a Letter of Response, stating the matters that are agreed and those that are not agreed, with reasons. The claimant's solicitor then formalises the Letter of Claim by stating the Particulars of Claim. A formal Defence is then entered. Witness statements are exchanged at that point, and both parties become aware of what the witnesses to the alleged events would say under oath. Expert evidence is exchanged and detailed schedules of financial losses and expenses suffered by the claimant and future expenses associated with the injury are drafted. Counter schedules are usually produced challenging the extent of the losses. These schedules can be very long and complex documents. Offers to settle the claim may be made at any time, and the claimant will be advised on whether or not to accept.

If the case is not settled out of court, a trial will follow. The entire process is carried out under the control of the court, established by the Civil Procedure Rules and the Protocol for the Resolution of Clinical Negligence Disputes (which encourages the use of alternatives to litigation), and strict timetables must be adhered to. At any stage there may be an offer in writing under Part 36 of the Civil Procedure Rules to settle. The decision of the judge may be followed by the appeals process.

---

168   Civil Procedure Rules 1998 and Protocol: see flow-chart in the pre-action protocol for the resolution of clinical negligence disputes.

Conclusion: reflections on the figures

It has been observed that 'the figures regarding tort liability are very slippery'.[169] In the course of this chapter it will have become apparent that this is something of an understatement in the context of clinical negligence, as it is difficult to identify reliable, definitive evidence concerning the number of medical errors and claims occurring throughout the UK as a whole. Even if reliable data were available, as is always the case in analysing all statistics, great care is required when attempting to draw conclusions from figures. At present it is virtually impossible to make sense of the data on the volume of claims, the levels of compensation and the number of errors in the healthcare context. Official sources are riddled with contradictory information and there is a lack of clarity throughout the information system. To take but one example – the following statement appears on the NHSLA website:

> Currently, fewer than 2% of the cases handled by the NHSLA are litigated in court, with the remainder being settled out of court or abandoned by the claimant. Where appropriate we participate in mediation or other forms of alternative dispute resolution (ADR).

Yet in the NHSLA Annual Report and Accounts, the position is stated as follows:

> Only 4% of cases on average go to court, including settlements on behalf of minors. 96% are settled by means of ADR.

Although it is likely that the figures supplied by the CRU relating to the number of clinical negligence claims are the most reliable, it is not a simple matter to relate this to the data held for each separate devolved area of the UK by the organisations handling claims (and the CRU itself recognises that claims involving clinical negligence may be difficult for them to deal with because it is necessary to determine how much of the benefit was paid as a result of the negligence – not an easy task when the claimant may well have been ill before the event and afterwards from other causes).[170] Nor can the figures be readily understood in the context of the number of errors made annually in healthcare. Many of the sources of information about the level of compensation are complex and are less useful. Data is collected for different purposes by different organisations, and such statistics as are gathered are used

---

169   Wier, T., 'A Compensation Culture?' Talk to the David Hume Institute on 30 October 2003.
170   DWP, 'CRU Guidance for Advisors, Complex Cases', 2007.

in support of a range of different propositions. Even the definitions of errors and the methods by which they are measured differ in different jurisdictions, in different institutions and at different times. Although there may be valid explanations for the complexity of the data, the plethora of statistical sources and differing approaches to analysing them must surely enable those who have an interest in concealing information to do so. The single fair indicator from the mélange of figures is that the average value of each claim is rising as the total amount being paid in compensation is rising significantly. The expected effect in the long term must be a very serious cause for concern.

The Government is aware that there is little public confidence in statistics, following a major project undertaken in 2004 to assess public confidence in British Official Statistics, which concluded that there was a perception that the Government manipulates statistics[171] for its own purposes. In order to build public confidence in the data relating to errors and claims in health-care, it is essential to establish an institution, which will collect information centrally for the entire UK, and present it openly in a coherent form that is easily understood. It is very difficult to engage in evaluation of the clinical negligence litigation system unless there is reliable data on which to make meaningful conclusions.[172] This is not the case in other spheres of public life. In housing, for example, clear statistics are available for the whole of the UK about the state of the housing stock, which can be accessed with ease.[173]

The only clear conclusions that can be drawn at present are that the available data on claims is unhelpful; the definition of error is unhelpful in the context of evaluating the proportion of actionable errors resulting in claims; the number of errors far outweighs the number of claims for a variety of reasons, some legal or procedural and some simply based on the vicissitudes of human nature; the process of litigation is complex and costly; and it is likely that many deserving claimants are never compensated for their suffering. Although some illuminating empirical work has already been carried out, the reasons why relatively few claims are being made are certainly worthy of investigating further.[174] In any event, the high incidence of adverse events means that a comprehensive system of no-fault compensation for medical injuries is out of the question.

171 Kelly, M., 'Public Confidence in British Statistics', 28 February 2005, London, United Kingdom Office for National Statistics.
172 See Dewes, D., Duff, D. and Trebilcock, M., *Exploring the Domain of Accident Law: Taking the Facts Seriously* (Oxford University Press, Oxford 1996).
173 See e.g. the English Housing Condition Survey, January 2007.
174 See Genn, H., *Paths to Justice: What Do People Think About Going to Law?* (Hart Publishing, Oxford, 1999).

Chapter 2

Reasons for the increase in claims

Who is to blame?

Introduction

Many ideas have been developed in the course of speculation about the rising level of claims against healthcare organisations. There has been much conjecture about, but little research[1] into, the causes of the increase in the number of legal claims for accidents and illness generally in the UK since the mid-twentieth century. This chapter explores some of the possibilities and what some commentators claim to be myths perpetrated over recent years about the underlying reasons for increased litigation. Among the potential causes in the healthcare context is the intense media interest in stories about human suffering and the scandals of medical malpractice. The received wisdom, prevalent among non-lawyers, is that the UK is following the US experience,[2] which has shown spiraling litigation for many years, fuelled by media coverage. Human psychology may also have a place in the jigsaw.[3] However, this is too simplistic a view, as the legal system in the US lends itself more readily to a high volume of claims and to excessively high awards of compensation.[4]

Other possible factors are the increased expectations of patients that their treatment will be successful; greater complexity in diagnostic and therapeutic procedures; the development of new medical technologies that allow greater potential for error; publicity given to high awards of damages that

---

1   Probably the most useful source of information based on research is to be found in Harris, D., MacLean, M., Glenn, H., Lloyd-Bostock, S. and Fenn, P., *Compensation and Support for Illness and Injury* (Oxford University Press, Oxford, 1984).

2   In fact, the statistics reveal that personal injury compensation payments amounted to only 0.6 per cent of GDP in the UK, one the lowest figures in the civilised world. In the US, the figure was 1.9 per cent of GDP. See 'Better Regulation Task Force Report Better Routes to Redress', May 2004, p 16.

3   Vincent, C., Young, M. and Phillips, A., 'Why Do People Sue Doctors? A Study of Patients and Relatives Taking Legal Action', *Obstetrical & Gynecological Survey* 50(2): 103–05, February 1995.

4   Sage, W. and Rogan, K., *Medical Malpractice and the US Health Care System* (Cambridge University Press, Cambridge, 2006).

may encourage people to bring claims if they believe that they could have victims of clinical negligence; a changed relationship between doctors and patients[5] that could well have resulted in a less deferential attitude on the part of patients; and factors involved in the developing NHS itself, such as the introduction of the new complaints system in 1996. In the legal context, changes in the litigation system towards the end of the twentieth century reduced the practical obstacles for claimants, as funding for claims became more readily available and more specialised solicitors were better qualified to advertise and advise on clinical negligence claims. The legal profession may have played a significant role in prompting a rise in the number of claims, along with 'ambulance chasers' and 'claims farmers', who have led to more claims being initiated.[6]

Reflections on the causes of the rise in claims

In the later years of the twentieth century the quality of healthcare became an issue for more public debate, assisted by incursions of the mass media into UK households through television, radio, and newspapers, and inspired by documentary television programmes highlighting incidents of medical malpractice. As early as 1974 it had been suggested that the NHS should be prepared to acknowledge and accept greater responsibility on a public level for its policies and errors, and to welcome more open discussion.[7]

Malpractice scandals, medical stories, and the role of the media

A catalyst for changed attitudes lay in Ian Kennedy's Reith Lectures in 1980,[8] through which he generated a movement towards greater patient involvement in decisions about their healthcare. In 1991 the first Patients Charter[9] was introduced. This raised patients' expectations about the quality of services and led to criticisms of the NHS if it proved unable to deliver on some of its promises. One of the commitments in the Patients Charter was that all patients had the right to have their complaints investigated and to receive a full and prompt written reply – a promise that led many to seek information about problems with their treatment.

5   See Giesen, D., 'Medical Malpractice and the Judicial Function in Comparative Perspective', *Medical Law International* 1(1): 3–16 at p 4.
6   But see Lewis, R., Morris, A. and Oliphant, K., 'Tort Personal Injury Claims Statistics: Is There are Compensation Culture in the United Kingdom?' (2006) *Torts Law Journal* 14(2): 158; republished (2006) *Insurance Research and Practice* 21(2): 5–14, in which the authors cast doubt upon the significance of the introduction of advertising by solicitors and CFAs as a cause, at least in recent years.
7   Klein, R., 'Accountability In the Health Service', *Political Quarterly* 1974.
8   Kennedy, I., *The Unmasking of Medicine* (George Allen & Unwin, London, 1981).
9   An off-shoot of the Citizens Charter introduced on the initiative of John Major in 1991.

Medical malpractice scandals have recently been highly publicised, and it is possible that they could have fuelled speculation that many more people were injured by the negligent, or indeed deliberate, acts of doctors than had previously been thought possible, with the result that more people are prepared to question their treatment in the courts. The Bristol scandal and the subsequent inquiry and report on paediatric heart surgery in Bristol reviewing the deaths and injuries suffered by children in Bristol Royal Infirmary,[10] followed by the Alderhey and Shipman Inquiries, highlighted shortcomings in the NHS that would have been unthinkable in its early years. A large number of claims were made as a result of these scandals, most being settled out of court, and the public was alerted to the possibility that many more cases of malpractice exist than ever come to light. As has been pointed out by Merry and McCall Smith:[11]

> The desire to blame leads to official inquiries and in many cases to legal proceedings. In many parts of the world, this has gone hand in hand with a marked increase in medical litigation, reflecting public concern over the level of iatrogenic harm.

The healthcare professions have been subjected to numerous criticisms in the course of these inquiries. Sir Ian Kennedy's criticisms in the Bristol Inquiry Report focused on poor organisation, failure of communication, and lack of leadership. The report of the Shipman Inquiry, chaired by Dame Janet Smith,[12] was very critical of the General Medical Council (GMC), the body responsible for regulating doctors. Harold Shipman was convicted of 15 murders in 2000, but the inquiry concluded that he had probably killed at least 200 more patients during his career. The following damning comment castigating the healthcare professions was made in a national newspaper by a solicitor who represented the families of many of Shipman's victims:

> Blunders, loopholes, shortcomings and cover-ups were exposed by Dame Janet Smith's public inquiry. ... Doctors have become accustomed to believing that they deserve privileged treatment.[13]

The coverage of these and other medical stories, such as the media-generated MMR vaccine scare, and the doubts planted in the mind of the public about the reliability of expert witnesses, have generated more publicity than it is

---

10   Learning from Bristol: Report of the Public Inquiry into Children's Heart Surgery at the Bristol Royal Infirmary 1984–95, www.bristol-inquiry.org.uk/final_report.index.htm
11   Merry, A. and McCall Smith, A., *Errors, Medicine and the Law* (Cambridge University Press, Cambridge, 2001) p 1.
12   www.the-shipman-inquiry.org.uk/5r
13   Alexander, A., 'Where is the political will to save us from bad doctors?' *Guardian*, 19 April 2005.

possible to mention here, and the trend does not abate. One recent example is the attention given by the media to the Health and Safety legislation which was used against the NHS as a means of expressing public disapproval of a Trust which failed to supervise two junior doctors whose gross negligence resulted in the death of a patient.[14]

The increasing size of compensation awards is a source of endless fascination for the media and this is one factor that the Office of Fair Trading blamed for the rise in the number of claims since the 1980s.[15] The role of the media in reporting medical malpractice stories is explored more fully in Chapter 4.

Legal procedural change

Throughout the last decades of the twentieth century, it had been recognised that the litigation system in the UK was costly and inefficient to the extent that it could not be relied upon to deliver justice.[16] Claimants in clinical negligence cases were acknowledged to be in a substantially weaker position than defendants, who were often 'repeat players' within the system and could afford to pay top-class experienced lawyers to handle claims against them, and many claimants in personal injury cases gave up easily or were under-compensated.[17] Defendants were in possession of most of the factual evidence, such as patients' records and inside knowledge of events which often occurred when the claimant was unconscious, anaesthetised, weakened by illness or otherwise unaware of what was happening.

In 1996, under the auspices of Lord Woolf, following a detailed investigation of the civil litigation system undertaken throughout England and Wales, a radical report was produced,[18] which resulted in what became known as the Woolf Reforms, a series of major procedural reforms including new protocols for the conduct of the pre-trial process. A significant comment in the Report was that 'the civil justice system was failing most conspicuously to meet the needs of litigants' in clinical negligence cases.[19] The Civil Procedure Rules 1998 (CPR), which cover civil litigation in the County Court and High Court, have now been implemented, and by April 2007 had been subject to 44 amendments, allowing the Rules, in theory, to keep pace with substantive legal developments and social and procedural requirements.

---

14   See e.g., the extensive coverage on BBC News, 11 April 2006.
15   Analysis of Current Problems in the UK Liability Insurance Market (OFT, London, 2003).
16   Royal Commission on Civil Litigation and Compensation for Personal Injury, *Report of the Royal Commission on Civil Liability and Compensation for Personal Injury*, Cmnd 7045, 1978, London, HMSO.
17   Harris, D., MacLean, M., Glenn, H., Lloyd-Bostock, S. and Fenn, P., *Compensation and Support for Illness and Injury* (Oxford University Press, Oxford, 1984).
18   Lord Woolf, 'Access to Justice: Final Report to the Lord Chancellor on the Civil Justice System in England and Wales'.
19   Ibid., para 2.

The Clinical Disputes Forum was established in 1997 as a means of bringing together medical and legal professionals with a view to pooling expertise and ensuring greater efficiency in handling cases involving clinical negligence (previously known as medical negligence). This body devised the Protocol for the Resolution of Clinical Negligence Disputes, which sits alongside the Rules and aims to encourage good practice in clinical negligence proceedings by creating a climate of openness and reducing the previous mistrust in healthcare disputes. The Protocol is an interesting example of cooperation between the professions, and it advocates the settling of disputes without going to court through alternative dispute resolution and the use of the complaints system.

Since the implementation of the CPR, judges have greater control than previously over the progress of litigation, and many more claims are settled out of court because financial pressures are brought to bear on those who pursue claims or defend them unnecessarily. Expert witnesses are also under stronger control, and their duties are set out clearly in the Rules.[20] According to figures released by the NHSLA for England, 96 per cent of the cases that it handles are settled out of court through a range of methods of 'alternative dispute resolution'. From its own analysis of clinical claims that it handled, the NHSLA over a ten-year period, found that 38 per cent of claims that had been initiated were abandoned by the claimant, 43 per cent were settled out of court, 4 per cent were settled in court, and these were mostly court approvals of negotiated settlements, and at that time 15 per cent remained outstanding. Fewer than 50 clinical negligence cases a year were contested in court.[21]

Since the CPR encourages early settlements, it is possible that victims of clinical negligence have been encouraged to bring claims by lawyers who are aware that it is considerably less expensive for NHS organisations to settle smaller claims out of court, albeit for lower sums of compensation, than to allow claims to proceed to trial, with the attendant risk of costs penalties if the value of the claim exceeds that of the costs. The decision as to whether to offer to settle or proceed to trial has become the province of claims and complaints managers in NHS Trusts, in cooperation with legal advisors from the NHSLA or equivalent. There are some cases, of course, in which it is ultimately necessary to defend claims in the longer term interests of the NHS, even though the least expensive option would have been to settle the claim at an early stage. An example given by Baroness Hale in her article on the subject of the compensation culture is *Ward v Commissioner of Police for the Metropolis*[22] in which a claim was made by the patient against the police and a hospital in connection with his detention under s 135 of the Mental Health

20   CPR, Part 35.
21   NHSLA Annual Report 2006.
22   *Ward v Commissioner of Police for the Metropolis and St Helier NHS Trust* [2005] UKHL 32, cited by Baroness Hale in 'What's Wrong with the Compensation Culture', *Clinical Risk*, 2007; 13: 60–64.

Act 1983. Although the hospital made a decision on commercial grounds not to defend the case, its managers were later persuaded to resist the claim in the interests of longer term financial savings. That case is exceptional. Healthcare professionals at the centre of disputes have little input into decisions about the progress of the defence. This can be a cause of bewilderment and dissatisfaction for them, and indeed is arguably a breach of their rights under Art. 6 of the European Convention on Human Rights 1950.[23] The result of all these developments could well have been dissatisfaction among healthcare professionals.

The role of lawyers

Writing in 1999, Ferudi suggested that the growing compensation culture could be explained by ever-watchful and enterprising lawyers, who, anxious to increase their business, have presented arguments over the years that enhanced the scope of liability and were accepted by the courts.[24] The response of lawyers to that criticism was that they were simply offering their clients access to rights created by law, and that the most effective means of preventing litigation was for public sector bodies in particular to take care to prevent accidents, and not to waste taxpayers' money by fighting every case to the bitter end.

Within the adversarial legal system operating in the UK, many of the initiatives for developing the common law emanate from the lawyers who prepare and present cases to the courts. It is lawyers who suggest to judges the possibility of developing new avenues of compensation or expanding existing means of compensating claimants. Not only has this activity resulted in the increased value of awards, but the ingenuity of specialist lawyers has also meant that new avenues for bringing claims have been successfully explored. This is discussed in more detail later in this chapter in relation to the expansion by the courts of liability in tort. To take but one example, it has recently been predicted that a deluge of claims by patients infected with MRSA can be expected, because lawyers are beginning to realise that the most appropriate cause of action in such cases lies within the regulations governing the control of hazardous substances (the COSSH Regulations) which form part of the health and safety regime introduced towards the end of the twentieth century. It can be difficult to establish causation and attribute blame in negligence claims involving hospital infections because it is seldom known precisely when a person becomes infected, so there have been few successful claims or settlements for injuries caused by MRSA or other infections, and none has involved an admission of liability.

It is believed that the new approach, relying on the traditional clinical negligence claim, coupled with a claim for breach of statutory duty, will improve the

---

23   The right to a fair trial.
24   Ferudi, F., 'Courting Mistrust – The Hidden Growth of a Culture of Litigation in Britain' Centre for Policy Studies, April 1999.

prospects of success for claimants. Under the COSHH (Control of Substances Harmful to Health) regulations, employers must control exposure of their employees and visitors to hazardous substances, and it is at least arguable that MRSA falls within this statutory definition, as the regulations cover biological agents such as bacteria and other micro-organisms.[25] A significant advantage of bringing a claim for breach of statutory duty based on the COSHH Regulations is that the burden is on defendants to prove they are meeting the statutory requirements. The handful of claims based on this new approach is being settled out of court, as defendants' insurers wish to avoid publicising the fact that this is a fertile ground for litigation. Leading firms of solicitors, including Irwin Mitchell, Anthony Collins and Hugh James, report that they are now handling a significant number of MRSA cases in which COSHH is cited. The NHSLA and the DoH have refused to comment on the issue. In December 2004, according to the *Daily Telegraph*,[26] two prominent personal injury firms of solicitors reported that they had taken instructions from 70 patients, and one was receiving as many as six new inquiries each week. In the whole of 2000–01, the last period for which statistics are available, only 45 cases were pursued under the basic law of negligence. As public awareness grows, more claims can be expected, and more are likely to be successful if the new approach is adopted.

The impact of legal advertising

Since the mid-1980s it has been possible for lawyers to advertise for clients, and this has led to greater specialisation among firms of solicitors.[27] It is now necessary for solicitors to demonstrate their competence to practise in the field of clinical negligence in order to obtain certification of competence for legal aid purposes that they are capable of providing an efficient service to clients wishing to claim against the NHS. Only around 1 per cent of UK solicitors are franchised to apply for public funding of a clinical negligence case, and to become a Law Society panel, member solicitors are required to submit a detailed application giving information about their ability and experience, and outlining the resources available within the firm for handling clinical negligence claims. Among an impressive list of areas of the competence required are the investigation of potential claims, drafting of documents to be used in court by experts and by counsel, research of legal and medical issues, assessment of potential damages payments, and knowledge of complaints and clinical procedures.

Like doctors, solicitors are required to update their knowledge and skills on a regular basis. The result of these professional developments is that there are now highly competent specialist firms able to offer competent advice to

25   Harpwood, V., *Medical Law Monitor*, December 2006, p 7.
26   9 December 2004, p 15.
27   For the most recent guidance, see Law Society Code of Conduct 2007.

clients wishing to bring claims for clinical negligence. Better networking among lawyers has enabled them to increase their knowledge and skills in claims handling. Where large numbers of potential claimants are connected to a particular source of illness or injury, this networking affords claimants access to more efficient means of initiating claims and better understanding of the issues involved through well-publicised information. The process of advertising has proved beneficial for claimants since they are able more easily to identify the firms specialising in personal injury and clinical negligence claims.

The concept of 'claims farming' is not new. Solicitors have for some years placed advertisements in hospitals, on notice boards and illuminated signs, and this has been a source of revenue for NHS Trusts, which are required to balance their books.[28] As is the case in virtually all business environments, solicitors and claims management companies are in competition for clients and need to advertise for business. Lord Falconer, in a speech made in 2005,[29] blamed aggressive advertising by claims farmers and solicitors for fuelling what he described as the 'have a go' culture that has developed in the UK. There has indeed been a growing industry of organisations that have been variously described, among other things, as 'accident management companies', and 'claims farmers'. These bodies actively seek out potential claimants and offer to handle claims for them on a 'no-win, no-fee' (contingency fee) basis. They organise medical experts and other expert witnesses and offer services to solicitors by providing funding for the initial expenses involved in making claims. Although some of these companies have now foundered amid considerable criticism, their very existence helped to raise the profile of personal injury litigation and encourages people to claim.

Restating views expressed in the Better Regulation Task Force Report in 2004[30] (which denied the existence of a litigation crisis), Lord Falconer said:

> There is no place for advertising that raises false hopes of unrealistic or unachievable personal injury compensation awards. Practices which basically encourage people to 'have a go' are distasteful and pernicious. In our response to the BRTF report new guidance has already been issued about personal injury claims advertising in hospitals. It may be that such guidance needs to go to other public bodies.

While there may be some truth in the notion that the persuasive powers of advertisers encourage people to bring claims against the NHS, there are few professionals who are willing to pursue doubtful claims under a no-win, no-fee arrangement.[31]

28   Pollock, A., *NHS plc: The Privatisation of Our Healthcare* (Verso, London, 2004).
29   22 March 2005 at the Jolly Hotel London at a Health and Safety Executive event.
30   Report of the Better Regulation Task Force: Compensation Culture: Exploding the Urban Myth, May 2004.
31   See Lewis *et al.*, fn 2, supra.

Despite the improvements introduced into the litigation system as a result of the CPR, the Better Regulation Task Force Report in 2004,[32] which was critical of the culture that generated what it regarded as misplaced fears in potential defendants, blamed the increase in claims on a combination of factors closely connected with the legal system and management of claims:

> The current perceived problems can be put down to a combination of factors, all of which occurred at around the same time. These were the abolition of legal aid for most personal injury claims; the introduction of conditional fee arrangements; the appearance and growth of claims management companies.

Although legal aid was abolished in 1999 for claimants in general personal injury claims, it was retained for clinical negligence claimants. However, the threshold for qualifying is very low, and only the less financially secure can benefit from state funded financial assistance to support clinical negligence claims. Many people under the age of 18 years fall into this category, and the system has facilitated the bringing of claims on behalf of infants suffering injuries at birth. Research indicates that in 1999, children's claims amounted to approximately one-quarter of all legally aided clinical negligence applications.[33]

The potential dangers of conditional fees were recognised by the Courts long before they were introduced in the UK. Lord Scarman in the *Sidaway*[34] case said:

> The danger of defensive medicine developing in this country clearly exists – though the absence of the lawyer's 'contingency fee' (a percentage of the damages for him as his fee if he wins the case but nothing if he loses) may make it more remote.

Contingency Fee Arrangements (CFAs) are now available for potential claimants who do not qualify for assistance from the Legal Services Commission. These arrangements for funding claims were given official blessing by the Government to fill the gap left by the withdrawal of legal aid from personal injury and other litigation. A few years later, blaming the reduced availability of legal aid and the introduction of CFAs for the accelerating compensation culture, Skidmore *et al.*,[35] describe the development as 'a great illustration of unintended consequences when great ideas go wrong'. Not sur-

---

32   Report of the Better Regulation Force, 'Better Routes to Redress' May 2004 at p 12.
33   Masson, J. and Orchard, A., 'Children and Civil Litigation, Research Report Department of Constitutional Affairs 10/99' (1999) cited in 318 *BMJ* 830 (27 March).
34   *Sidaway v Board of Governors of Bethlem Royal Hospital* [1985] AC 871, at p 873.
35   Skidmore, P., Chapman, J. and Miller, P., *The Long Game: How Regulators and Companies Can Both Win* (Demos, London, 2003).

prisingly, unwilling to blame its own intitiative, the Government does not accept this analysis, stating in 2006:[36]

> The Government welcomes the [Select] Committee's conclusion that CFAs have not directly caused the perception of the compensation culture.

Despite such protestations, a direct effect of the introduction of CFAs was a change in the market for claiming, with the growth of claims farmers and consequent advertising, which one survey found had stimulated demand for compensation services.[37] Popularly known as 'no-win, no-fee' agreements, CFAs have the advantage of enabling people who could not otherwise afford to finance claims for clinical negligence, to litigate. Following a series of cases[38] in which these arrangements were questioned by the courts, the regulations governing them were simplified and modified in 2005. Basically, the system operates in such a way as to allow those who do not qualify for legal aid to bring claims for clinical negligence by only paying the lawyers involved if the claim is successful. The claimant may still have to pay the costs of the successful party and any other costs, such as court fees or the fees for medical reports, known as disbursements. Insurance known as 'after-the-event insurance' can be arranged to cover this risk, and claimants may have to pay the insurance premium, though such premiums may be recoverable if a costs order is made against the opposing party. According to Baroness Hale, the Government's decision to charge the uplift and the claimant's insurance premium costs to the defendant had been the cause of higher settlement costs[39] and resulting 'turf wars'.[40] The success fees available to lawyers representing clients under CFAs are now more modest. Nevertheless, this has not always been the case, and there are a large number of claims management organisations, somewhere around 500,[41] in the business of encouraging people to bring personal injury claims, which were heavily criticised by the Better Regulation Task Force and by Tony Blair in his speech on the Compensation Culture:[42]

---

36   Government's Response to the Constitutional Affairs Select Committee Reports: Compensation Culture and Compensation Culture NHS Redress Bill, para 17, Cmint 6784, April 2006.
37   In a Norwich Union Survey in 2004 23 per cent of those who were asked thought that no-win, no-fee advertisements on television were raising people's expectations of what they were entitled to, Norwich Union, 18 May 2004.
38   *Callery v Grey* [2002] UKHL 28.
39   Baroness Hale of Richmond, 'What's Wrong with the Compensation Culture' (2007) *Clinical Risk* 13: 60–64.
40   *Callery v Grey* [2002] UKHL 28.
41   The Government estimated in 2006 that as a starting point, 500 claims management businesses would seek to register under Regulations made pursuant to the Compensation Act 2006, Department for Constitutional Affairs, Compensation Act 2006, Regulation of Claims Management Services, Consultation on the Application Form for Seeking Authorisation, 2006.
42   Reported in the *Guardian*, 26 May 2005.

Claims farmers capture claims and typically sell them on to solicitors, sometimes having already signed the consumer up for a package of insurance. Many claims farmers indulge in high pressure selling and aggressive marketing including approaching vulnerable people in public places, such as hospitals. Many consumers have been misled into making claims where their cases are weak.

Claims management companies have been criticised by a wide a range of sources, and the emphasis has been on their advertising techniques and tendency to pressurise people into initiating claims. Widespread mis-selling of insurance products and high pressure sales tactics, accompanied by misleading advertising, were some of the failings identified by Citizens' Advice in 2004.[43] More recently, evidence has emerged that solicitors are beginning to compete with claims management companies for their place in the market by advertising free i-pods, 110 per cent compensation or cash rewards of £300 to claimants whose cases they agree to handle. This practice, frowned upon by Lord Falconer, is to enable solicitors in an ever more competitive marketplace to avoid paying introduction fees to claims management companies.[44] However, there is evidence, following investigative journalism,[45] that many claims management companies are in financial difficulty. The infamous Claims Direct collapsed in July 2002 and The Accident Group went into administration in May 2003. The Compensation Act 2006 has introduced a regime for regulating these organisations,[46] including they way in which they advertise, but some commentators believe that their influence is less damaging than has been supposed, since although they might well have encouraged people to make inquiries about the possibility of claiming, no solicitors would be prepared to take on cases that had little or no hope of succeeding.[47]

AvMA welcomed CFAs for clinical negligence claims in cases where the claimant does not qualify for legal aid, as in their view these arrangements do improve access to justice. However, according to AvMA, they *'have not yet come near to meeting their full potential'*, and the vast majority of clinical negligence claims are still brought by those who are eligible for legal aid.[48] The main reason identified by AvMA for this is the prohibitive cost of after-the-event insurance policies to cover the claimant against the costs of the defence, should they lose. Nevertheless, taking into account the average time lag between date of incident and date of claim, the peak in the number of clinical negligence

43   'No Win, No Fee, No Chance', op. cit.
44   As described on BBC Radio 4 programme 'You and Yours', 27 March 2007.
45   See BBC programme: 25 years of Watchdog.
46   www.claimsregulation.gov.uk provides comprehensive information on the requirements.
47   See e.g., Radio 4, 'You and Yours', 7 March 2007.
48   This is supported by the work of Fenn, P. *et al.*, 'The Finding of Personal Injury Litigation', para 5.2 Making Amends: A Report by the Chief Medical Officer (2003), 71.

claims is easily attributable to CFA's. This was not taken into account by Lewis *et al.* when they researched this matter (see Chapter 1, fn 23).

Writing in 2004, around the time that the Government was planning to take action to regulate claims farmers, Jon Robbins summed up the position as follows:[49]

> Conditional fees are a fiendishly complicated way to achieve a very simple effect. Lawyers can be surprisingly poor communicators and the increasing number of intermediaries in the form of claims management companies interposing themselves between the client and lawyer further muddies the waters.

He added that:

> some clients ended up with nothing or very little, as excessive insurance premiums could wipe out any compensation.

He stated:

> Many people sign up for what are in reality insurance products without any clear understanding of what they mean. One early study of CFAs revealed that of 40 clients interviewed, only one understood how his claim was funded.

The potential for more claims within the developing NHS

The establishment and later development of the NHS is itself a reason why claims have increased in number. The NHS has long been recognised as one of the great British institutions, despite the many problems that it has faced from almost the very beginning. Planning for the NHS commenced even before the Second World War had ended, and both main political parties had developed schemes for comprehensive healthcare provision, though the plan that succeeded was of course that of the Labour Government elected at the end of the Second World War.[50] The NHS has been accorded an important place in every party manifesto since then.

Before the NHS, free access to medical care was available to most people in regular full-time employment, but not usually to their families. Most hospitals charged for treatment, but poorer members of the community could sometimes be reimbursed. Psychiatric patients were incarcerated in institutions, frequently for life, and elderly people who could not care for themselves, and whose relatives were unable or unwilling to help, were housed in former workhouses called Public Assistance Institutions.

---

49   Robbins, J., *Affordable Law* (Jon Robbins, Lawpack Publishing, 2004).
50   For a detailed history of the NHS, see Rivett, G., *From Cradle to Grave: Fifty Years of the NHS* (King's Fund ISBN 1 85717 148 9).

The new framework for comprehensive healthcare provision offered by Aneurin Bevan involved the nationalisation of municipal and voluntary hospitals and the establishment of a network of regional hospitals. The NHS was funded almost entirely from central taxation, and anyone resident in the UK, even on a temporary basis, was eligible for NHS treatment and referral to hospital if necessary. The most important, and at the time the most attractive element of the early NHS, was that care was free at the point of delivery.[51] Following the austerity of the Second World War, the general public received the compre-hensive new health service with gratitude and there were few ordinary consumers of healthcare who questioned the success of the NHS, which had brought about improvements in the general health of the population through mass screening and vaccination programmes, improved maternity and child health services, free primary care, free hospital treatment, and (initially) free prescriptions. The pattern of enhanced healthcare provision continued throughout the rest of the twentieth century with a hospital build-ing programme, greatly improved facilities, technology and equipment, and the introduction of advanced medical treatments and techniques.[52] Grateful patients were reluctant to sue doctors in this environment at a time when there was a strong culture of deference to professional people.

As ever greater demands were made on the system from many different directions, complaints and criticisms began to emerge. An important feature of the NHS is that almost from its inception, it has been changing and developing.[53] The rate of change has increased exponentially in recent years, with successive Governments making political capital out of commitment to improving the NHS,[54] but the most far-reaching changes have taken place since 1990. A White Paper published in 1989, entitled 'Working for Patients', became law in the NHS and Community Care Act 1990, and was recognised almost universally as a thinly disguised attempt to deal with the problems of funding the increasingly expensive provision of healthcare, of growing waiting lists and increased demand. The new framework was meant to be designed to meet the needs of consumers of healthcare and to defeat the pre-existing bureaucracy by the introduction of an internal market and greater competition,[55] which could, theoretically at least, reduce costs and improve the quality of services.

---

51 Prescription charges were introduced later.
52 See Webster, C., 'Fifty Years of the NHS', (1998) *History Today*, www.historytoday.com, July.
53 See Salter B., 'The Politics of Change in the Health Service' (Macmillan, London, 1998).
54 Tony Blair gave as the main reason for his refusing to leave office until the last possible minute his commitment to seeing though further changes to the NHS, in an interview with John Humphries on the BBC Radio 4 Today programme, 2 February 2007.
55 The Conservative Government was anxious to prevent anti-competitive practices in all walks of life, including healthcare, which it considered to be against the public interest. See Monopolies and Mergers Commission 'Services of Medical Practitioners: A Report on

Under the modified system that was introduced during the 1990s, Central Government continued to fund the NHS out of taxes, but self-governing NHS Trusts were created to run and manage hospitals, ambulance services, and other healthcare services. Health Authorities, and larger (fund-holding) GP practices purchased services for their patients within this increasingly competitive market. This approach formed the basis for the healthcare system in the twenty-first century, though there have been further modifications. It was within this context that it became apparent that the time was ripe for the introduction of a new complaints system. In 1996, following a report and recommendations made by the NHS Complaints Review Committee (the Wilson Committee), the new complaints system was established.

When New Labour entered office in the late 1990s the NHS structure was rapidly ostensibly rationalised to correct flaws that had emerged in the previous system, though many of the changes were superficial window-dressing. The rhetoric of the new Government referred to the need to sweep away bureaucratic and wasteful competition within the NHS, but in reality there were few very radical changes to the structure that had been established by the previous Government[56] apart from the abolition of GP fund-holding in the internal market and its replacement with another system involving commissioning of healthcare services. There have been attempts to distance responsibility for healthcare decisions from the Central Government Department of Health by the establishment of organisations such as NICE, the Healthcare Commission, and more recently, Foundation Trusts.

Rapid developments have also ensued since the 1990s in the general environment in which medicine was practised. New technologies and better education of the public, with increasing numbers of people entering higher education, meant that patients became more demanding and less deferential; cost-effectiveness in treatment became increasingly important and ethical issues arising in the context of healthcare were discussed more openly. Health promotion, environmental issues, screening programmes and the prevention of illness began to be given priority, as the relationship between income, occupation and health became clearer. Key areas of concern, such as heart disease, diabetes, and cancer were targeted for funding and research. Fewer people were admitted to hospital for long-term care, and day surgery became more widespread as medical technology became more advanced. Despite this, waiting lists for treatment continued to grow and there was constant speculation about the state of NHS funding. Since the year 2000, the problems involved in funding and streamlining the NHS have continued to generate

the Supply of Services of Registered Medical Practitioners in relation to Restrictions on Advertising', Cmnd 582, 1989, London, HMSO.

56 See White Paper, 'The New NHS: Modern, Dependable', Cmnd 3807, 1997, London, HMSO.

further reforms,[57] many of which focus on the need to improve patient safety, though a large underlying element in that agenda is an attempt to reduce claims for clinical negligence by injured patients.

Healthcare is now treated much as a large commercial enterprise,[58] in that context patients are more willing to claim against it. It is unsurprising that hospitals have adopted the habit of allowing solicitors and claims management firms to advertise their services on hospital premises – for a fee. This practice was criticised by the Better Regulation Task Force in its Report of May 2004, and is now regulated by the Compensation Act 2006, but such advertisements as the one it cites: 'Did the doctor or nurse make you worse? If so you can claim compensation'[59] could well have been responsible in part for encouraging patients to pursue claims against healthcare organisations.

Giving patients a voice: patient-centred care and the NHS complaints system

One of the objectives of the reforms of the 1990s was to achieve 'patient-centred care' within the NHS.[60] That phrase has been repeated on many occasions since the reorganisation of the NHS, and is still[61] highlighted as a major policy objective.[62] On the initiative of the then Prime Minister, John Major, the Patients Charter, reflecting the notion of the 'empowered client' in the related Citizens Charter, encouraged patients to complain by asserting their so-called 'rights' in health care. One such right, which was not enshrined in the law at that time, though that position has since changed,[63] was stated to be the right to full information about the treatment that patients receive.

The role of law in recent years has been to facilitate both choice and freedom of expression in the context of healthcare,[64] and part of this process has been the legal reshaping of the complaints procedures to allow patients to express their concerns more effectively. It is no coincidence that the report of The Wilson Committee, published in 1994, was entitled 'Being Heard', nor that one of the objectives of the Committee was to facilitate the process of complaining by providing individual patients with an effective voice. Latterly,

---

57   The NHS Plan, DoH, 2000.
58   See Pollock, A., *NHS plc* (Verso, London, 2004).
59   Better Regulation Force Report, May 2004, op. cit., p 25.
60   The White Paper 'Working For Patients' published in 1989 emphasises this focus.
61   See e.g., Creating a Patient-led NHS – Delivering the NHS Improvement Plan 2005, www.dh.uk/asset
62   The NHS Plan published in 2000 claims to be designed to give patients 'more power, protection and choice than ever before'.
63   *Chester v Afshar* [2004] UKHL.
64   See Longley, D., *Healthcare Constitutions* (Cavendish Publishing, 1996).

initiatives have been introduced to offer the public the opportunity to express their views on a much larger scale,[65] and to involve patients in healthcare by introducing public and patient involvement initiatives, but the individual consumer of healthcare services with personal grievances was the first priority in the early years of the last decade. It was therefore necessary to facilitate the process of complaining and to rationalise the complex systems for making complaints that existed at the end of the 1980s.

The introduction of a new NHS Complaints System in 1996 may have led some people to use the complaints system as a means of obtaining information on which to base claims. General awareness of the possibility of bringing claims may have encouraged patients to complain.

It has been suggested that many claims arise as a result of the claimant's desire to understand precisely what went wrong, to identify who was responsible for the errors that led to the injury, and to receive an apology and an assurance that the event will not be repeated. The theoretical need for an explanation, which was one of the driving forces behind the recommendations that led to the development in 1996 of the new and comprehensive complaints system,[66] can be satisfied in a variety of ways. The complaints system, revised in 2003, does provide a means by which explanations can be obtained, but there is evidence that once a claimant has received information about the errors that were made, even coupled with a carefully framed apology, a claim may follow hard upon it, so that the complaints system becomes a route to litigation.[67] Common sense might suggest that the raising of patients' awareness of the possibility that some error may have been made in the course of their treatment would lead some to seek financial recompense.

The rise of medical consumerism: a rights-based culture in healthcare

One factor in the rise in claims against doctors could well be increased claims consciousness of, and different views about the vicissitudes of life, as Ham *et al.* comment:[68]

> One possibility is that there may have been a cultural change towards greater insistence on the right to be compensated for life's misfortunes and an increased distrust of the assumed skill and honour of professionals.

65   National Survey of NHS Patients, DoH 2000.
66   'Being Heard', Report of the NHS Complaints Review Committee 1994, para 111.2.3.
67   See Harpwood, V., *NHS Complaints: A Route to Litigation.*
68   Ham, C., Dingwall, R., Fenn, P. and Harris, D., 'Medical Negligence, Compensation and Accountability (1988)', cited in Kennedy, I., and Grubb, A., *Medical Law* (3rd edn, Butterworths, London, 2000), p 541.

It is not only claims against healthcare professionals that have risen in number in recent years. Similar trends have been identified in relation to all other professions.[69]

Healthcare complaints and litigation should be viewed in the context of a changing pattern of attitudes towards claims in society as a whole, because although many of those who complain insist that they are not interested in receiving compensation, complaints are nevertheless closely related to more positive forms of compensation-seeking. Information which might not otherwise be readily available can be obtained relatively easily in the course of the investigation of a complaint, and there is anecdotal evidence, at least, that some solicitors advise clients to complain before they decide whether a viable claim exists.

An important factor in the challenge to medical paternalism has been the rise of the consumer movement in the healthcare context. 'Consumerism' in terms of a 'movement' developed on a large scale after the Second World War in Western commercial culture. Collective action by consumer groups, coupled with the operation of competition and market forces,[70] succeeded in introducing significant changes in the law to afford greater protection to consumers of goods and services.[71] The Consumers Association was formed in 1957, followed by the National Consumer Council in 1975. Consumers collectively demanded greater freedom of choice, and fuller information and protection from unconscionable contract terms. The classical contract in which both parties had equal bargaining power had been discredited by the 1970s.[72] By that time, most commentators recognised that in practice contracts were complex transactions, the terms of which were frequently dictated by Government intervention as well as by the contracting parties themselves.[73] It was accepted that without statutory intervention, consumers as individuals had minimal power and little choice, being forced to accept terms imposed upon them by more powerful contracting parties. Within the public sector, individual consumers were afforded greater respect and the benefit of more competitive services and wider choices by sweeping statutory innovations brought about during the later Thatcher era, when a variety of public services,[74] including

69   Ibid., at p 542.
70   See Cranston, R., *Consumers and the Law* (Weidenfeld & Nicolson, London, 1984, p 10, et seq.).
71   E.g. The Unfair Contract Terms Act 1977, The Supply of Goods and Services Act 1982.
72   Macaulay, S., 'An Empirical View Of Contract' (1985) *Wisconsin Law Review*, 465; Beale, H. and Dugdale, T., 1975, 'Contracts Between Businessmen: Planning and the Use of Contracual Remedies', 2 *British Journal of Law and Society* 45; Atiyah, P.S., *An Introduction to the Law of Contract* (4th edn, Clarenden Press, Oxford, 1989).
73   See Friedman, W., *Law In A Changing Society* (Stevens, London, 1975).
74   See Walsh, K., Deakin, N., Spurgeon, P., Smith, P. and Thomas, N., 'Contracts for Public Services: A Comparative Perspective,' in 'Contract and Economic Organisation', Campbell, D. and Vincent Jones, P. (eds) Socio-Legal Studies Series, Dartmouth 1995.

healthcare, was privatised and 'marketised,' becoming more competitive as a consequence.

In 1948, the establishing of the NHS paved the way for a change in the attitude of patients towards doctors. As healthcare was provided free at the point of delivery, over time this came to be accepted as the 'right' of every individual, leading in more recent years to claims on that very basis.[75] The state provision of healthcare and the development of programmes of public health led to regular open debate in Parliament on healthcare issues. In these early decades of the NHS, claims were unusual, not least because the likelihood of succeeding in a claim was small, partly because of judicial attitudes, but also because there were many practical obstacles for patients in bringing claims. Judges were protective of doctors, as is evidenced by Lord Denning's famous comparison between the medical negligence claim and 'a dagger at the doctor's back'[76] and by less-well publicised statements such as that cited by Charles Lewis in *Medical Negligence a Practical Guide*,[77] where he quotes J. Finnemore in 1953 as follows:

> There is considerable onus on the court to see that persons do not easily obtain damages simply because some medical or surgical mistake is made.[78]

It was difficult for patients in the early days to find competent lawyers to assist them, and experts willing to testify for them. There were problems in obtaining evidence because healthcare staff tended to close ranks to protect one another, patients' records were difficult to obtain, and were frequently incomplete or misleading. The procedural rules applicable at the time did not allow for early disclosure of witness statements. It is not surprising that the Pearson Commission Report in 1978[79] found that there were in the region of 500 medical negligence claims annually that were being referred to legal advisors, but that 305 were abandoned and only 175 were successful, a success rate in medical negligence claims of only 35 per cent.[80] This was compared with a success rate of around 60–80 per cent for other negligence claims reaching court. These figures might have been predictable, but what is more interesting is that even though the trend is towards increased claims

---

75   *Rogers v Swindon NHS Primary Care Trust* [2006] EWCA Civ 392.
76   *Hatcher v Black, The Times*, 2 July 1954.
77   (6th edn, 2006, Tottel Publishing, West Sussex), p 3.
78   *Elder v Greenwich and Deptford Hospital Management Committee, The Times*, 7 March 1953.
79   Royal Commission on Civil Liability and Compensation for Personal Injury Cmnd 7054, 1978, London, HMSO.
80   *Report of the Royal Commission on Civil Liability and Compensation for Personal Injury*, ibid., vol 2, paras 237–39.

for medical accidents in England, after the introduction of the CPR and the Protocol for the Resolution of Clinical Negligence Claims, the success rate for claimants is currently only 76 per cent.[81]

Despite the general trends towards consumerism and the formation of Community Health Councils (now abolished in England) as early as 1974[82] to provide a voice for patients, it was not until the 1990s that patients were given fuller recognition as consumers of healthcare and were offered easier access to more information about their medical condition and treatment. During this decade the structure and nature of healthcare delivery within the NHS was fundamentally refashioned, and greater emphasis was placed on local decision-making within the new market regime. Implicit in the notion that patients should be accorded greater consideration, as consumers, were some important assumptions. First, that patients should have access to more information about the state of the NHS, their medical conditions and treatments that might be available to them; second, that they should have an effective voice to make their grievances known; and third, that their complaints should be addressed, dealt with to their satisfaction, and information should be fed back into the system to bring about improvements in the quality of care.

Further developments have since emerged from Europe, including the Nice Charter of Fundamental Rights, which was to become part of the "European Constitution" – though of course this has yet to be adopted by the UK. The European Charter of Patients' Rights[83] forms the basis of the declaration of 14 patients' rights currently considered to be at risk; namely the right to preventive measures, access, information, consent, free choice, privacy and confidentiality, respect for patients' time, observance of quality standards, safety, innovation, avoidance of unnecessary suffering and pain, personalised treatment, the right to complain, and the right to receive compensation. The Charter develops these themes, and the preamble to this document states that it is intended to 'reinforce the degree of protection of patients' rights in the difference national contexts and can be a tool for the harmonisation of national health systems'.

As has been seen, it became easier for claimants to obtain practical help and advice towards the end of the twentieth century as a result of an improved market for legal services, resulting in the growth of specialist firms of solicitors which had gradually developed expertise in handling claims for clinical negligence. After changes in professional rules permitted solicitors to advertise their services, members of the general public became more aware of the possibility of obtaining compensation for medical injuries. In addition, the charitable organisation originally called Action for Victims of Medical Accidents, now entitled Action against Medical Accidents, was responsible for improving the

---

81   National Audit Office, 'Handling Clinical Negligence Claims in England', 2005.
82   These organisations.
83   Basis document, Rome 2002.

prospects of patients injured in the course of receiving healthcare. However, of those patients bringing claims, in many instances because they were supported by public funds, a relatively small percentage were successful.[84]

The emergence of a general rights-based culture in society is reinforced by the Human Rights Act 1998, which came into force on 2 October 2000, giving force to the European Convention on Human Rights in UK law. This is yet another factor that drives the courts to recognise individual entitlement and encourages recourse to law.[85]

A new doctor–patient relationship?

Clinical autonomy and the consequent respect for the medical profession has a long history. Under the model favoured by the Ancient Greeks, the doctor was perceived as a beneficent paternalist, possessing a highly valued body of specialist skills and knowledge denied to outsiders. Constraints on the doctor's freedom of decision-making were those imposed by the medical profession itself in accordance with its own code of ethics and its own perception of what were the best interests of patients.[86]

The psychology of the doctor–patient relationship is a subject worthy of a monograph in its own right, and there has been much speculation about the emotional power with which specialised knowledge and skill imbues the doctor in the eyes of a sick and vulnerable patient.[87] There was a long-held assumption that external regulation of any kind was unacceptable to the medical profession, and that self-regulation would be carried out competently. Patients were not entitled, as a matter of course, to information about their medical conditions and treatment. Few had challenged this paradigm which reflected and reinforced respect for, and deference to, doctors, and regulation of the medical profession remained in the hands of the GMC and the Royal Colleges even after the NHS was established in 1948. Even the most senior judges demonstrated a deference to the medical profession which some would argue was unjustifiable in their interpretation and development of the defence established in the Bolam case.[88] However, developments during the second half of the twentieth century introduced greater concern for the autonomy of the

---

84   In 1996 Michael Jones cited 25 per cent as the number of clinical negligence claimants who are successful. Jones, M., 'Medical Malpractice In England and Wales – A Postcard from the Edge' (1996) *European Journal Of Health Law* 109.

85   See Cane, P., *Atiyah's Accidents, Compensation and the Law* (7th edn Cambridge University Press, Cambridge, 2006) p 194.

86   Pellagrino, E.D. and Thomasma, D.C., *For the Patients' Good* (New York and Oxford, 1900), p 3.

87   See Lewis, C., *Medical Negligence: A Practical Guide* (6th edn, Tottel Publishing, West Sussex, 2006) p 2.

88   *Bolam v Friern Hospital Management Committee* [1957] 1 WLR 582, [1957] 2 All ER 118 (1957) 1 BMLR 2.

patient, and new attitudes threatened to circumscribe significantly the doctor's traditional and jealously guarded freedom to practise with the minimum of external intervention.[89]

By the end of the twentieth century, following the series of highly publicised medical errors,[90] doctors were no longer treated with the same reverence as had been accorded to them by previous generations. Better educated and more affluent patients demanded respect from their carers, and were prepared to complain more freely and to claim compensation if they were injured as a result of clinical negligence. The old culture of deference to doctors has, it is claimed, been replaced by a new approach, which indicates that many patients are no longer in awe of doctors. According to Lord Woolf this approach has reached the courts, as he commented in 2001:

> Until recently the courts treated the medical profession with excessive deference, but recently the position has changed. In my judgment it has changed for the better.[91]

Lord Woolf attributed the change in attitude, inter alia, to that notion that the courts have become less deferential generally to authority,[92] and that we are moving towards a rights-based society. He concluded that the Human Rights Act has had a significant impact on the development of the law in this respect. He emphasised that recent scandals, citing the Bristol and Alderhey reports, have meant that judicial confidence in healthcare professionals has been undermined. Another factor regarded as important by Lord Woolf was the increase in the number of cases involving ethical complexities, which meant that some cases could not be decided in terms of clinical judgement alone.[93]

Other commentators[94] who have considered the doctor–patient relationship from a sociological perspective, have identified the concept of compliance[95] as key to the earlier deference shown to doctors, placing patients in a pupil-headmaster relationship with their doctors. However, as the same writer explained in 2001:

---

89   For an excellent critical analysis of self regulation in healthcare, see Stacey, M., *Regulating British Medicine: The General Medical Council 1992* (Chichester, Wiley, 1992).
90   Learning from Bristol: the report of the public inquiry into children's heart surgery at the Bristol Royal Infirmary 1984–95 www.bristol-inquiry.org.uk/final_report.index.htm
91   Lord Woolf, 'Are the courts excessively deferential to the medical profession?' (2001) 9 *Medical Law Review* 1.
92   See also Lord Bingham in *Chester v Afshar* [2005] 1 AC 134, see fn 112.
93   Ibid.
94   See Karpf, A., *Doctoring the Media: The Reporting of Health and Medicine* (Routledge, London, 1998).
95   Karpf, A., *Guardian Unlimited* (Friday, 20 July 2001).

The past decade has also seen a profound change in the ways in which we think about medical care. While the demystification of the medical profession is a good thing, there's a danger that we replace the idealisation of doctors with their demonisation. ... What the Kennedy inquiry might ideally help produce is a new kind of implicit contract between doctor and patient: doctors trade in some expectation that patients will deliver themselves uncritically, compliantly, into their care.[96]

In the private healthcare sector a more aggressive consumer rights approach might be expected,[97] but empirical research suggested that within that sector, tensions exist which constrain the relationships between doctors and patients and prevent too strong a shift towards a lack of respect for doctors.

Access to information and enhanced choice

With the creation of the NHS, patients were able to choose their GPs and were given the opportunity to seek a second opinion if the consultant to whom they were referred did not provide then with satisfactory answers to health concerns. In the world of commerce, a concept, which has been belatedly adopted by public sector healthcare organisations, is that of the need to provide information to consumers and users of services. It had been recognised for some time by commercial organisations that only if adequate information is available to consumers will they be able to make rational choices, and in some instances businesses have been forced to make public detailed information about their products and services. The Consumer Protection Charter of the Council of Europe[98] recognises that principle, which, as Ross Cranston observes, can be justified economically because it facilitates competition, 'one of the necessary conditions for which is that consumers possess a high degree of knowledge about products and services in the market'.[99]

In the healthcare context, common sense dictates that before patients can make adequate decisions about their treatment, they need to be provided with information about the treatment and services they receive. For many years after the NHS was established, information was not readily available to patients.

If patients are to be regarded as consumers and treated with dignity, it follows that they should be entitled to detailed information about their medical conditions and prognoses. Many patient organisations began to demand openness and full information about available treatment options, about crucial matters such as the performance and competence of their doctors, about

96   Ibid.
97   Wiles, R., Higgins, J. (1996) 'Doctor–Patient Relationships in the Private Sector: Patients' Perceptions', *Sociology of Health & Illness* 18(3): 341–56.
98   Res. 543, in Eur. Consultative Assembly, 25th Session, Texts Adopted (1973) p 2 C(I).
99   Cranston, R., op. cit., at p 278.

success rates for surgery, and about the state of the NHS in general. It was argued by some commentators that sick, elderly, and otherwise vulnerable people should not be treated in the same way as commercial consumers, and that healthcare should be regarded as a caring profession rather than an industry or commercial enterprise. Nevertheless, the Thatcher reforms had spelled an end to the traditional approach by creating competitive internal markets for healthcare provision[100] and new management structures within the NHS, and by giving a central focus to patients[101] as consumers.

Despite considerable progress in the UK[102] towards establishing rights of access by patients to their medical records through common law developments, statutory provisions,[103] and quasi-statutory intervention,[104] there were by 1990, and still are, despite further reforms, certain circumstances when information about health status can be withheld.[105] It has not been until the very last years of the twentieth century that progress towards greater openness has been furthered in the UK following the implementation of the Human Rights Act 1998.[106]

All of the late twentieth century developments served to further the view that healthcare is a competitive sector, and reinforced the sad fact that in modern times, the ideology of healthcare is the ideology of the market, in which the concept of accountability accompanies official rhetoric about consumer choice. In the commercial world, and in relation to other public services outside the healthcare sector, consumers had become aware of the existence of greater competition and of their ability to exercise their preferences freely. However, in the healthcare setting, the reality was that the individual patients at the start of the 1990s were probably unaware that they had any power to exercise choice. This state of affairs was probably true for patients at the end of the

---

100 See Longley, D., 'Diagnostic Dilemmas: Accountability in the National Health Service' (1990) *Public Law* 527.

101 As is demonstrated by the White Paper that preceded the 1990 legislation was entitled 'Working For Patients'.

102 Other common law jurisdictions have developed different approaches, see e.g., Dickens, B. (1994) *Canadian Bar Review* 234.

103 Data Protection Act 1998; Access to Health Records Act 1990; Access to Medical Reports Act 1988.

104 A Code of Practice on Openness was introduced in the NHS on 1 June 1995, by which patients may request access to medical records and to other information held by NHS bodies.

105 E.g., Data Protection Act 1998 Part IV; also *R v Mid Glamorgan Family Health Services Authority ex p Martin* [1995] 1 All ER 356 CA.

106 The European Convention on Human Rights 1950 Art 8(1) states that every individual has a right to respect for his family life, and in *Gaskin v United Kingdom* this was held to include personal information relating to health. Clearly, the right of access to medical records cannot be absolute, but there is a potential problem if the gatekeepers of records are doctors themselves. In *Gaskin*, where access to information provided in confidence to social services had been sought, it was held that there had been a breach of Art 8, because there was no system of independent review by which access (or its denial), could be monitored, when consent of the person providing the information had not been obtained.

decade, influenced as they probably were by the mass media. Reports dwelt on medical errors resulting in serious injuries to patients, on controversial cases in which individuals were denied the treatment they sought,[107] and on an NHS in which long waiting lists and staff shortages resulted in patients being left on trolleys in draughty corridors, or even worse, outside in ambulances waiting for a bed to be vacated. Although healthcare was locally driven in the internal NHS market established by the 1990 legislation, the individual patient was offered little opportunity to choose anything.

The concept of 'quality' in healthcare

Although the concept of 'Total Quality Management' was first developed in the 1950s, and had been widely adopted in industry in developed countries over the following decades, the idea was applied only slowly to healthcare. The NHS may have escaped rigorous scrutiny because of the traditional deference accorded to doctors by society in general, and despite early attempts to monitor standards of medical practice through self-regulation and the voluntary system of confidential inquiries, patient satisfaction was not a significant factor in quality assurance until the early 1980s.[108] This was despite the fact that in the commercial world, closely related to the notion of quality is the implication that standards should be assessed in the light of the ability of an organisation to satisfy the expectations of its consumers.

The structural reforms of the 1990s initiated new funding regimes and systems of quality management in the NHS through the introduction and evolution of medical and clinical management, which was based on the concept of feeding back information to improve the quality of healthcare.[109] However, it was not until the changes introduced under the Health Act 1999 that the compulsory imposition, monitoring, and enforcing of uniform quality standards throughout the NHS was established. The Care Standards Act 2000 now imposes a similar regime in the private healthcare sector.

At the same time a solution was sought to the funding problem in the NHS by the placing of greater emphasis on value for money by the promotion of cost-effective treatment. Evidence-based clinical guidelines, which had been used with increasing frequency during the early part of the decade, became a central focus for delivering quality care and for ensuring that the same standards applied across the entire NHS. The National Institute for Clinical Excellence, now the National Institute for Health and Clinical Excellence (NICE) began its task of commissioning and disseminating guidelines in key areas of healthcare

---

107   *B v Croydon Health Authority* (1994) 22 BMLR 13.

108   Ahmed, A., *Review and Practice in Medical Care-Steps for Quality Assurance* (George McLaughlan, Nuffield Press, London).

109   Crombie, I.K., Davies, H.T.O., Abraham S.C.S. and Du V. Florey, C., *The Audit Handbook: Improving Healthcare Through Clinical Audit* (John Wiley & Sons, Chichester, 2006).

and of making recommendations to the Government aimed at ensuring that clinically effective and cost-effective treatments are delivered to patients. In any system that places great emphasis on quality and maintaining high standards, risk management is of course of crucial importance, and a rigorous system of risk management has been achieved through the implementation of clinical governance, internal audit, external audit by the NHSLA and the WRP, and through the monitoring of standards of care by the Commission for Health Improvement, now known as the Healthcare Commission. Equivalent bodies have been established in the devolved areas of the UK.[110] The MHRA also has a role in monitoring standards of products, such as blood and medical devices used throughout the NHS. Reporting systems are being established throughout the NHS to ensure that errors are brought to light and dealt with as soon as possible. A crucial aspect of risk management is that mistakes are recorded and action is taken to ensure that they are not repeated. Complaints and claims clearly play an important part in this process and that is one reason for encouraging them. NHS Trusts have clinical governance and risk management committees with an overview of standards in the organisation and a role in ensuring that quality and safety requirements are met.

The role of the courts

Judges are now less supportive of the medical profession than they were during the early days of the NHS. No longer does the sympathetic approach of Lord Denning offer almost guaranteed security to doctors faced with negligence claims.[111] For many years, the rigid application of the *Bolam* defence by the courts enabled doctors to escape liability for negligence if they were able to produce expert evidence to support them in establishing that they had acted in accordance with a practice accepted as proper by a responsible body of medical opinion. Judges were reluctant to choose between two bodies of expert medical opinion, and this approach, established in 1957 by a High Court decision,[112] was endorsed by the House of Lords,[113] creating powerful protection for the medical profession. When the House of Lords modified the *Bolam* test in *Bolitho v City and Hackney Health Authority*[114] to allow greater discretion to judges to reject expert opinion, which they regarded as logically indefensible, there was little prospect that the new approach would result, instantaneously, in dramatic developments. The concept of a 'responsible body of opinion' was more clearly defined, and claimants who might otherwise have been advised not to pursue a matter might now be advised to continue.

110   E.g. Health Inspectorate Wales (HIW).
111   See *Hatcher v Black* (*The Times*, 2 July 1954).
112   *Bolam v Friern Hospital Management Committee* [1957] 1 WLR 582, [1957] 2 All ER 118 (1957) 1 BMLR 2. See Chapter 6 for a fuller account.
113   *Whitehouse v Jordan* [1980] 1 All ER 650.
114   [1997] 4 All ER 771 HL.

Another important development in recent years, following the implementation of the Human Rights Act in 2000, has been the reluctance of judges to strike out claims on the blanket basis that no duty of care is owed, and this has led to an increase in the number of cases going to trial.[115]

Though there have been few cases since 1997 in which a claimant has benefited from the application of the Bolitho test, there may be many which have been settled out of court, and in theory at least, the balance has been redressed in favour of claimants to some extent. The precise effects of Bolitho are impossible to measure, since the reasons for settlements are not publicly recorded, and liability is routinely denied, but there is a possibility that the change has been for the better from the claimant's perspective, and has to some extent encouraged claims. In the area of consent to medical treatment and related claims for negligence, there is no doubt that the law has been adapted to the patient's benefit as a result of the Bolitho approach, and that 'medical paternalism no longer rules'.[116] Successful claims in this area of law are likely to result in further litigation, and lawyers are able to advise clients more positively in the light of the emergent culture in which the focus is on the possibility of demanding redress when errors are made. The Human Rights Act 1998 was implemented on 2 October 2000, and human rights issues are now raised in a range of medical law cases. Although the general public may not be fully aware of the impact of the Human Rights Act, lawyers certainly should be, and it is possible that the Act has had some impact on the accelerating level of claims during the first few years after it became law.

Baroness Hale, in her analysis of the compensation culture, considers the ways in which the courts might have contributed to the rise in claims during her own professional lifetime.[117] The tort of negligence is continuing to evolve and expand to encompass areas which would not have been contemplated 50 years ago. A striking example from medical law is the case of *Chester v Afshar*[118] which goes some way towards establishing a 'new' tort of failing to inform a patient of potential risks and side-effects of treatment without the need to prove injury or damage. Against these developments, however, it is necessary to observe that the judiciary tends to be conservative and that once a new line of negligence liability has been developed, this caution frequently results in a withdrawal from radical positions, so restricting further developments.

---

115   *Osman v UK* (2000) 29 EHRR 245; *Barrett v Enfield* [2001] 2 AC. Although the European Court has withdrawn to some extent from the extreme position in the Osman case, it has been left open as to whether using the duty principle could infringe the claimant's right to an effective remedy in the national courts for breaches of the Convention when the conduct of the defendant also constitutes breach of a Convention right.

116   *Per* Lord Steyn in *Chester v Afshar* [2005] 1 AC 134 at para 16.

117   Baroness Hale of Richmond, 'What's Wrong with the Compensation Culture', *Clinical Risk* (2007) 13: 60–64.

118   [2005] 1 AC 134.

This approach is to be observed in relation to liability for psychiatric injury,[119] wrongful conception,[120] public authority responsibility,[121] economic loss,[122] and even mesothelioma[123] – some of the very areas identified by Baroness Hale in her analysis as illustrative of the expansion of tort liability. Nevertheless, the courts do continue to pursue new possibilities presented to them by ingenious lawyers, such as those identified above in relation to claims for injuries suffered as a result of hospital infections.

Internet access

Internet access has opened new avenues of information to patients about a wide variety of medical conditions and available treatments, and about the possibility of bringing claims. This raises the notion that we are becoming a nation of 'cyberchondriacs'. Reports by the Healthcare Commission on NHS organisations are freely available on line. Guidelines issued to doctors by NICE and other organisations such as Royal Colleges, NHS Trusts, and patient pressure groups are freely available to patients on the internet, and those whose treatment does not meet expectations may attempt to claim damages for negligence if they do not recover from illnesses as well as they had hoped. The number of websites providing information about clinical negligence in the UK is surprising.[124]

Many are sites of firms, journals, solicitors and claims companies offering information about how to claim and where to obtain advice. To take an example at random, a website was found without difficulty which provides advice on the errors that can be made in diagnosing the need to investigate further an abnormal cervical smear. The site lists possible diagnostic and screening errors, provides an online form to complete to apply for no-win, no-fee funding or legal aid. The same site supplies a long list of other potential medical errors.[125]

Increased understanding of types and causes of injury

Even outside the internet, better general knowledge and social awareness[126] of illnesses, injuries and their causes may well have led people to understand their injuries and attribute blame for them more accurately than in the past. This is reflected in some of the claims brought outside the limitation period where claimants have discovered for the first time, after talking to friends,

---

119   *Alcock v Chief Constable of South Yorkshire Police* [1992] 1 AC 310.
120   *McFarlane v Tayside Health Board* [1999] UKHL 50.
121   *JD v East Berkshire Community Health NHS Trust* [2005] UKHL 23.
122   *Adams v Bracknell Forest BC* [2004] UKHL 29.
123   *Barker v Corus* [2006] UKHL 20.
124   A Google search for 'clinical negligence' yielded 681,000 hits.
125   www.hospitalnegligence.co.uk
126   See Lewis *et al.*, op. cit., fn 5, at p 170.

watching television documentaries or noticing advertisements by solicitors, that they are suffering from a condition that can be traced to negligence.[127] For example, the rise in claims for psychiatric injury and hospital-acquired infections could be ascribed to this recently developed social awareness. Information about medical malpractice, patient safety, risk management, consent to treatment and data protection in healthcare can also be obtained with ease. Anecdotal statements from clinicians suggest that many patients are better informed about treatment options, and that increasing numbers of them attend consultations armed with information printed from medical sites. Those who are not given the treatment they demand for themselves and their relatives are now more likely to take their claims to the courts.[128] Unsurprisingly, Lloyd Bostock concluded in the course of their survey of claimants in the Oxford area, that people are more likely to bring claims once they become aware that they might be able to obtain compensation for their injuries.[129]

The increase in claims

It is at least arguable that the increase in claims, which costs the NHS a large amount of money each year, is itself responsible for an upward spiral from which it will be difficult to break free. The inescapable logic is that because claims have increased, less funding is available for patient care. This results in greater expenditure on risk management, more cost-cutting on staff training and safety equipment, creeping privatisation by the contracting out of essential services such as cleaning and laundry, and therefore more mistakes.[130] It is surely no coincidence that, as Allyson Pollock suggests, hospital cleanliness has not been helped by over-reliance on poorly paid contract cleaners with no allegiance to the NHS, as has been confirmed by the Health Protection Agency and the Association of Infection Control Nurses.[131]

Charting the causes by time-line

The changes which may have given rise to the increased level of clinical negligence claims since the 1980s can be understood graphically by examining the time line that appears on the next two pages. It will be immediately observed, allowing for the interval between incident and claim that one of the main triggers appears to be the implementation of conditional fee agreements through the good offices of the Lord Chancellor.

---

127 *Norton v Corus UK Ltd* [2006] EWCA Civ 1630; *A , B & Ors v Nugent Care Society (Formerly Catholic Social Services (Liverpool)* [2006] EWHC 2986 QB.
128 *Re Wyatt* [2005] EWCA Civ 132; *Evans v Amicus and Ors* [2004] EWCA Civ 727.
129 Lloyd Bostock, S., 'Fault and Liability for Accidents: The Accident Victim's Perspective, in Harris, D., MacLean, M., Glenn, H., Lloyd-Bostock, S. and Fenn, P., *Compensation and Support for Illness and Injury* (Oxford University Press, Oxford, 1984).
130 Pollock, A., *NHS plc: The Privatisation of our Healthcare* (Verso, London, 2004).
131 *Health Service Journal* (11 December 2003,) p 5, cited by Pollock, A., supra, p 52.

TIME LINE

1984   Advertising by solicitors permitted for the first time.

1990   Courts and Legal Services Act gave the Lord Chancellor power to make contingency fees lawful for certain types of litigation.

1995   The Contingency Fees Arrangements Regulations were introduced by which the Lord Chancellor made it practicable to use CFs in personal injury, human rights and insolvency cases. Lawyers could charge success fees but at a higher rate than they would normally charge and the claimant would have to pay if successful.

1996   New NHS Complaints System introduced.

1998   *Wells v Wells*. House of Lords decision meant that damages would be assessed to provide higher lump sum awards. Legal Aid was withdrawn for personal injury, defamation, and corporate matters. It was enacted that legal aid should be refused if conditional fee agreements was considered to be a 'more appropriate' form of funding. Legal Aid (Prescribed Panels) Regulations 1998. Only solicitors with special expertise allowed to handle clinical negligence claims, so increasing the likelihood of successful claims.

1999   Law Commission Report No. 257 suggested that awards of general damages were too low.

2000   The Contingency Fees Agreement Regulations (2000) were introduced to fill the gap in access to justice left by the withdrawal of civil legal aid, by allowing the successful party to recover the success fee from the losing party, under certain formalities. If a success fee was included, it would be a percentage of the lawyers' costs, is recoverable from the paying party, as is an insurance premium paid by the claimant to cover the risk of losing the case, provided that certain formalities are complied with. *Heil v Rankin*. Court of Appeal decision, acting on the Law Commission's comments, introduced phased increases in general damages, resulting in an overall increase for the NHS of around 50% in damages awards for pain and suffering.

2000   Human Rights Act 1998 came into force.

2001   Report of Bristol Inquiry 2002. First Report of Shipman Inquiry 2003. Second Report of Shipman Inquiry.

2004   Fourth and Fifth Reports of Shipman Inquiry 2000–2004. Rapid increase in the number of claims management companies offering no-win, no-fee services. Citizens Advice Bureaux reported problems arising from growing number of claims management companies. Better Regulation Task Force Report highlighted problems resulting from pressure on consumers by Claims Management Companies Clementi Report of the Review of the Regulatory Framework for Legal Services in England and Wales. Recognition of the need for formal regulation of claims management companies.

2005   Sixth Report of Shipman Inquiry. Speeches by Lord Falconer and Tony Blair claiming that there is no compensation culture in the UK. The Regulatory Impact Assessment accompanying the Compensation Bill estimated that there were roughly 400–500 claims management companies operating in the UK.

2006   Compensation Act to regulate claims farmers. 2006: NHS Redress Act to control NHS spending on clinical negligence claims.

Figure 4 Time line showing key events in relation to number of claims indicated in Figure 5

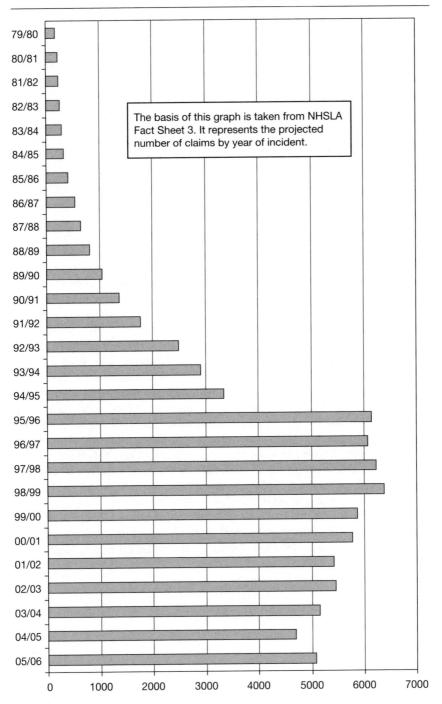

Figure 5 Projected number of claims by year of incident

Conclusion

It is clear from the discussion in this chapter that there are many complex reasons for the accelerating rate of claims in the UK for clinical negligence towards the end of the twentieth century and the early years of the twenty-first century. It may be possible, through empirical research, to identify with greater certainty some of the factors responsible, but too little research has been undertaken on this matter to date, and suggestions are based on intuition rather than hard facts. Although commentators have suggested a wide range of reasons, no single factor can feasibly be identified as the main cause. The multifactorial nature of the problem allows only for the possibility of considering the relative weighting of the potential factors. The size of compensation awards increased as a result of judicial policy, easier access to law created by the policies of successive Governments which have now perhaps returned to haunt them, and a general climate of consumerism generated by the media could all be highly motivating factors for claimants. The media influence has been significant, as have cultural changes, new developments in the delivery and structure of healthcare, better access by patients to information about medical treatment, and more efficient rules concerning the bringing and funding of claims. It would be the supreme irony if the rising volume of claims and cost of compensation, resulting in sensationalist media reports and cost-cutting in the NHS, were to be identified as the cause of an ever-spinning upward spiral of claims and rising costs.

In many ways the Government has been the author of its own misfortune by facilitating the introduction of CFAs which in turn resulted in an explosion in the number of claims management companies. It hardly seems rational to abolish legal aid except for the poorest, and then to blame the public for responding to what is in fact commission-based compensation culture. These factors, combined with the reduction in the discount rate following *Wells v Wells*, led to media reporting of stratospherically high awards and constant advertising in the media by solicitors and claims farmers, which led to more claims... and so on. It is understandable that the Government should be anxious to persuade the public that there is no compensation culture. There is clearly a strong case for wide-ranging empirical research to increase understanding of the underlying causes of the high volume of claims for clinical negligence.

Chapter 3

The compensation culture in healthcare

Myth or reality?

The previous chapters indicate that there is a general public understanding, and a perception among healthcare professionals, that the number of claims involving medical errors is rising. Despite numerous assertions supporting this view, there are some commentators who consider that current evidence indicates that suggestions of a litigation crisis in healthcare in the UK may be unfounded[1] and that there is a wide chasm between the perception of the public and the reality of the situation. In terms of personal injuries claims as a whole, there is strong evidence that there is indeed a widely held belief that the UK has developed a society in which people are making false claims for compensation.[2] The history of the rise in the volume of claims has been considered in Chapter 2, against the background of a growing consumer rights culture and the developing NHS. The alleged role of the media in perpetuating the notion of malpractice litigation escalating out of control, and the true extent to which litigation concerning medical error is increasing, will be examined in the following chapter. Over the past decade serious articles in heavy-weight newspapers have carried headlines such as 'The litigation bug brings Britain down in a fever of greed',[3] claiming that there is a litigation epidemic that has forced public sector organisations, including the NHS, to adopt defensive practises that undermine their efficiency. This chapter will focus on the gap between myth and reality within what is perceived to be the current compensation culture. It is possible that some organisations have an interest in promoting the view that the levelling in the number of claims is an indication that there is no compensation culture in the UK, and that the law should be reformed, while

---

1   See Chapter 2 for detailed figures, but note e.g. that in 2005–06, 5,697 claims of clinical negligence and 3,497 claims of non-clinical negligence against NHS bodies were received by the NHSLA. This compares with 5,609 claims of clinical negligence and 3,766 claims of non-clinical negligence in 2004–05, NHSLA Annual report 2006.

2   'See Effects of Advertising in Respect of Compensation Claims for Personal Injuries', Department for Constitutional Affairs 2006.

3   Article by Frank Furedi, a sociologist at the University of Kent in Canterbury, *The Times*, 17 January 2000.

others stand to gain from asserting that claims are continuing to rise. The chapter will consider whether or not lawyers, claims farmers, the healthcare professions, the insurance industry, big business, politicians, the Government, or the media are responsible for perpetrating misapprehensions.

Is there a compensation culture in the UK?

The closing years of the twentieth century, according to received wisdom, witnessed the growth of what has been described as a 'compensation culture' across the whole spectrum of professional services in the US and Western Europe, though it has been in healthcare that the largest rise in claims has occurred.[4] In his analysis of the position in the UK at the end of the last century, Frank Ferudi estimated that the rapid growth of what he described as the 'compensation culture' in Britain could cost the country almost £7 billion a year in damages and lawyers' fees.[5] He urged Parliament, in his pamphlet published by the Centre for Policy Studies, to place an upper limit on damages, and claimed that the UK was following a trend that had been set in the US. Citing some of the more bizarre instances of successful legal claims, Ferudi blamed the legal profession for the situation. He drew attention to the cases of Vincent Kemp, who was awarded £500,000 after tripping over a kerb stone when he was extremely drunk and sustained serious spinal injuries after falling into the path of a vehicle, and of the junior doctor who received a £465,000 settlement from an NHS Trust after a needle-stick injury that resulted in 'needle-stick phobia', which brought her career to an end. He urged the Government to consider limiting the scope of liability for psychiatric injury, asserting that litigation is contrary to the public interest, giving as an example the litigation bill for obstetrics, which amounted to £264 million in 1995–98, when the cost of employing 250 consultant obstetricians in England and Wales at that time was a mere £15 million a year.

It is difficult to determine precisely what is meant by the terms 'compensation culture' and 'litigation crisis', which are frequently used interchangeably, and there are some obscure statements suggesting that there is a large gulf between the perception and the reality of the compensation culture and litigation crisis. Yet these concepts appear to be influencing the political agenda and have already resulted in two major new UK statutes – the NHS Redress Act 2006 and the Compensation Act 2006 – both of which are designed to deal with problems arising from a perceived claims culture.

---

4   See Ham, C., Dingwall, R., Fenn, P. and Harris, D., *Medical Negligence: Compensation and Accountability* (1988).

5   Ferudi, F., 'Courting Mistrust – The Hidden Growth of a Culture of Litigation in Britain', Centre for Policy Studies, April 1999.

As the writer of a letter to 'The Actuary' commented in November 2005:

> The money that the BRR describes being spent by local authorities is real. The claims that the BRR describes being fed into the system are real. The adverts that the BRR describes promising untold riches if you're lucky enough to have an accident are real. That sounds like reality to me, not perception.

Baroness Hale tackled this issue in an article published in Clinical Risk after the first draft of this chapter had been written,[6] in which she states that there appears to be a great deal of confusion as to what the term 'compensation culture' means. As she sensibly points out, there can surely be no objection, within a tort-based system, to people wanting to claim compensation for injuries suffered at the hands of tortfeasors. Like Kevin Williams,[7] and in keeping with some of the conclusions in the preceding chapters of this book, she is concerned about the poor quality of the statistical evidence that makes the task of data analysis very daunting. In her view, the main objection appears to be the view that the fear of litigation has produced risk-averse behaviour in a number of areas of human activity, including healthcare.

Another more serious objection, since it is virtually impossible to devise a means of dealing with it, centres on human nature – that people who are injured will now inevitably consider claiming compensation whether or not they deserve to be compensated. This approach to life is not new,[8] but assertions have recently been made that the attitude is developing apace. The existence of a compensation culture was considered in some depth in a report produced by the Better Regulation Task Force (BRTF) in 2004. Its May 2004 Report, entitled 'Better Routes to Redress', cites in its introduction headlines such as 'The culture that is crippling Britain'[9] and 'Blame culture in road to suicide'[10] as examples of what it calls the 'urban myth' of a compensation culture which is overwhelming the UK. The report continues obliquely:

> The term 'compensation culture' is not used to describe a society where people are able to seek compensation. Rather, a 'compensation culture' implies that a decision to seek compensation is wrong. ... It suggests greed rather than people legitimately enforcing their rights.

6   Baroness Hale of Richmond, 'What's Wrong with the Compensation Culture', *Clinical Risk* (2007) 13: 60–64.
7   Williams, K., 'State of Fear: Britain's Compensation Culture Reviewed', *Legal Studies* (September 2005) 25(3): 498–514 at p 503.
8   E.g., see the short story by Guy de Maupassant in which a peasant woman who is superficially injured is set to claim a lifetime of financial support from the person who caused her injury.
9   *Daily Mail*, 21 February 2004.
10   BBC News website, 6 January 2004.

The authors, in a spirit of self-contradiction, since they deny that a compensation culture exists, argue that the '*have a go*' culture[11] encourages people to pursue misconceived or trivial claims, and that this has led to a drain on public sector resources, higher insurance premiums and overcrowded courts. In fact the document is riddled with contradictions – on the one hand claiming that there is no compensation culture, without clarifying what the term means – and on the other giving a number of instances of what it regards as unjustifiable claims and the way in which the country is being crippled by the risk-averse attitude of public authorities. For example:

> Local authorities are spending a great amount of money dealing with all the claims they receive. Every claim made, however frivolous or vexatious … has to be handled.

And again:

> One large local authority we met estimated that, for highway liability claims alone, it will have spent over £2m. … Multiply this by the 409 local authorities … it comes to a staggering figure.

There are two main concepts underpinning the debate as to whether there is a compensation culture in the UK, but to confuse matters, in the BRTF Report and in the speeches of senior ministers, the two concepts appear to be conflated. The first is the statistical evidence relating to the number of claims and the cost of defending them and paying successful claimants. This is based, in so far as the statistics are reliable, on fact. The second concept is more nebulous, and by definition more difficult to assess. That is what apparently underpins the popular belief that the UK is gripped by a frenzy of claims – the notion of a culture of claiming compensation whenever possible. It is important to distinguish between the two concepts, and while the rise in the number of claims may have levelled, it may still be the case that there is a continuing popular belief that too many people take every opportunity to pursue legal claims.

The Government failed to make this crucial distinction when Tony Blair and the TUC[12] claimed in 2005 that the compensation culture was a mere myth perpetrated by the media, concentrating on the fact that the number of claims has reached a plateau, but failing to recognise the fact that there is still a culture within which there is a strong focus on naming, blaming, and

---

11   This heavily loaded expression was used in the BRTF Report of May 2004.
12   Paton, N. (May 2005) 'Compensation culture is a myth', www.management-issues.com.

claiming compensation. It is surely no coincidence that since Tony Blair and Lord Falconer made their speeches denying the existence of a compensation culture, the number of articles in UK newspapers concerning clinical negligence has in fact doubled.[13]

The position, frequently overlooked, is that although fraudulent and frivolous claims are to be frowned upon, there is nothing morally reprehensible, given the fault-based nature of tort, about using the system legitimately in order to obtain compensation for injuries caused by the fault of another.[14] The BRTF did acknowledge this in its Report[15] that:

> It has got to be right that someone who has suffered an injustice through someone else's negligence should be able to claim redress.

However, the general tenor of the report concentrates on denouncing those who fuel the perception of a compensation culture and its main emphasis is on tackling the problem of unscrupulous claims farmers, in order to 'make the system better' for genuine claimants.

It seems that there is no generally accepted definition of the term 'compensation culture'. In terms of popular understanding, it can be seen as a state in a society in which it is acceptable for anyone who has suffered an injury to seek compensation by means of litigation from some person or organisation connected with the injury, even if the injury is trivial or has a tenuous connection with the alleged wrong. The term is usually used in a pejorative sense.

In the US, the leading writers on the topic define it as follows:[16]

> The term litigation crisis refers to something that is very murky and very vague. There have been increasing allegations from politicians and pundits and editorialists that litigation is spinning out of control in American society. The verbs often used are 'skyrocketing,' 'exploding,' 'mushrooming.' The focus is on personal injury litigation, employee claims, discrimination claims.

---

13 See Chapter 5.
14 For a snapshot illustrating what is happening in the USA, see Monbiot, G., 'The risks of a killing – compensation culture is a myth – ask the thousands who will die this year from asbestos', *Guardian*, 16 November 2004.
15 Op. cit., p 4.
16 McCann, M., In an interview with *Lawyers' Weekly USA* (2004), shortly after the publication of his co-authored book, Haltom, W. and McCann, M., *Dis-torting the Law: Politics, Media and the Litigation Crisis* (University of Chicago Press, Chicago and London, 2004).

Lowe *et al.*[17] define it narrowly as:

> The desire of individuals to sue somebody, having suffered as a result of something which could have been avoided if the sued body had done their job properly.

A more realistic and acceptable definition would adopt a wider approach[18] to indicate that if indeed there is a growing body of claims, it could be accounted for by individuals who may not have suffered a high degree of harm in situations falling short of what would amount in law to negligence, though it may involve careless conduct of some kind. A more complete definition would encompass the attitudes and perceptions of people in general that there is a growing tendency to claim compensation for the slightest damage. If a compensation culture can be taken to include a general belief, however misplaced, that there is a growing number of claims, and public awareness of an entitlement to receive monetary compensation for harm suffered at the hands of professionals, it is difficult to accept that no compensation culture exists in the UK at present. This is so irrespective of the economic basis of any expectation. It must also be remembered that expectations of the general public in the UK tend to be derivative of those in America where the cultural expectations and the financial rewards are more evenly matched, though even there, despite some spectacular compensation payments to claimants,[19] it appears that in healthcare at least,[20] relatively few claims are made in relation to the number of errors causing injury.

The Report entitled 'No Win, No Fee, No Chance', which appears to have influenced the thinking of Government, was published in 2004, and its author took the view that seeking compensation for injuries was not a social problem; nor was it a sign of the emergence of a 'compensation culture', but simply the process of realising a civil and legal right, which if not addressed could contribute to social exclusion.[21]

Lord Falconer, in 2005, described the term 'Compensation culture' as a catch-all expression meaning different things to different people:

---

17   Lowe, J., Broughton, J., Gravelsons, B., Hensamn, C., Rakow, J., Malone, M., Mitchell, G. and Shah, S. (2002), 'The Cost of Compensation Culture', report of a working party of the Faculty of Actuaries.

18   Fenn, P., Vencappa, D., O'Brien, C. and Diacon, S., 'Is There a Compensation Culture in the UK? Trends in Employers' Liability Claim Frequency and Severity', Centre for Risk and Insurance Studies, Nottingham Business School.

19   E.g., to women who succeeded in obtaining compensation for illness and injury allegedly caused by breast implants.

20   See Baker, T., *The Medical Malpractice Myth* (University of Chicago Press, Chicago, 2004).

21   Sandbach, J., 'No Win, No Fee, No Chance', CAB evidence on the challenges facing access to injury, para 3, December 2004.

It's the idea that for every accident someone is at fault. For every injury, someone to blame. And perhaps most damaging, for every accident, there is someone to pay.

The problem, he said, did not concern legal niceties, but rather the fact that people who are 'having a go' hinders normal business development, with the result that the law has shifted into a new era that favours spurious claims. He added that this misperception is very damaging to business and to society as a whole.

Paradoxically, some evidence for the existence of a compensation culture is cited by BRTF, despite its denials, which reports that one UK local authority spent 10 per cent of its roads budget on defending claims for compensation. Ironically those figures were cited by the Chair of the BRTF in the process of arguing that there is no compensation culture in the UK.[22] Personal experience of the author, in the course of regular conversations with doctors and other healthcare professionals, suggests that almost all healthcare professionals are under the strong impression that patients are all too ready to claim compensation on the slightest pretext. Simply on the basis of a 'show of hands' at more than 50 meetings with healthcare professionals in the course of the past five years, it is possible to conclude that there is an almost unanimous view on the part of those questioned that there is currently a litigation crisis in healthcare in the UK. However, AvMA examined the question of a compensation culture in relation to clinical negligence,[23] and concluded that no such culture exists in that context.

The quality of the evidence

If the work of the courts is taken into consideration – and by case analysis it is possible to form a view on developments – the general scope of liability in some areas of tort has expanded in recent years; a factor that would suggest that we are living in a compensation culture. For example, a growth area of litigation lies in claims for psychiatric injury caused by work stress, and instances of stress, depression and anxiety have doubled since 1990 to an annual number of 563,000, according to the Health and Safety Executive.[24] The general range of situations in which compensation is awarded has also increased, as in the medical law case of *Chester v Afshar*.[25] Thus, some of the older tort defences have been disallowed over recent years, to the extent that individuals who consent to their injuries and even some who have been guilty

22 'Better Routes to Redress', May 2005.
23 Evidence by AvMA to the Commons Select Committee on Constitutional Affairs 2005.
24 Corporate Health and Safety Plan 2005–06.
25 *Chester v Afshar* [2004] UKHL 41, see Chapter 3.

of criminal activities[26] have succeeded in their claims for compensation.[27] On the other hand, the courts have also limited the scope of liability in an area of medical law that had been settled for many years – that of claims for the up-bringing of a healthy child born after a failed sterilisation operation.[28] There is evidence that the courts take into account the policy arguments concerning economic factors and distributive justice, and it should not be forgotten that in *Donoghue v Stevenson*[29] itself there were signals that an impending compensation culture was in the minds of the dissenting judges. Nevertheless, it is difficult to draw definite conclusions, since as Lord Steyn noted in *McFaralane v Tayside Health Board*:

> tort law is a mosaic in which the principles of corrective justice and distributive justice are interwoven.[30]

As far as general personal injury claims are concerned, it is difficult to assess the accuracy of the figures relied upon by the BRTF in its Report. As Kevin Williams points out, since the phasing out of legal aid for personal injury claims, with the exception of claims for clinical negligence, data recorded on the number of personal injury claims, including those involving clinical negligence, is of limited help, and the same is true of the Judicial Statistics, which have collected only a fraction of the true numbers.[31] The BRTF based its conclusions on statistics obtained from the CRU, which did indicate, conveniently, a fall in the number of claims over a three-year period, though its approach fails to supply information about longer term trends, and the data it supplies is by definition limited to cases in which the claimant has been in receipt of benefit.[32] Moreover, Datamonitor provides figures that demonstrate no consistency.[33] Lewis *et al.* are critical of the present situation in which any attempt to make a serious evaluation of the data is undermined by the dearth of consistent and reliable statistical information.[34] In their helpful analysis of the CRU figures, they point out that it was not until 1997, when benefits paid to claimants could be recovered from all compensation

26   *Revill v Newbury* [1996] QB 567.
27   *Reeves v Commissioner of Police* [1999] 3 All ER 897, in which damages were available for a suicide.
28   *McFarlane v Tayside Health Board* [2000] 2 AC 59.
29   [1932] AC 562.
30   Op. cit., at para 165.
31   Williams, K., 'State of Fear: Britain's Compensation Culture Reviewed', *Legal Studies* (September 2005) 25(3): 498–514 at p 503.
32   See Chapter 2.
33   Ibid., p 504.
34   Lewis, R., Morris, A. and Oliphant, K., 'Tort Personal Injury Claims Statistics: Is There a Compensation Culture in the United Kingdom?' (2006) *Torts Law Journal* 14(2): 158; republished (2006) *Insurance Research and Practice* 21(2): 5–14.

payments (even those below the previous £2,500 limit), that the reporting requirement was extended to all claims.[35] The same is not true of the figures relating specifically to public sector clinical negligence claims,[36] which are now monitored reasonably accurately, at least as far as claims against NHS Trusts are concerned.[37]

Despite more accurate collecting of data on clinical negligence claims, different figures are quoted in different contexts. For example, in Hansard,[38] the figures taken from the NHSLA Report and Accounts for 2004 differ from those produced by the CRU,[39] and even the NHSLA's own figures appear contradictory because they are presented at different times according to different criteria.[40]

The data relating to hospital infections provide an interesting example of the complexity of official information made available to the public. MRSA and *Clostridium difficile* are thought to have been responsible for more than 5,400 deaths in 2005, a rise of 2,000 since the previous year according to figures published by the Office for National Statistics in 2007. The sharpest rise was in *C. difficile*, which showed a 69 per cent increase on death certificates. Deaths from MRSA rose 39 per cent. Yet, an announcement by the HPA, which was established as a Special Health Authority by the Government just a few weeks before these figures were released, stated that MRSA is 'in downward trend', and that there has been another reduction in MRSA levels in England, which are 'down by 5.0 per cent from the same period in 2005'.[41] It is difficult for most people to reconcile such contradictory statements. Although one report relates to the incidence of hospital-acquired infections, and the other to the number of deaths that they caused, only the more discriminating members of the public would take the trouble to consider the details in depth, and it is understandable that scepticism abounds.

Who asserts that there is a compensation culture: who denies its existence?

Claims that the country is in the throes of a compensation crisis have been made by a variety of organisations, and it is only recently that these assertions have been challenged. A range of different organisations may have interests

---

35   Ibid. The authors emphasise that the Department of Social Security estimated that, as a result of the £2,500 limit, around half of all claims were not recorded at all.
36   See Chapter 2 supra.
37   See Chapter 2.
38   HC 149, HMSO 2005.
39   See Chapter 2.
40   Ibid., fn 26.
41   HPA March 2007.

in encouraging litigation, while others are anxious to dispel any notion that there is a claims crisis in the UK.

The insurance industry

The insurance industry and actuarial profession have been arguing for some time that there is a general compensation culture in the UK, and that UK businesses are being restricted by the fear of claims and by dealing with the increasing volume of litigation, to the extent that they are diverting valuable resources away from their core business and into claims handling and risk management. Many of the allegations concern the entire range of compensation claims rather than those concerning clinical negligence in particular, but they are meaningful in so far as they refer to the culture which is prevalent in the UK at present.

Lord Levene, chairman of Lloyds, in a speech to an insurance forum in the City of London[42] echoing Lord Falconer's views, claimed emotively that:

> There is strong evidence that the compensation culture is starting to plunder the UK economy.

He stressed that this was not simply an insurance crisis but also a national economic problem.

Aon, one of the UK's leading broking and risk management organisations, conducted a survey of UK companies and public bodies, and published its findings in 2004.[43] It concluded that 75 per cent of those surveyed believed that there was a trend towards increased claims which was creating an unsustainable burden for industry and commerce. Sixty-two per cent of companies included in the Aon survey anticipated an increase in the cost of claims which would directly affect their business, and 60 per cent expressed the fear that too much management time was being devoted to dealing with compensation-related matters, creating inefficiencies and distractions. Forty-nine per cent of companies expressed the view that the compensation culture was diverting financial resources from other fields of activity. Smaller companies (with fewer than 500 employees and a turnover of under £25 million) reported that they rarely had claims brought against them by employees. Aon concluded that there is hard evidence of a compensation culture in the UK. However, the research appears to be have been based on somewhat impressionistic

---

42   Cited in Zurich Financial Services web publication January/February 2006, 'The Strange World of Tort Cases'.

43   'Blame, Claim and Gain: The Compensation and Blame Culture: Reality or Myth?' AON, 27 July 2004.

criteria which do not specify the kinds of claims or volume of the increase involved. Nevertheless, such a statement from so eminent a source must have had resonances for the Government, and it is hardly surprising that the Prime Minister and others have issued statements to contradict this view, though there is little evidence to support either view.

In May 2004, the Norwich Union, a branch of the Aviva Group, the largest insurer in the UK, concluded after its own survey that the compensation culture had become a fact of life in the UK today.[44] That report found that 96 per cent of the public surveyed believed that people in the UK are more likely to seek compensation than they were 10 years ago, and 10 per cent of those blamed the US influence, while a further 5 per cent identified the media as creating the perception that compensation is worth claiming and relatively easy to obtain from large companies, public bodies and the NHS. The methodology used in the survey may well be open to question, since the questions were posed to members of the public on the assumption that a compensation culture does indeed exist in the UK. Despite that potential flaw, the results of the survey are interesting, because the public appeared to be unhappy with the culture and wanted measures to be introduced to reduce the level of claims.

Zurich Financial Services, in an article published in 2006[45] detailing some outlandish and bizarre tort claims, concludes that despite arguments to the contrary, the compensation culture is 'alive and well in the US, firmly embedded in the UK, and ready to 'leapfrog' into Europe'. Many of the assertions in that article, such as the cancellation of public firework displays because of the fear of claims, are unsupported by firm evidence. The article cites the speech by Lord Levene,[46] in which he claimed that the US compensation culture had spread to the UK and was costing more than £10 billion a year, rising annually by 15 per cent.

The report of a working party of the Institute of Actuaries presented to the General Insurance Convention in 2002 and entitled 'The Cost of a Compensation Culture'[47] highlighted its finding that the majority of the people it surveyed consider that although they would not claim compensation from a neighbour or employer for personal injuries, they would have no such compunction about bringing a claim against the NHS or a local authority. Referring in particular to claims against the NHS, the working party concludes that 'this is one area where the compensation culture has taken root.'[48]

The same report points to what it describes as a recent change in society which has provided virtually every area of consumer activity with an ombudsman to hear and monitor complaints, saying:

---

44   News item in the *Insurance Journal*, 19 May 2004.
45   January/February 2006, 'The Strange World of Tort Cases'.
46   Speech to a UK insurance forum in the City of London.
47   See fn 7.
48   Op. cit., fn 7, para 2.3 B.

This is a further tilting of the consumer protection environment towards individuals and further embeds the right to compensation in the national psyche.

A contention contained in the report, which has been made fairly frequently elsewhere, is that as a society we are progressing away from the stoical 'stiff upper lip' attitude traditionally attributed to the British as a national characteristic (though on what grounds it is difficult to determine), towards:

a country where every mishap leads to a complaint. ... A potential consequence of compensation culture is that the rich tapestry of life gets dumbed down and reduced to bland, humourless interactions, which is what we fought a war for.

The research base upon which this type of speculative statement is predicated is insubstantial, the survey having been conducted among actuaries and their friends, and the authors of the report confess that their own costings are imprecise and that they rely on some 'heroic assumptions.'[49] However, the Institute of Actuaries went on to report that there is indeed a growing compensation culture, which involves claims amounting to a total cost of around £10 billion a year, which is about 1 per cent of GDP. Yet the UK Government appears to have embraced the idea that the blame culture is prevalent.[50]

As far as the insurance industry is concerned, at least in relation to the commercial world as opposed to organisations such as local authorities and the NHS, which are their own insurers, it is important to be aware that the cost of insurance premiums depends in part on the level of claims that are made. In the NHS, the cost of defending claims and paying compensation is a drain on the public purse at a time when NHS Trusts are having trouble balancing their books and staff are being dismissed in order to save money, with obvious adverse effects on patient care.[51]

The OFT took the view[52] that some insurers:

Rely heavily on anecdotal evidence of a worsening environment in order to justify price increases, quoting individual cases of highly speculative claims.

49   Op. cit., para 4.1.
50   Better Regulation Task Force, 'Better Routes to Redress' May 2004, p 15.
51   See *The Times*, 29 June 2006.
52   'An Analysis of Current Problems in the UK Insurance Market', OFT June 2003, cited by Williams, K., in his excellent article, 'State of Fear: Britain's "Compensation Culture" Reviewed' *Legal Studies* (2005) 25(3).

In the US, all clinical negligence claims are dealt with by insurance.[53] Although it may not be particularly helpful to draw on the US experience in this context, extensive research conducted there leads to the conclusion that the insurance industry is content to perpetuate the myth that large numbers of patients are prepared to bring claims on the least pretext, and that a very high percentage of them are awarded large sums by way of compensation. In reality, research demonstrates that the reverse is true.[54]

In the field of nursing, however, the UK system does bear some similarity to that in the US in relation to the current controversy concerning independent midwives, and it is very likely that the changes described below can be ascribed to the so-called compensation culture in the UK and to the media publicity given to high awards for damages birth injuries. Until 1994, all midwives were covered by an indemnity scheme of the Royal College of Midwives (RCM), irrespective of where and how they worked. Midwives working in the NHS could also be assured that their employers would be vicariously liable for them in the event of claims. Then the RCM withdrew insurance cover from independent midwives in 1994, and only a few insurers were prepared to cover them. The result was a rise in premiums of up to £18,000 per midwife per year. In 2001, following a rise in the number of claims and the cost of defending them, the last insurance provider withdrew from the market and there has been no insurance cover available to independent midwives. The issue has been further complicated by a proposal in 2003 by the NMC to make insurance cover a 'requirement' for registration, with the result that it became an official recommendation. Now all midwives practising without insurance have an obligation to ensure that their patients are made aware of the fact that they are uninsured. In effect, this means that any client of an uninsured independent midwife takes upon herself the financial risk of supporting herself or her child if they are injured as a result of the midwife's negligence. No midwife could afford to pay from her own pocket the cost involved in providing care and support for a brain-damaged child. In a more recent development, independent midwives have been informed by the Chief Nurse that the Government is intending, in legislation, to make professional indemnity insurance a prerequisite for registration. The European Parliament is considering similar legislation.

---

53   See Baker, T., 'Medical Malpractice and Insurance Reform', in Sage, M. and Kersch, R. (eds) *Medical Malpractice and the US Healthcare System*, p 267 (Cambridge University Press, Cambridge, 2006).

54   E.g. Danzon *et al.* Chicago Study, 1985, op. cit.

Multi-national companies and employers generally

George Monbiot stated the position of manufacturing industry in a Guardian article in 2004:[55]

> Compensation culture has usurped political correctness, welfare cheats, single mothers and new age travellers as the right's new bogeyman-in-chief. According to the Confederation of British Industry, the Conservative Party and just about every newspaper columnist in Britain, it threatens very soon to bankrupt the country.

He argued that it is in the interests of politicians who aim to support manufacturing industry to contend that there is something unsavory about claiming for illnesses and injuries suffered as a result of work accidents.

Multi-national companies stand greatly to gain from discrediting people who have genuine claims. The compensation payable to victims of asbestos is likely to reach record levels if all those who are bringing claims succeed. Any doctor or lawyer who has advised a claimant suffering from mesothelioma will confirm that this illness has devastating effects on its victims and their families. Yet, as George Monbiot so aptly points out:

> Compensation culture is a convenient bogeyman because it allows big business to associate its victims – such as the 3,500 people who die every year in Britain as a result of exposure to asbestos – with scroungers and conmen.

There are those who lay some of the blame for the increase in claims for clinical negligence in the US at the door of the insurance companies.[56] However, the boom and bust cycle experienced in the medical insurance business does not apply in the same way in the UK where NHS Trusts are their own insurers and where those who are not employed by Trusts are members of the defence organisations.

Lawyers and claims farmers

The compensation business is a useful source of income for many lawyers. It was estimated that in 2001, of the £900m compensation paid by the NHS, around £300m was paid to lawyers in fees,[57] so it not surprising that the present system of compensation for healthcare negligence is regarded as inefficient by

---

55   Monbiot, G., 'The risks of a killing', *The Guardian*, 16 November 2004.
56   Baker, T., *The Medical Malpractice Myth* (University of Chicago Press, Chicago and London, 2005).
57   Lowe *et al.* supra, fn 7.

many commentators. This sentiment was echoed by David Davis MP in his comment on the House of Commons Public Accounts Committee Report on clinical negligence claims in 2002:

> The report provides firm evidence that the only people winning from the system are the lawyers.

There are numerous websites containing statements by UK solicitors to the effect that claims are increasing in volume and that clinical negligence is widespread. Not only do these advertise the increased volume of claims and the likelihood that there are many injuries that go uncompensated, but they also draw attention to areas of medical practice in which negligence is common place.[58]

Such assumptions extend beyond the realm of legal practitioners. At least as recently as 2003 it was possible to find alarmist statements by academic lawyers supporting the opinion that medical malpractice claims are rising in number. For example: 'Malpractice litigation in England is increasing apace'.[59] The same theme was repeated by other legal academic writers,[60] perhaps before it had become widely apparent that there had been a levelling in the number of claims.

It seems that judges, too, are under the impression that there is a compensation culture in the UK. In 2003, Lord Hobhouse, in the House of Lords, in *Tomlinson v Congleton BC*[61] – not a medical law case, but one concerning the liability of occupiers for injury to trespassers – commented:

> The pursuit of an unrestrained culture of blame and compensation has many evil consequences.

Again, in *Gorringe v Calderdale MBC*[62] Lord Steyn argued that:

> the courts must not contribute to the creation of a society which is premised on the illusion that for every misfortune there is a remedy.[63]

---

58   www.hospitalnegligence.co.uk
59   McHale, V.J., 'Medical Malpractice in England', *European Journal of Health Law* (2003) 1: 135.
60   See, e.g., Mason, J.K. and Laurie, G.T., *Law and Medical Ethics*, (2005), 7th edn 2006, para 9.1.
61   [2003] 1 AC 46, para 81.
62   [2004] UKHL 2, cited by Williams, K., in 'State of Fear: Britain's Compensation Culture Reviewed' *Legal Studies* (2005) 25(3): 499.
63   Ibid., at para 2.

Lord Woolf, in an article published in 2001, referred to a developing 'malpractice crisis'.[64] Analysis of the case law on clinical negligence and personal injuries indicates that the fear of a flood of claims is frequently argued in court[65] and expressed by judges as a possible reason for not allowing the law to develop too far in favour of claimants, and even when that view is not explicitly stated, it may be used to explain judicial caution behind a large number of decisions.[66]

Action Against Medical Accidents (AvMA)

AvMA is a registered charity, representing patients as consumers of healthcare, which has more than 20 years' experience of work in the field of clinical negligence, and which has focused on the need to develop more effective ways of resolving disputes arising from medical incidents. Part of its remit is to provide support for those who are affected by clinical negligence. This organisation has achieved some real successes over the years and is one of the most authoritative organisations in terms of reflecting the views of patients who have been caught up in the tangled web of clinical errors and claims. In its evidence to the Select Committee on Constitutional Affairs when the NHS Redress Bill was under consideration, AvMA made this statement:[67]

> Does The Compensation Culture Exist? In relation to clinical negligence, the answer to this must be an unequivocal 'no'. The Department of Health for England estimates that there are over 850,000 medical accidents a year in English hospitals. Research evidence suggests that a third of these involve clinical negligence. Yet, the NHS Litigation Authority received only 5,609 new claims in 2004–05.

Clearly, this statement was made in the light of a definition of 'compensation culture', which approached the issue from the perspective of the number of claims, rather than the public perception more generally, ignoring the fact that over the past 20 years there has been a rise of 1,200 per cent in the number of claims. The statement continues in a vein which would please the Government:

> AvMA believes that if anything, there is an 'anti-compensation culture' when it comes to the NHS.

---

64   Lord Woolf, 'Are the Court Excessively Deferential to the Medical Profession?' (2001) 9 *Med Law Review* 1.

65   *Gregg v Scott* [2005] UKHL 2; *White v Chief Constable of South Yorkshire* [1999] 2 AC 455.

66   See especially, the law relating to psychiatric injury caused by negligence.

67   AvMA evidence to the Select Committee on Constitutional Affairs, November 2005.

However, the statement goes on to make a further pronouncement that is unlikely to please the policy makers:

> In view of the low take up of claims, we believe that this area should be prioritised for improving access to justice rather than making it harder (which is what various reforms to the Legal Aid scheme have done).

The media

Headlines in the media have perpetuated the view that there is a claims culture in general and a medical malpractice crisis in particular, and spectacular headlines sell newspapers. The Final Report of the Bristol Inquiry noted that:[68]

> Stories of scandal and malpractice seem to dominate the media coverage of the NHS.

Take, for example, just two of the many statements which would have caused consternation and alarm – the BBC News headlines on 2 May 2002, 'NHS Negligence Claims Soar', or the more inflammatory 2006 *Times* headline,[69] '£2.8 million award for prisoner who tried to kill himself', followed by a front page article opening with the words:

> Compensation payments to prisoners have doubled in the last year to more than £4 million, while the total legal bill to the prison service has reached £20 million a year.

Such statements, which are based on fact and made by respectable media sources, will inevitably lead the general public to the view that there is a litigation crisis in the public services. As the Better Regulation Task Force commented:

> Quoting statistics will not win the arguments while the papers run compensation culture stories.[70]

Despite the plea of the BRTF for senior commentators and for those in positions of influence to be more responsible about the way they report matters, following the pronouncements of the House of Lords in *Tomlinson v Congelton BC* [2004] 1 AC 46, *The Times*, in December 2005,[71] carried a

---

68   Chapter 22, para 24, 'A Culture of Openness'.
69   *The Times*, 19 May 2006.
70   Report of BRTF. S 3, 'The Compensation Culture: It's All in the Mind', May 2004, p 18.
71   *The Times*, 6 December 2005.

report about a woman who had been awarded £2.8 million in a claim against the ambulance service, which it reported to have been guilty of 'a catalogue of errors'. The report continued:

> A mother who took an overdose while suffering from post-natal depression has won £2.8 million from the ambulance service which, she claims, arrived too late to save her from permanent brain damage.

The Trust agreed to pay the damages but denied liability, while admitting that a justifiable delay in the arrival of the ambulance.

The role of the media in promoting advertising is significant in relation to the growth of claims management companies which have in turn led more people to claim for injuries arising from medical and other accidents.[72] The role of the media is explored more fully in Chapter 4 of this book.

Healthcare professionals

It appears that no research results have been published specifically to elucidate whether healthcare professionals believe that there is a compensation culture in the UK. Opinions of doctors and other healthcare professionals on this matter would no doubt be based on figures relating to the increasing volume of claims during the 1990s and the very early years of this millennium which have been widely publicised in the media. Details of the levelling in the number of claims against the NHS have not been disseminated on a large scale, and the earlier impressions appear to prevail.[73] Such impressions are no doubt reinforced by media coverage of errors and claims, the existence of organisations such as the NPSA, the Healthcare Commission and NICE, and the emphasis within the NHS on clinical governance, critical incident reporting and other mechanisms designed to identify errors and at the same time to reduce the number of claims. In the course of an informal survey of 300 specialist registrars in Wales conducted by the author in the course of CPD training over a period of four years between 2002 and 2006, it transpired that 92 per cent thought that claims were continuing to rise, 8 per cent did not know, and 96 per cent said that they carried out defensive practices.[74] Doctors are quick to emphasise the view that their clinical freedom has been curtailed by the need to follow guidelines that appear to have been introduced in part as a means of preventing claims.[75]

---

72   'See Effects of Advertising in Respect of Compensation Claims for Personal Injuries', Department for Constitutional Affairs, 2006.
73   See Pollock, A., *NHS plc* (Verso, London, 2004), p 50.
74   Defined as 'treatment examination or other procedures which were not considered necessary in the patient's clinical best interests, but were designed primarily to prevent claims'.
75   Pollock, A., op. cit.

The New Labour government

It is only relatively recently – since the BRTF Report of 2004 – that the UK Government has made serious attempts to communicate to the general public the message that we are not in the grip of a compensation culture. Examples of an earlier approach abound. Frank Dobson, then Secretary of State for Health in the Blair Government, is famous for his statement in an interview for Newsnight, the highly respected BBC television current affairs programme, in 1998:

> The best place for a lawyer is on the operating table. Lawyers are milking the NHS of millions of pounds every year – money that would be better spent on patient care.

An allegation of this nature, made with such vehemence, would have a significant impact on public opinion, and however vigorously politicians attempt to promote the case to the contrary, it is difficult to shift assumptions once they have become rooted in popular culture.

Another instance is to be found in a speech delivered in March 2004,[76] by Stephen Byers. Commenting on figures which indicated that claims against schools had risen to £200 million a year, and claims for medical error against the NHS had risen from £1 million in 1974 to £477 million in 2003, he said:

> Money is being taken away from saving lives and educating our children to pay for a compensation system in which the real beneficiaries are the lawyers and accident management companies.

He continued:

> There has been little public debate about the growth in this blame, claim and gain culture. Yet the consequences for our society are dramatic. We see it with playground equipment being fenced off; hanging baskets being taken down as a health hazard; teachers being advised to no longer supervise school outings.

He was later accused of jumping on the compensation culture band wagon for political ends.[77] Some of the successful claims outside the sphere of clinical negligence have been blamed on the raft of safety regulations emanating from

---

76   Speech delivered in Birmingham on 10 March 2004 and reported on BBC News on the same day and cited but contradicted in the BRTF Report, May 2004, op. cit.

77   See response by Tom Jones, Solicitor, Thompson's, at the same conference: 'Blaming injured people, their lawyers and by default the trade unions who back claims for the financial difficulties of the NHS is a cheap shot.'

Europe which have been introduced to improve conditions in the workplace. Significantly, the Blair Government has promised to reduce the amount of regulation affecting UK workplace activity, including healthcare, dismissing it as 'red tape' that stifles innovation and development. This appears to ignore the fact that health and safety regulations[78] have been responsible for major improvements in the rate of accidents and illnesses sustained in the workplace over the past 30 years.

As far as hospitals are concerned, as is explained in Chapter 2, new approaches taken by claimants' lawyers have meant that patients as well as NHS employees have benefited from the workplace regulations which apply to a broad spectrum of people, including visitors to places of work. Claimants who suffer illnesses and injuries arising from MRSA and other hospital-acquired infections might well have an enhanced chance of success if they claim for breach of statutory duty coupled with the traditional negligence claim, rather than relying on negligence alone.[79] There have been allegations that there is a deliberate attempt to obscure the true figures relating to infection rates and data relating to successful claims by avoiding the associated publicity by means of out-of-court settlements,[80] in order to prevent a further flood of claims against the NHS. This is especially significant given the reported rise during recent years in the number of deaths as a result of MRSA and *C. difficile* contracted on NHS premises.

The fact that successful claims have been the by-product of regulation intended for other purposes should not detract from the important progress that has been made in the field of accident prevention in the course of the past thirty years or so. Outside clinical negligence, there is some evidence that claims within the NHS are increasing in number – for example, equal pay claims supported by the trade unions are rapidly rising following the implementation of Agenda for Change, the new NHS pay structure for non-clinical staff, to the extent that the NHSLA has been given an extended remit for handling this burgeoning area of litigation. Claims for previously underexplored types of injury are also increasing, with psychiatric injury caused by alleged work stress, child abuse, and – outside the healthcare sector – damage to educational opportunity and sports injuries featuring increasingly in recent cases.[81]

The assertions made until the time of the speech by Stephen Byers in March 2004 were quickly countered in a major political offensive at the highest level

---

78   Health and Safety at Work, etc. Act 1974 and the many regulations made under it.
79   Under the COSHH regulations, employers must control exposure of their employees and visitors to hazardous substances in order to prevent ill health. It is at least arguable that MRSA falls within this statutory definition, as the regulations cover biological agents such as bacteria and other micro-organisms. Such claims are being settled out of court at the time of writing. See Chapter 2, fn 24.
80   See Madeleine Brindley, 'Legal approach to open floodgates on MRSA Claims', *Western Mail*, 1 December 2006.
81   See Jane Stapleton's prescience in 'In Restraint of Tort', in Birks, P. (ed.) *The Frontiers of Liability* (Oxford University Press, 1994), vol 2, p 84.

by senior members of Government and their friends and relatives. Senior members of Government were clearly pleased to embrace many of the ideas expressed by the BRTF. Although this organisation describes itself as an independent advisory body set up in 1997 'to advise the Government on action to ensure that regulation and its enforcement are proportionate, accountable, consistent, transparent and targeted', appointments to the BRTF are made by the Minister for the Cabinet Office. It is supported by a team based in the Cabinet Office and is clearly very close to the heart of Government. Indeed, it acknowledges that it has become 'a very influential body in influencing the Government's policy on regulation'. Every Government department is now required to report on its 'regulatory performance' and the BRTF will analyse these reports.

The Prime Minister Tony Blair mustered all his forces, including the services of his wife Cherie Booth[82] in her professional capacity, in his efforts to convince the public that the notion of a compensation culture is little more than a myth perpetrated by the media. Paradoxically, Cherie Booth's comments, made at the launch of a book that she had co-authored on the liability of public authorities, were responsible for accusations in the *Daily Mail* that she is fuelling compensation claims against hard-pressed local authorities, the police, the emergency services and the armed forces, with columnist Richard Littlejohn suggesting that the book be renamed 'How to Milk the Compensation Culture'.

In a long address delivered on 22 March 2005 at a Health and Safety Executive event, Lord Falconer of Thoroton, the Constitutional Affairs Secretary and Lord Chancellor, made a carefully planned attack on the concept of a compensation culture. Lord Falconer was anxious to emphasise, despite evidence to the contrary over the past 30 years,[83] that the courts are consistent in the way that they approach claims, and that the public in general is misled into believing that the courts have begun to award compensation in new ways. He promised that the Government would be committed to responding to what he described as 'these misperceptions' by preventing the practices that feed them and improving the efficiency of the litigation system for genuine claimants. Criticising the practice that has developed among solicitors and others of advertising for clients, he said:

> We need to look closely at the practicality and the process for how we could do this, but we may need to take legal powers to stop some of this advertising.

82   See Dyer, C., 'Booth hits back at compensation culture', *Guardian* 28 February 2006.
83   It is impossible to deny that the Health and Safety framework has made it easier for claimants to succeed in obtaining compensation for personal injuries, and continues to do so.

It was in the same speech that he gave a commitment to the provisions which have now been introduced by the Compensation Act 2006 in an effort to regulate claims management companies and solicitors. He also promised to consider ways in which rehabilitation services could be improved to provide better opportunities for genuine claimants to be dealt with satisfactorily. Alternative dispute resolution would also be explored as a means of ensuring justice for the deserving claimant.

Tony Blair's own speech made in May 2005[84] to the Institute for Public Policy Research think-tank highlighted the BRTF views. The Prime Minister sought a 'sensible debate' about what he saw as a culture that put public services in danger of taking a wholly disproportionate attitude to the risks that people should expect to run as a normal part of everyday activities. Although he recognised the value of the many regulations introduced to ensure safety in the workplace and other fields of human activity, he deplored the 'plethora of rules, guidelines, responses to "scandals" of one nature or another that ends up having utterly perverse consequences'. Referring to Julia Neuberger's book 'The Moral State We're In',[85] he reflected on the absurd situation cited by the author of an old person falling on the floor who cannot be given assistance because the present regulations decree that care workers cannot help them to their feet without the use of suitable equipment. He also criticised the approach of some scientists to risk, citing the case of the MMR vaccine scandal as an example of a single piece of research that was responsible for a scare which, contrary to the vast weight of evidence to the contrary, made parents believe that a tried and tested method of vaccination used globally was unsafe. He emphasised that there was proof of the fact that between 2000 and 2005 the overall number of accident claims fell by 5.3 per cent, and that accident claims against public sector bodies, including doctors, fell by overall by 7.5 per cent. However, he was anxious to make the point that 'public bodies, in fear of litigation, act in highly risk-averse and peculiar ways'. The costs of tort claims in the UK in 2000 were 0.6 per cent of GDP, which is the lowest of any developed nation except Denmark. In that same year the cost of all tort litigation in the UK as a percentage of GDP was less than a third of that in the US.[i]

Tony Blair's response to the problem was to propose that the compensation culture be replaced with a 'common sense culture'. Blaming the media for the claims culture, he called for 'a proper, serious debate with the media about how some of these issues are addressed and how the public is better informed.'

84   Reported in the *Guardian*, 16 May 2005.
85   Harper Collins, London, ISBN 978-0-00-721499-0.

Using the speech as a starting point for the introduction of the Compensation Bill, he promised to implement the recommendations made by the BRTF and to regulate the work of 'claims farmers' who capture claims and typically sell them on to solicitors, indulging in high pressure sales techniques. He announced that the Compensation Bill would also clarify the existing common law on negligence 'to make clear that there is no liability in negligence for untoward incidents that could not be avoided by taking reasonable care or exercising reasonable skill.' The Bill is now an Act, and strangely, the measure to which he referred relating to the standard of care in negligence does no more than re-state the common law position.[86]

The Prime Minister made a commitment to ensuring that valid claims are settled as quickly as possible without the need for court proceedings, citing the much-repeated claim that what the public frequently demand is not money but acknowledgement of error and non-recurrence of the same type of injury. He predicted that what was then the NHS Redress Bill would allow for quicker redress to patients in respect of the low monetary value clinical negligence claims, and real alternatives to litigation.

In what appeared to be casting around for solutions, Tony Blair referred to the need to engage the public more directly and to explore new ways of involving them in the debate on matters of scientific uncertainty. Since that speech was made, the HFEA has engaged in public consultations, and NICE has continued to progress its established citizens' council to discuss medical decision-making.

The Government has an obvious interest in ensuring that the level of claims against the NHS and other public bodies remains under tight control, lest as Tony Blair melodramatically claimed in his speech, things go wrong, 'with the capacity to do serious damage to our country'.

John Tingle reflected a similar view in his comment:[87]

> Patients continue to sue the NHS for nurses' and doctors' negligence, steps must be taken to attack the 'compensation culture', which may be encouraging some of them to mount spurious claims that block up the system, cause unnecessary expense and stress and lead to defensive clinical practice.

The BRTF[88] reinforced the Government's approach:

> The Government is determined to scotch any suggestion of a developing 'compensation culture' where people believe that they can seek

86   See Compensation Act 2006 s 1.
87   *British Journal of Nursing* (9 September 2004) 3(16): 938.
88   'Tackling the Compensation Culture: The Government's Response to the Better Routes to Redress', November 2004, op. cit.

compensation for any misfortune that befalls them, even if no-one else is to blame. This misperception undermines personal responsibility and respect for the law and creates unnecessary burdens through an exaggerated fear of litigation.

There are good reasons why the Government should want to suppress the notion of a compensation culture as reflected in a rising level of claims. Tax payers' money is used to fund public services, and the Government has promised to improve education services and the service provided by the NHS. It is vital to the credibility of a government which has come under severe criticism for its failings in both areas, to deal effectively with threats to their financial stability, and the findings of reputable academic researchers support the Government's standpoint. For example, Fenn *et al.*, at an Association of British Insurers conference in 2005, examined the conflicting claims of the BRTF and the actuarial profession, and concluded that the compensation culture is a matter of public misconception and does not really exist, at least as far as claims for employers' liability are concerned, as there was evidence that in the employment sector claims were falling.

More recently, in keeping with the Government's view that litigation should be discouraged, Lord Falconer made the surprising suggestion that:

> If you can't get legal aid and an efficient service from the civil courts, perhaps it's time to consider the alternative: forgiving and forgetting.[89]

A strong tactic for politicians in the battle for credibility is to blame the system – in this instance lawyers, claims managers, the litigation system and media reporting of legal cases. As Haltom and McCann revealed in their highly acclaimed work[90] on the media influence on public perceptions of tort law, a complex political agenda may be unwittingly fed by the media. Despite all its efforts, the Government is likely to encounter real difficulties in convincing the nation that there is no compensation culture. Research into public attitudes indicates that people tend to trust other professional groups far more readily than politicians, and attempts to dislodge such preconceptions can be futile, as there is evidence that widely held beliefs are generally difficult to change.[91] The contradictory data produced by official bodies is likely to increase general suspicion that the truth is being hidden and exacerbate public cynicism.[92]

---

89   BBC Radio 4, 'Law in Action', 27 February 2007.
90   Haltom, W. and McCann, M., *Dis-torting the Law: Politics, Media and the Litigation Crisis* (University of Chicago Press, Chicago and London, 2004).
91   Renn, O. and Levene, D., 'Credibility and Trust in Risk Communication', in Pasperson, R.E. and Stallen, P.J.M. (eds) *Communicating Risks to the Public: International Perspectives* (Kluwer, Dordrecht, 2003).
92   See data relating to hospital infections, supra fn 27.

Why disapprove of a compensation culture?

Although it is generally supposed that a compensation culture is bad for the country and for individuals, it may carry certain benefits. For example, the threat of litigation may operate as a general deterrent and an incentive to improving safety, and the cost of taking sensible precautions may be lower than the cost of compensating the injured. This might be particularly true in the context of healthcare and is a principle which has generated an extensive programme of risk management.[93] It may also lead to the establishing of carefully considered guidelines by which to measure the standard of care – another feature of medical law. As Lord Bingham has acknowledged:

> I cannot accept, as a general proposition, that the imposition of a duty of care makes no contribution on the maintenance of high standards.[94]

It is possible that the introduction of safety measures (in part imposed by the Government implementing EU Directives, and in part implementing risk management procedures), which cannot be separated entirely from the fear of liability, has played a role in reducing accidents in industry, healthcare and on the roads.

Seeking compensation may have certain advantages. It enables defendants to learn from their mistakes; it encourages reflection on errors and the introduction of safer practices; it is a mechanism by which healthcare staff are made accountable for malpractice and it is means of vindication and financial support for those who are injured. Set against these advantages are the numerous disadvantages, which are perceived by the healthcare professions, lawyers[95] and the Government to outweigh the advantages by a significant margin, and there is now a widely held view that litigation is to be avoided wherever possible, chiefly because it is time-consuming, a drain on valuable resources and can be counter-productive in terms of defensive medicine and the stress it places on healthcare professionals.

Conclusion

Haltom and McCann, authors of the classic work on the supposed litigation crisis in the US,[96] concluded that perception and reality are so widely separated in relation to the state of their civil litigation system that rational debate about the topic is nearly impossible. In the UK, assumptions made by

---

93   See Chapter 6.
94   In the Court of Appeal in X (Minors) v Bedfordshire CC and M (A Minor) v Newham LBC [1994] 2 WLR 554.
95   See Lord Woolf's Final Report on the Civil Justice System.
96   Haltom, W. and McCann, M., *Dis-torting the Law: Politics, Media and the Litigation Crisis* (University of Chicago Press, Chicago and London, 2004).

the Government challenging the existence of a 'compensation culture', and those made by healthcare professions who fear litigation, suggest that there is something reprehensible about claiming for negligent medical treatment, but there are powerful arguments in favour of compensating those who suffer injury as a result of medical errors. Yet the data suggests that the number of incidents in which patient safety has been compromised far exceeds the number of claims. The studies conducted in the US and Australia revealed that, as in the UK today, despite a high number of adverse incidents, only a small proportion resulted in the bringing of legal claims.[97] Inevitably there are some organisations, including the Government, which have an interest in promoting the idea that too many people, even those who deserve to be compensated, are making claims, and that this movement is creating a climate which is damaging the economy and the morale of the nation; that much of the blame for this lies with the legal profession and so-called 'claims farmers'. These charges lose sight of another social evil, in that at present there is no efficient and accurate system for identifying and preventing errors, and alongside it, no definite system for ensuring that those who deserve compensation are informed that they have been the victims of negligence so that they can proceed with relative ease with the process of recovering financial support, at least as long as the present tort system continues to exist.

It should not be forgotten that a welcome side-effect of the rising number of claims, far from being unproductive risk-averse behaviour as the Government asserts, has been the introduction of more effective risk management and measures to ensure patient safety. As Tom Baker, discussing the defensive medical problem in the US,[98] states:

> With two exceptions … none of the researchers who have studied defensive medicine have claimed that they are able to separate the bad, wasteful effects of malpractice lawsuits from the good, injury-preventing effects.

Clinical governance and risk management might well be thinly disguised attempts to manage the rising number of claims, but they do have the official approval of policy makers and legislators in the UK, and there is evidence that the number of errors being detected in the healthcare setting is relatively stable.

The arguments that rage between politicians and others about whether there is a compensation culture are to some extent irrelevant. As long as compensation is available, and in view of the fact that claims for clinical negligence are now 1,200 per cent higher in number than they were 20 years

97 President and Fellows of Harvard College, The Harvard Medical Practice Study, 'Patients, Doctors and Lawyers: Medical Injury, Malpractice Litigation and Patients Compensation in New York (Cambridge, MA, 1990).

98 Baker, T., *The Medical Malpractice Myth* (University of Chicago Press, Chicago, 2005).

ago, there will be a compensation culture. The potential still exists for a further rise in the number of claims as a result of population growth and possibly even, some would argue, because of the less rigorous training requirements for consultants which are in the process of being introduced.[99] The pertinent questions are: how deeply is the compensation culture entrenched and how can it be managed effectively?

99   Department of Health 'Modernising Medical Careers', 15 April 2004, see comments by the BMA, February 2007.

Chapter 4

Perpetuating the myth
Should we blame the media?

Introduction

This chapter examines the role of the media in reporting medical stories, and accounts of clinical negligence and error in particular, and considers assertions that irresponsible media reporting can be blamed for fuelling what Lord Falconer called 'have a go' attitudes to compensation in the UK.[1] The question is whether the media are engaged in a 'feeding frenzy' centred on the NHS, or whether they are bringing to the attention of the public matters of serious concern, in a climate of freedom of expression for which the UK is famous throughout the world. This is supported by the human rights framework and Freedom of Information Act 2000 which, although criticised as being too restrictive, has enabled journalists to obtain some highly sensitive information about the NHS. It is logical that negative media reports may lead to negative publicity for healthcare organisations, and it has been suggested that stories about malpractice and the volume and level of claims have been exaggerated by the popular media. The result is that many NHS Trusts and healthcare organisations now employ press officers to handle difficult publicity and encourage the reporting of success stories. Government departments, including the Department of Health, have had press officers and 'spin doctors' ever since New Labour came into power, and Health Ministers' announcements are obviously drafted by civil servants with public opinion firmly in mind – a study of which is worthy of a doctorate in its own right. That does not mean that there is no cause for concern about the number of errors in healthcare and the volume of claims, but the position becomes self-authenticating because of the role of the media in reporting healthcare malpractice stories.

Fact or melodrama?

Given the volume of media reports about healthcare malpractice, there can be little doubt that the media view is that members of the public are

1   22 March 2005 at a Health and Safety Executive event.

fascinated by tales of misfortune, negligence, illness, injury and vast awards of compensation. If sex can be introduced into the equation, it seems that the press are unstoppable. The more salacious the better, as the wide coverage of the recent more general personal injury case of Stephen Tame[2] indicates – the claimant was awarded £3.2 million after suffering a head injury at work, which caused him to experience an increase in his sex drive, and to be sexually disinhibited and unfaithful to his wife. Many of the reported errors and claims concern high awards of money, always an attention-grabbing topic. Thus, as Haltom and McCann argue,[3] in relation to the US position, the media in reporting personal injury cases unwittingly create a picture of the legal system which fits closely with the highly critical and moralistic agenda of those who wish to promote tort reform. This is also true of the UK's New Labour Government.

Some of the coverage of high awards in general personal injury cases in *The Times* in 2005, to take but one day's example, is illustrative of the approach that can be taken even by a serious broadsheet.[4] Under a headline entitled 'Compensation Culture', the following cases were listed:

- Lorraine Capener, 53, a mortuary technician, received £15,000 from an employment tribunal in October after developing a morbid fear of death
- A soldier injured when he fell from an army lorry as he 'windsurfed' on the tailgate, received £75,000 from the MoD
- A Scots policeman won £2,000 after being bitten by his own dog; another got £5,000 for exposure to 'excessive' noise while on motorcycle duty
- Karl Jones, a fraudster, was awarded nearly £248,000 in 2003 after suffering from erectile dysfunction when he slipped in a jail shower
- Marvin Pomfret received £75,000 in 2002 after blaming his violent criminal career on his attendance at a school for children with learning difficulties
- The mother of an unruly teenager who suffered from anxiety after he was expelled for taking a knife to school won £11,000 from Greenwich council.

The *Daily Telegraph* on 15 March 2007 contained the following:

£8.5m for woman paralysed crossing the road … A woman who was run down on a pelican crossing when she was a child received £8.5 million yesterday in what is thought to be one of the highest ever injury compensation awards.

2   *Tame v Professional Cycle Marketing Ltd* (QBD, 19 December 2006).
3   Haltom, W. and McCann, M., *Dis-torting the Law: Politics, Media and the Litigation Crisis* (University of Chicago Press, Chicago and London, 2004).
4   *The Times*, 6 December 2005.

A cursory glance at the news reports of personal injury awards indicates that the higher the award, the more reportable it is, yet it is difficult to criticise this as irresponsible journalism even if the cases selected are somewhat surprising, since they are all based on verifiable facts, and even the Government admits that those who are genuine tort victims deserve to be compensated for their injuries and losses.[5]

Among many examples of articles about healthcare claims in regional newspapers is a report in December 2006, *The Western Mail*,[6] a Welsh newspaper, which carried a story outlining successful recent claims for injuries caused by MRSA, using the COSHH Regulations, under the headline, 'Legal approach to open floodgate on MRSA claims.' It continued:

> The number of patients successfully pursuing claims after contracting MRSA could skyrocket under a fresh legal approach. Solicitors are now using the same laws that protect building site workers from harmful chemicals to make claims for compensation. An increase in claims could see already cash-strapped NHS trusts forced to pay larger premiums to the Welsh Risk Pool, which covers the cost of legal action on behalf of the NHS.

On the topic of cleanliness, or the lack of it, in the healthcare setting, the media have been forthright in exposing serious shortcomings, with headlines like:

> Patient who overcame leukaemia killed by a dirty hospital shower[7]

> Dentist accused of urinating in surgery' sink[8]

In relation to the lack of skill on the part of junior doctors, the following headline appeared in the *Independent*:

> Danger: white coats – Doctors call it 'the killing season': the time in August when keen, but as yet unskilled, young medics are first let loose on the wards. Be very afraid.[9]

5   See Tony Blair's Speech, May 2005, to Institute of Public Policy Research.
6   Brindley, M., *Western Mail*, 1 December 2006.
7   *The Times*, 22 March 2007, p 7.
8   Ibid.
9   Sokol, D., *The Independent*, 2 August 2004.

It is not difficult, then, to find negative and sensationalised coverage of medical stories. The accounts in the popular media of the Bristol and Shipman cases abound with examples of sensationalism, but all of them contained matters of pressing public importance. In the years following the Bristol cases, there has been a shift in public attitudes towards less deference to the medical profession than was shown in previous years,[10] and the media are discovering more and more medical scandals with which to 'entertain' us. The medical press abounds with articles on the topic or media coverage,[11] attempting to throw light on the rash of malpractice stories in the popular press. One author drew some examples from the popular press of the day,[12] citing The *Sun* newspaper's dramatic stance in its report of the activities of a certain Dr Walmsley, a GP on trial for sexual offences:

What the hell is going on? Countless women have suffered mutilation, horrifying internal injuries and been psychologically traumatised.

Reviewing statements made by patients, the coverage continued:

'He ought to be castrated,' and 'I'd like to string him up and cut him to bits,' said another.

The *Independent*, by any standards a more moderate newspaper, was also quoted in relation to the same doctor:

In a medical scandal that is being described as potentially worse than the Bristol heart babies tragedy, more than 100 women may have been injured by an incompetent surgeon who was allowed to continue operating unchecked for more than a decade.

Describing Dr Walmsley, *The Times* on 18 November 1987 stated with high drama:

For 17 years Gerald Walmsley had preyed on young female patients at surgeries in Yorkshire and Kent as he subjected them to indecent assaults on his consulting room couch.

It has been suggested that as a society we are now less afraid of challenging doctors than in earlier years, but that there may also have been a

10   See Lewis, C., *Medical Negligence: A Practical Guide*, p 2 (6th edn, Tottel Publishing, West Sussex, 2006).
11   See e.g., Abbasi, K., 'Medicine and the Media: Butchers and Gropers', Student *BMJ*, February 1999.
12   Ibid.

fundamental change in the relationship between the medical profession and the media, so that post-Bristol, 'doctors are now fair game like everyone else'.[13]

The NHS as a whole is also under fire in the national newspapers. Take, for example, an article in the *Observer*[14] reporting a King's Fund Report on NHS spending, which contained this text:

> A damning report by the highly respected health think-tank, the King's Fund, reveals that productivity in the health service has actually declined, despite the huge injection of cash.
>
> The report reveals that only 30 pence in every £ of the Government's record NHS budget has been aimed at directly improving patient care. As well as salaries, the rest has gone on a growing bill for clinical negligence payouts and rising drug costs. The King's Fund report, based on the most detailed and authoritative analysis yet of Labour's trebling of health spending, will make difficult reading for government ministers alarmed at criticism of the impact of their health reforms.

Serious television and radio documentaries are presented convincingly, yet they can be unbalanced and unfairly critical of healthcare professionals.[15] In a review of a BBC programme in the QED science series, one medical writer[16] complained:

> The programme makers say the story is based on real life, but certainly the plot had all the features of a classic Clint Eastwood 'I'm gonna fight 'till I get justice' movie. The father (the hero of the drama) nearly smokes himself to death ... He is helped in his search for the truth by a black charge nurse, who whispers that all is not what it seems, and a young female solicitor. ... The rest of the characters – oleaginous solicitors, pompous barristers, stupid judges, indifferent hospital managers, arrogant consultants, ignorant junior doctors, crass intensive care nurses – all play out their stereotypes like characters in a Punch and Judy show.

13   Abassi, K., 'Medicine and the Media', Student *BMJ*, February 1999.
14   Campbell, D., Revill, J., Temko, N., 'Patients miss out as NHS cash floods in', *Observer*, 18 March 2007.
15   Essex, C., 'Medicine and the Media: Who can we blame?' (A Critique of 'Law Suits and Liniment', Radio 4 Trilogy) (1997) 315 *BMJ* 688.
16   Bulstrode, C., 'Medicine and the Media: The Traumas of Casualty Departments' (1997) 315 *BMJ* 196.

Responsible media practices, freedom of information and public concerns

It is undeniable that some of the accounts carried in popular newspapers are sensationalist, but there are many examples of responsible media reporting of medical malpractice.

Recent examples

A classic example of good media practice is the story reported in the *Sunday Times*[17] under the headline 'Hospitals botch 300 births a year'. The article that followed was the result of serious investigative journalism facilitated by the Freedom of Information Act 2000, which exposed a situation in the NHS that requires further investigation by the Government and urgent remedial action. Yet Tony Blair and Lord Falconer, in keeping with the spirit of their drive to suppress the compensation culture, would no doubt regard this as scaremongering which might ultimately deter people from having babies. In fact, it is responsible reporting of a subject which needs to be brought into the open in order to inform the public. Accidents, which are blamed on staff shortages and inadequate monitoring of women in labour, do lead to very high awards of compensation, and to higher costs to the public purse in terms of special education, continuing health problems and social services costs. It is a matter of genuine public interest that in the five years covered by the data under investigation there were 2,763 claims relating to obstetrics, of which 6 per cent–10 per cent are estimated to be by mothers who had their reproductive organs damaged.

Despite a commitment to freedom of expression through the Human Rights Act 1998 and the Freedom of Information Act 2000, the Government is now so displeased by the activities of the media in covering issues concerning health and other public matters that the political climate has changed to the extent that the Department of Constitutional Affairs is taking steps to restrict the scope of their investigations.

The very fact that senior members of the Government have reacted so strongly as to criticise the operation of the Freedom of Information Act 2000, a flagship piece of legislation for New Labour which came fully into force in 2005, is testimony to the success of journalists in uncovering and reporting issues such as obstetrics deaths, which are embarrassing for the Government. Lord Falconer has described the Act as 'the single most significant act of any government in improving transparency, accessibility and accountability'. Ironically, the *Independent* reported[18] more recently that Lord Falconer, at the Lord Williams of Mostyn Memorial Lecture, told journalists to stop using the

---

17   Rogers L., 'Hospitals botch 300 births a year', *Sunday Times*, 27 August 2006.
18   *Independent*, London, 22 March 2007, 4th edn.

Freedom of Information Act to 'mount fishing expeditions aimed at uncovering stories about the Government', saying that the Act was intended for the public, not the media. Lord Falconer referred to Government-commissioned research, which proved that journalists account for some 16 per cent of the total cost of Central Government requests under the Act, costing around £4 million. This misses the very point that the media are using the Act to inform the public about important matters which the Government appears anxious to hide. The director of the Campaign for the Freedom of Information, Maurice Frankel, told the same newspaper:

> They may be right that the press is out to get them, but that is the nature of our democracy. What they don't seem to recognise is that the media publishes material from which the public benefits.

The *Daily Mail* later reported that MPs are very concerned about Lord Falconer's approach, because in their view 'Tony Blair's former flat-mate, Lord Falconer who is unelected', has no right of his own to restrict legislation that was passed by Parliament.[19] According to *The Sunday Times*, a newspaper once famous for its high quality investigative journalism, those who attempt to use the Freedom of Information Act already face 'bureaucratic stonewalling'. There is already a large backlog of complaints being dealt with by the Information Commissioner about attempts to block investigations.

Tales from the past

Responsible investigative journalism has been the impetus for unearthing many matters of serious concern about the state of the NHS, and has resulted in some of the most far-reaching healthcare reforms of recent years. The exposure of the Thalidomide tragedy is an early illustration of the power of the press in the medical arena to bring about changes in social attitudes to compensation. *The Sunday Times*, by exposing the fact that inadequate tests were performed to assess the safety of the drug, with catastrophic results for the children of women who had taken thalidomide during the 1960s, was ultimately able to obtain compensation for a large number of victims of the drug.[20] Over the next decades there followed numerous exposures by the media of medical scandals and injuries to patients, culminating in the Bristol heart babies cases and the Harold Shipman murders, many of which were initially unearthed by investigative journalists and some of which resulted in the establishing of major public inquiries[21] and radical reform of the law

19   *Daily Mail*, 21 March 2007.
20   See Evans, H., 'Attacking the Devil', *British Journalism Review* (2002) 13(4): 6.
21   'Learning from Bristol', the report of the public inquiry into children's heart surgery at the Bristol Royal Infirmary 1985–95; the Shipman Inquiry Reports.

to improve safety in healthcare, ensure proper regulation of the healthcare professions, and among other developments, to recognise patient autonomy.

Of all these examples, the most noteworthy media intervention was in the Bristol case. After years of concerns by staff, on 14 February 1992, *Private Eye* published the first article that referred to cardiology and cardiac surgery in Bristol. This was followed by another on 27 March, and yet another on 8 May. It was the *Eye*'s coverage of the situation on 9 October in the same year that exposed the true extent of the situation, with the words:

> The sorry state of paediatric cardiac surgery at the United Bristol Healthcare Trust has been confirmed by an internal audit over the last two years' operations. The results of procedures to correct two congenital heart abnormalities (Tetralogy of Fallot and transposition of the arteries) were especially poor.
>
> James Wisheart, chairman of the hospital management committee and medical advisor to the trust board, is required to maintain standards of medical practice at UBHT. Curiously he has not felt it necessary to inform the trust board or the trust's purchasers of these findings. Could it be because he is also associate director of cardiac surgery?[22]

Commenting on this later, Phil Hammond, a doctor who was instrumental in exposing the Bristol story to the media, was to say:[23]

> The largest ever public inquiry into systematic failure in the NHS, chaired by Professor Ian Kennedy, has just been published. It centred on the poor results for child heart surgery in Bristol between 1984 and 1995, and how the surgeons were allowed to continue unchecked for years. But concerns about Bristol were first made public nine years ago, in a satirical magazine and at an Edinburgh fringe show.

After the Bristol story was taken up by the mainstream media in 1995, Phil Hammond participated in BBC2's series, 'Trust Me, I'm a Doctor', which brought to the attention of the public similar scandals to that in Bristol across a range of medical specialties.

Another infamous scandal which was reported widely by the media concerned Rodney Ledward, a gynaecologist, who was given sufficient leeway to condemn himself in an interview on the Radio 4 Today Programme,[24] the flavour of which is captured in these words:

---

22   Final Report of Bristol Inquiry Annex A, Chapter 27, para 134.
23   Hammond, P., 'Killing Fields and Other Doctor's Tales', *New Statesman*, 21 July 2001.
24   BBC News, 'The Rodney Ledward Interview', 8 June 2000.

Interviewer: Now, you have been described by some of the papers as a butcher and as a rogue gynaecologist, what do you feel when you read comments like that about yourself?

Rodney Ledward: Well I just feel sorry for the press because I've read a thousand and one other things, I've got a yacht and a stud farm and a few other addendums to my life so I just. ...

Interviewer: The report also says that you would see patients dressed up in jodhpurs and riding boots and with a riding whip?

Rodney Ledward: Yes ... it's not a whip it is a crop and if you go riding you have a riding crop.

Ledward had been struck off the medical register in 1998, and his activities led to the Ritchie Inquiry and Report[25] that ran to almost 400 pages. It was the media coverage of Ledward's activities that led 500 women to come forward with evidence about their treatment at his hands. Other shocking accounts followed concerning the injuries caused to women by Richard Neale, another gynaecologist.

The media also played a central role in informing the public that organs taken from dead children had been retained over a long period of time. The publication of the report of the Redfern Inquiry resulted in the following sensationalist headlines:[26]

'Horror of organs hoard' (*Evening Standard*); 'The basement of horrors' (*Independent*); 'The baby butcher' (*Daily Mirror*); 'He stripped the organs from every dead child he touched' (*Guardian*); 'My Baby's Body was on a Dirty Table in 36 Jars' (*Sun*).

There followed a large number of claims by distressed parents. Helen Rickards discovered from a television documentary that her daughter's heart had been retained after a post-mortem examination following cardiac surgery at the Bristol Royal Infirmary, which led her to seek information from the hospital about her daughter's medical records. A Bristol Heart Children Action Group was established, which called a press conference to allow the public to be informed about the retained hearts. Soon, the hospital received more than 600 enquiries from parents.

In 2002 the Report of Media Analysis of the retained organs story,[27] set up to study how the media was delivering the message of the Retained Organs

25   An Inquiry into Quality and Health Within the National Health Service, arising from the actions of Rodney Ledward, Department of Health 2000.
26   Quoted by Sir Hugh Pennington in his account of the Royal Liverpool Children's Inquiry Report 2001.
27   ROC Media Analysis Report, January 2001–April 2002.

Commission (ROC), concluded that the media coverage of the work of the ROC was not exceptionally high – only around 100 mentions in a 15-month period. However, it also noted that the media had covered the matters widely and had 'left no stone unturned'.

The news story that led to saturation coverage by the media was of course that of Harold Shipman and the events surrounding his denunciation, trial, multiple murder convictions and suicide in prison. There were attempts by investigative journalists, some of them successful, to identify murders that Shipman had committed over a long period of time.

Other media reports of medical malpractice events include incidents of cruelty at nursing homes for the elderly,[28] deaths resulting from failure to monitor patients[29] or as a result of misdiagnosis,[30] incompetent doctors and nurses,[31] concerns about the quality of expert evidence given in court by doctors,[32] manipulation of waiting lists[33] and other targets, and financial mismanagement in the NHS[34] to name but a few. The media have also exposed malpractice and incompetence among lawyers[35] and claims management companies.[36]

On a rather different note, the media have been instrumental in raising the public profile of moral dilemmas concerning medical law matters such as resource allocation,[37] life-sustaining treatment for babies,[38] clinical trials,[39] euthanasia,[40] assisted suicide,[41] and abortion.[42] While coverage of these matters may not have led directly to claims, the reporting of the court proceedings involved would have generated an awareness of medical law processes in the minds of the public as a whole.

---

28   The website www.elderabuse.org.uk/media contains 28 press cuttings about elder abuse at nursing home in the month of October 2006 alone.
29   See accounts of the case of *R v HM Coroner for Inner London North ex p Touche* [2001] EWCA Civ 383 (QB.).
30   Hall, C., 'Mother died after delays and misdiagnosis', *Daily Telegraph* 14 March 2007.
31   See media coverage of the establishment of the National Clinical Assessment Authority.
32   The coverage of the case of Sir Roy Meadow described him with the title of 'the discredit' even before his case was heard by the GMC. There has been copious media coverage of other 'scandals' surrounding medical experts over the past few years.
33   E.g. 'Crackdown on waiting list fiddles', BBC News, 19 December 2001.
34   *Guardian*, 23 May 2002, 'Plan to ban scandal hit managers from the NHS'.
35   'You're never too old to be defrauded', *Guardian*, 4 April 2004.
36   See BBC Radio 4 'You and Yours' progamme – a series of exposures of aggressive selling tactics by claims management companies.
37   E.g. *R v Cambridge Health Authority ex p B (Minor)* (1995) 25 BMLR 5 to name but one instance.
38   E.g. *Re Wyatt (A child) (medical treatment: parents' consent)* [2004] Fam Law 866 and subsequent proceedings.
39   See extensive coverage of the Northwick Park incident in 2006.
40   See BBC News Special Report, 24 March 2007.
41   See wide ranging media coverage of the Diane Pretty litigation.
42   E.g. BBC News, 12 December 2005.

Criticisms of media coverage in the healthcare context

Criticisms abound of media reporting of healthcare stories. By and large the critics are drawn from the healthcare professions and the Government. Some of the criticisms are justified – if reports contain exaggeration and inaccuracies, or where grieving relatives are interviewed while still in distress. However, exposure of genuine concerns about the state of the NHS and analysis of the number of errors and claims are matters to which the public are entitled to have access, and can usually do so only through the work of investigative journalists.

The views of healthcare professionals

The views of one academic healthcare manager[43] about journalists at the time of the Bristol Inquiry were expressed forcefully:

> We are not being paranoid; 'they' – the journalists – really are out to get us.

Commenting on the media coverage as some of the scandals outlined above came to light, a *BMJ* article quoted copiously from daily newspapers,[44] pointing out that:

> Horror stories of medical incompetence, arrogance, and libidinousness have filled newspapers; broadsheets and tabloids have been united in their condemnation of a profession unable to regulate itself except when it's too late. ... Even Caligula would have blushed, but the press have feasted daily on the medical professions' misery: sex and violence sell. Nurses are good, doctors are bad; patients are pure, doctors are evil.

Chief among the objections voiced by the medical profession is the lack of scientific rigour demonstrated by the media, which can have a damaging effect on doctors and also, on occasion, on patients. Sir Hugh Pennington, commenting on the media coverage of the role of Alder Hey in the retained organs scandal, made the point that no donations had been received in some English research centres since the publication of the Redfern Report. He continued:[45]

43   Willis, J.A.R., 'The Pen is Mightier Than the Scalpel'. Commentary on the paper, 'Public trust, and accountability for clinical performance: lessons from the national press reporting of the Bristol hearing' (H.T.O. Davies and A.V. Shields, *Journal of Evaluation in Clinical Practice* 5, 335–42', http://www.friendsinlowplaces.co.uk/index.htm

44   Abassi, K., 'Butchers and Gropers – Media Coverage of Medical Malpractice', *BMJ*, 5 December 1998.

45   *LRB* (8 March 2001) 23(5).

It is clear from what they wrote that many reporters did not know, and still do not understand, that at a routine post-mortem the brain, heart, lungs, liver, intestines and kidneys are removed from the body, sliced, examined and then returned. This ignorance probably fuelled the outrage that followed Redfern's revelations and it may help, in part, to account for the view that Alder Hey was the worst disaster ever to befall the NHS.

The failure by the media to apply scientific criteria to reporting medical stories has been considered at some length by Ben Goldacre, a doctor who writes the 'Bad Science' column for the *Guardian*. In an article at the time of the MMR vaccine fiasco, one of the worst examples of confused thinking by the media[46] which resulted in a nationwide scare and the return of some very serious childhood infections, he reflected that it would be possible to spend a lifetime talking to the media about scientific and medical research without meeting a 'single one of the incompetent and nefarious journalists who were driving the MMR vaccination "scandal" for so long'. He called for an improvement in communication between scientists, journalists, and the public, with the observation that properly qualified science journalists seldom cover major science news stories. He quoted a survey in 2003 by the Economic and Social Research Council which had found that a mere 20 per cent of stories about the MMR vaccine were written by specialist correspondents. Parents were thus taking advice on immunology and epidemiology from 'lifestyle-columnists'.

The result of lack of scientific rigour and objectivity is the failure to produce reporting based on empirical evidence. Apparently authoritative pronouncements from so-called experts with an interest in promoting particular views abound. Goldacre's solution is based on common sense – simply that specialist journalists with science qualifications should write and report scientific stories. They are able to appraise scientific evidence and prevent the 'dumbing down' of medical coverage, as compared with the finance, sports pages, and literary pages.

The views of politicians

There is no shortage of criticism by politicians of the way the media handle coverage of clinical negligence and medical malpractice. The views of Tony Blair and Lord Falconer were outlined in Chapter 3. The House of Commons Constitutional Affairs Committee Report on the Compensation Culture[47] covered a wide range of topics, including the impact and side effects of conditional fee agreements and the role of the media in generating claims.

---

46 Goldacre, B., 'Media Scares: Where Are All The Science Journalists?' Education and debate (13 August 2005) 403 *BMJ* 331.
47 Third Report of Session 2005–06.

Selective media reporting of high value awards was one of the problems identified in the Report as a cause of risk aversion on the part of public bodies like the NHS.

The BRTF[48] adopted a theme that was later taken up by Tony Blair and Lord Falconer:

> Almost every day there is a report in the media ... suggesting that the United Kingdom is in the grip of a compensation culture. Headlines shout about people trying to claim what appear to be large sums of money for what are portrayed as dubious reasons

The Government has found it necessary to deflect possible criticisms of its approach to health policy by attempting to take control of what is published in the media. In the early days after New Labour came into Government, a powerful press office was established, which became famous for its spin, taking control over press releases. These little gems of Government spin developed linguistic uniformity, and did very little to fool the cynical journalists in the press pack. Although there were attempts to remedy this situation at a later stage, there remains an enduring party line approach implicit in all press releases concerning health, and to the present day they contain surprisingly similar language and style. As press releases on health reflect the Government's preferred interpretation of a news item or other story, journalists are understandably sceptical of their contents, and adopt them verbatim. Indeed, press releases have become almost counter-productive. The usual format of a press release is a statement about a new development giving the official ideological line which the Government wishes to promote, followed by a statement allegedly written by a Minister, often from a speech that is to be delivered the same day, and a set of explanatory notes for journalists.[49] The advent of the internet has seen the birth of the '*optimised press release*', intended not only for journalists but also for members of the public and professionals who tend to read them, and the result is that the press are no longer the gate-keepers of the information contained in them. This means that a wider, and possibly more gullible, audience is exposed to information which has the advantage to the Government of bypassing the editing process to which press releases would be subjected by journalists.[50]

The views of lawyers

Lawyers and judges who may have no political interest in making critical comments about the media do sometimes take the opportunity to express their

---

48   Better Routes to Redress, 2004.
49   For a wide range of examples, see Department of Health Press Releases Library.
50   Coldwell, I., 'The Ethics of Political Communication', Political Studies Association Conference, 7 April 2001.

views about media coverage of cases that come before the courts. If there is criticism from that quarter, it is frequently justified. An example of such criticism is the comment of Jean Ritchie QC in her report of the Inquiry into the activities of Rodney Ledward:

> Finally, we should say that we have been very troubled that many women have been damaged by the aftermath of Rodney Ledward's dismissal. They have been plagued by doubts and worry which has been fed by press attention and media reporting.[51]

One of the very real problems faced by doctors who are criticised by the media is that they are unable to defend themselves fully because of patient confidentiality, while their accusers have no such constraints. In the course of the appeal process and before his GMC hearing, Sir Roy Meadow, accused of incompetence in the evidence he gave at the trial of the late Sally Clarke, for the murder of her babies, was unable to comment in his own defence despite the adverse press coverage he was receiving at the time. He was bound by medical confidentiality and by the court rules. He has since argued that he was subjected to trial by the media. This had the inevitable effect of offering his critics a dominant position in the debate. Seldom was his name mentioned in the media without the epithet 'the discredited', even before the final sanction was imposed on him.[52]

The power of media-based advertising

As the analysis in the earlier chapters of this book demonstrates, there is evidence that in the closing years of the last century people in the UK experienced a compensation culture. This continued into the present millennium, with claims management companies aggressively targeting anyone with a potential cause of action, though the Government is in the process of introducing a range of measures to control the problem.[53] There are some commentators who have laid much of the blame for these developments on lawyers[54] but others, notably the BRTF,[55] are prepared to blame the media as well, especially media advertising by claims management companies.[56] Research on the US indicated that 73 per cent of people surveyed who had made a

---

51   Page 345, para 2.1.
52   Gooderham, P., 'Complaints About Medical Expert Witnesses in the United Kingdom' (2004) *Med. Law. International* 6(4): 297–325.
53   See the Compensation Act 2006.
54   Ferudi, F., 'Courting Mistrust – The Hidden Growth of a Culture of Litigation in Britain', Centre for Policy Studies, April 1999.
55   BRTF Report 2004.
56   See Aon Survey, July 2004.

claim against a doctor had been motivated to do so by a television commercial for a law firm.[57]

Advertising is an essential means of raising revenue for most media companies, and in a competitive market advertising can be responsible for persuading the public in a variety of directions. This is a powerful factor in the complex relationship between claims and publicity in general. This was an important influence on the views of the BRTF concerning claims management companies, and gave rise to a range of assumptions which are difficult to challenge. For example, Peter Cane states:[58]

> Claims management services are now widely advertised especially on TV. Such advertising, and increased media coverage of the tort system, have probably raised significantly public awareness of the possibility of claiming damages ... as well as expectations about the success of such claims.

The Government, concerned about the media influence on claims, commissioned research into the role of advertising, and a report was published in 2006.[59] The researchers concluded that there is no straightforward link between public attitudes and advertising, as the situation is extremely complex. However, it was apparent from the research conducted for the report that advertising, and especially advertising on television, is the main source of public awareness of personal injury claims, but the evidence suggested that advertising simply reinforces negative perceptions rather than creating new ones:

> Fanning the flames of a negativity which has its roots in media coverage and word of mouth.[60]

The chief problem lay, according to the researchers, in the quantity and frequency of advertisements, and the fact that media advertising reinforces misperceptions of the claims process. There is also a possibility that advertising normalises what might otherwise be a socially unacceptable activity – though if there is a legitimate claim for a genuine injury it is difficult to see why such a development should be frowned upon. People participating in the research had little idea from the advertisements that they were entering a

---

57   Huyke, L.I. and Huyke, M.M., 'Characteristics of Potential Plaintiffs in Malpractice Litigation' (1994) *Annals of Internal Medicine* 120(9): 792–98, p 793.
58   Cane, P., *Atiyah's Accidents, Compensation and the Law* (7th edn, Cambridge University Press, Cambridge, 2006, p 194).
59   'Effects of Advertising in Respect of Compensation Claims for Personal Injuries', Department for Constitutional Affairs 2006.
60   Ibid., p 40.

legal process by making a claim, having gained the impression that claiming was a game of some kind, and few were left with a clear impression of the length of time it takes to complete the claims process. The media, then, as a vehicle for advertising, must bear some of the responsibility for the higher volume of claims since the introduction of the no-win, no-fee system and the development of claims management companies. This is an indirect influence in a complex relationship between the media, the advertisers and the public.

The value of media analysis

The Government would argue that media reporting of compensation claims and the difficulties faced by organisations and companies in obtaining insurance cover may have warped to some extent the public perception of exactly how litigious UK society is in reality. The official line is that fear of litigation may be causing organisations to become risk-averse. However, setting sensationalism aside, it can also prompt improvements in health and safety, thereby reducing the number of claims. Insurers and the healthcare sector are under increasing pressure to predict new or emerging sources of claims, especially in the light of newly identified risks arising from conditions such as obesity and work-related stress. Organisations then have the opportunity to ensure that if claims cannot be prevented, they are handled fairly and that compensation is paid if is due. Millenson,[61] tracing innovation in medical error reduction to the shaming of the profession that occurred as a result of stories appearing in the US news media, comments that news stories about patient safety are giving rise to a similar process throughout the western world.

The media also play a vital role in humanising tragedies and bringing them before a wide audience in a way that law reports, which are not read widely by the public, are unable to achieve. The majority of claims do not reach court and would not be reported in any event if the media did not unearth them. The human interest in *The Times* report of the large number of errors at a maternity unit in a hospital is a recent example:

> The cost of such accidents is exemplified by cases such as that of Nathan Hughes. In May he was finally awarded £1.65m, plus £315,000 a year for life, to pay for his needs because the medical team delivering him 14 years ago at Rush Green hospital, northeast London, failed to notice he was being strangled by his umbilical cord.
>
> 'These disasters happen again and again,' said Eve, his mother. 'I found out later that the hospital where he was born was known by doctors as the "spastics factory" because of the number of birth injuries'.

---

61 Millenson, M.L., 'Pushing the Profession: How the News Media Changed Patient Safety into a Priority' (2002) *Quality and Safety in Health Care* 11: 57–63.

Although it may be inconvenient for the Government, and embarrassing for the NHS, that such reports appear, they can be regarded as useful sources of information about pressing social problems.

It is certainly possible to argue that there is an inherent value in the work of investigative journalists, though negative reporting is likely to remain a problem. Despite the many successful treatments that are carried out every year, awards to compensate victims of medical error are far more likely to generate interest, in part because of their spectacular nature, than everyday success stories which are too commonplace to be interesting.

The media have a habit of promoting good causes, and there are countless items about such people as sick children who are unable to obtain treatment in the UK, breast cancer patients who have been unable to obtain funding for essential drugs, victims of clinical trials that have not been properly conducted, infected blood products, inadequate smear tests and so on. It could be argued that by promoting these causes the media deflect claims away from the courts and help to defuse some of the problems created by the compensation culture, raising funds or pressurising organisations into providing treatment or even compensation which might not so easily have been forthcoming through the courts.[62]

The role of the media is crucial in disseminating vital information, and responsible, evidence-based journalism should not necessarily be blamed for increasing the number of claims. Indeed, it is laudable that deserving claimants are alerted by the media to the possibility of claiming.[63] The analysis in Chapter 1 suggests that many people deserving of compensation never receive an award. Even where little or no compensation would be forthcoming, there is a strong argument that the public interest needs to be served by the provision of information which might lead to improvements in future practices. For example, recent news reports[64] about a research study, which had concluded that many nursing home residents are allowed by staff to live in constant pain, alerted the public to the need for pressure to be put on the Department of Health to improve the situation. A new "dignity" policy has been introduced.

Another salient feature of media reporting is that legal professionals are kept informed about developments in their specialist fields. Information is disseminated in the specialist legal press as well as in daily news reports. Thus, for example, the spreading of knowledge about new avenues by which claims may be brought (for example the use of the COSSH Regulations as a basis for claims arising from infection with MRSA) is made possible – to the

---

62   On compensation for the Thalidomide victims see Cranston, R., *Consumers and the Law* (3rd edn, Cambridge University Press).

63   Yet another example of media-generated claims (though unrelated to the NHS) can be found in the wide dissemination throughout all the UK media in March 2007 of information about contaminated fuel supplies in the South East of England and how to claim compensation for damage to vehicles as a result. This served a useful social function.

64   BBC News report on 21 March 2007 of the Picker Institute research findings.

advantage of lawyers and their potential clients. Such developments may well not please NHS Trusts or the Government, but they are a means of achieving just solutions for deserving claimants.

The criticisms levelled at what is often regarded as sensationalising by the media in their coverage of medical malpractice stories begs the question as to whether such coverage will necessarily lead to all doctors being viewed with suspicion by their patients, thereby adding further to a deteriorating doctor-patient relationship. Although the Bristol Inquiry was critical of the arrogance of the doctors involved, and the Shipman Inquiry exposed the murderous activities of Harold Shipman, the public did not necessarily demonise every doctor practising in the UK. It can be all too convenient to blame the media for publishing sensational stories, offering justifiable criticism of a few proven bad apples within what is still a highly respected profession.

The medical profession as a whole is understandably sensitive to adverse publicity. A paper[65] produced soon after the GMC hearing of cases against the doctors in the Bristol case produced some interesting responses.[66] That discussion paper reviewed the reporting of the Bristol case in the quality and tabloid national newspapers over a five-week period at the time of the GMC's deliberations. The main themes emerging from the press coverage were discussed, and their implications assessed with a view to engendering future debate about clinical performance and accountability. The authors discovered that 184 items were published during the five-week period, and concluded that the reporting was:

> emotive and largely hostile, raising doubts about not just isolated lapses of care but also the possibility of more systematic failings.

Particularly worrying were the persistent themes of diminishing public trust and confidence in the medical profession,[67] though this lack of confidence has not been borne out by evidence in surveys of the public. The press coverage was criticised for its lack of balance, and the account of the Bristol Inquiry reported in the media was found to have been much over-simplified, provoking a series of letters[68] from indignant members of the medical profession to the

65 Davies, H.T.O. and Shields, A., Discussion paper: 'Public Trust, and Accountability for Clinical Performance: Lessons from the National Press Reportage of the Bristol Hearing', *Journal of Evaluation in Clinical Practice* (1999) 5(3): 335–42(8), Blackwell.

66 See for example, Willis, A.R. responding to Davies, H.T.O. and Shields, A.V., 'The Pen is Mightier Than the Scalpel'. Commentary on the paper: 'Public Trust, and Accountability for Clinical Performance: Lessons from the National Press Reporting of the Bristol Hearing' (H.T.O. Davies and A.V. Shields, *Journal of Evaluation in Clinical Practice* 5: 335–42).

67 See BMA 'Public Trust' surveys 2004 and 2005, outlined below.

68 See Dunn, P.M., Stirrat, G.M., Bolsin, S., Shortis, M., Winkler, E. and Cummings, M. 'Letters: More on the Bristol Case' (1999) *BMJ* 318: 1009–11.

BMJ. Willis, commenting on the perceived lack of balance, demanded that journalists be subject to revalidation and re-accreditation on the grounds that they have the power 'to do as much harm as any surgeon'. He argued powerfully:

> No society can afford to view with equanimity the demotivation and inhibition of its medical workforce by a hostile and uncomprehending press. Nor can it tolerate the deliberate distortion of complex issues of life and death, whether it be in support of narrow, pre-conceived ideas, or in a cynical search for sensation and circulation.

The same writer proceeded to indicate that some people have suggested 'even darker motives', citing the BMA head of communications Nigel Duncan, who used to be a Westminster lobby correspondent, as claiming[69] that politicians are using journalists to damage public respect for the profession in order to make way for controversial policy decisions.

Other studies conducted into the quality of media coverage of medical scandals have revealed that incidents such as the Alder Hey controversy can have a marked effect on scientific research, even research that has no relationship with the scandal under consideration.[70] The Alder Hey story concerned the retention of children's organs following post-mortem examinations – in many cases without the knowledge or consent of the parents at the time. Gruesome details were exposed, the emotive elements of individual case histories were emphasised, and various factions developed, with the scientific establishment portrayed as having offended public morals, thereby causing harm to grieving relatives. Fresh incidents came to light almost every day over a period of several months and the continuing nature of the scandal rapidly sold more and more newspapers.[71]

What do people believe anyway?

Research carried out since the 1940s indicates that the willingness of people to believe what the media tell them is directly related to the degree of confidence that they have in the source of the information,[72] rather than the

69   Wafer, A. (1999) 'Gotcha!' *BMA News Review*, 13 March, 40.
70   Seale, C., Kirk, D., Tobin, M., Burton P., Grundy, R., Pritchard Jones, K., Dixon-Woods, M., 'Effect of Media Portrayals of Removal of Children's Tissue on UK Tumour Bank', *BMJ* 2005, 331; 401–03.
71   For a more general analysis of the effect of media scandals, see Lull, J. and Hinerman, S. (eds), *Media Scandals: Morality and Desire in the Popular Culture Marketplace* (Polity Press, Cambridge, 1997).
72   Hovland, C.I., *Experiments in Mass Communication* (Princetown University Press, Princetown, 1949) and 'Reconciling Conflicting Results derived from Experimental and Survey Studies of Attitude Change' (1959) *American Psychologist* 14(3).

content of the message. Other important factors in what people believe are openness, and the 'emotional tone' with which information is presented. Doctors tend to score more highly on the trust and confidence scale than politicians, journalists and Government Ministers, but research indicates that as well as professional background, perceived competence, consistency and goodwill are important to the public. The Government has produced advice to those wishing to communicate information about health risks, in which it states that the perceptions of people in general of risks, such as the risk of being the victim of malpractice, are influenced by personal background and values.[73] According to the Department of Health,[74] a major story is more likely to develop if there is evidence of an attempted cover-up, conflict, questions about attribution of blame, human interest, a 'what next' element, the involvement of large numbers of people, high profile issues or personalities, and a link to sex or crime. Although the Government was specifically concerned in its advisory document about communicating public health risks, many of these factors are present, of course, in the history of medical malpractice and clinical negligence claims.

A poll, commissioned by the Department of Health and conducted by MORI concerning attitudes to medical regulation,[75] revealed that from the doctor's perspective media stories could have a negative effect on public trust in doctors as a profession, and the media were also blamed by doctors for creating unrealistic expectations in patients. On the other hand, another MORI poll conducted in 2004[76] after extensive media reporting of the most scandalous health stories reported in recent years – the Bristol and Shipman stories – showed that doctors are the people whom the public most trust, and that they are placed above teachers and judges in the minds of the public. At the bottom of the trust list were journalists, politicians and Government Ministers. MORI interviewed 2,004 adults at 196 sampling points, and data were weighted to the known national population profile. Ninety-two per cent of the sample said they trusted doctors to tell the truth, while only 22 per cent trusted politicians generally and 23 per cent trusted Government ministers. Journalists were the least trusted, at 20 per cent. By the following year, the figures were 90 per cent of people trusting doctors, who were again ranked top of the trust tables, with journalists, politicians and Government Ministers ranking equal bottom at 20 per cent.[77] This indicates a healthy scepticism, suggesting that the public are not as easily influenced by the media

73   Langford, I.H., Marris, C. and O'Riordan, T., 'Public Reactions to Risk: Social Structures, Images of Science and the Role of Trust' in Bennett, P.G. and Calman, K.C. (eds), *Risk Communication and Public Health: Policy, Science and Participation* (Oxford University Press, Oxford, 1999).

74   'Communicating About Risks to Public Health: Pointers to Good Practice', DOH 1999.

75   Attitudes to Medical Regulation and Revalidation of Doctors, Research Among Doctors and the General Public, July 2005.

76   BMA, 'Trust in Doctors', 2004.

77   BMA, 'Trust in Doctors', 2005.

as the media and the Government would like to suppose. In terms of error reporting, research in New Zealand[78] indicates that members of the public are more likely than healthcare professionals to believe reports about the number of errors. The reasons for this are unclear, but it has been suggested that the media, by reporting incidents of error in healthcare, have generated an interest in isolated but 'horrific' tales.

In any event, circular arguments inevitably arise in considering cause and effect; whether the media have influenced attitudes to the compensation culture, or whether the media is simply reflecting existing attitudes. Early research on the role of the media in effecting social control suggests some contradictions. On the one hand the media do influence public attitudes, but on the other, far from being independent, the media simply report the balance of forces within the society in which they operate.[79] It is clear that there has been a dramatic increase in the UK in media coverage of medical stories in general and clinical negligence litigation in particular, and the Government would have us believe that this has contributed materially to the litigation crisis. What is more difficult to determine is whether increasing litigation led to an increase in media coverage, or vice versa. This question is more complex than it appears, as there have been numerous other factors involved in the litigation spiral towards the end of the twentieth century. These were examined in Chapter 2.

Counting the media involvement

The work that deals in the greatest depth with the relationship between the media and the civil litigation crisis in the US is *Dis-torting the Law: Politics, the Media and the Litigation Crisis* by Haltom and McCann,[80] taking a broad perspective that focuses across a wide range of personal injury litigation in the US. The authors undertook an impressive analysis of almost twenty years' worth of media coverage, and considered not only the impact of the media on the public in relation to the creation of a 'litigation crisis', but also the role of the media in reporting views of the tort reform lobby. They discovered that there had been a dramatic increase in the media coverage of personal injury litigation – from 10 to 20 articles a year in five major national newspapers in the 1980s – to 500 or 600 a year by the late 1980s and early 1990s. They

---

78   Studies of errors and adverse events in healthcare: the nature and scale of the problem, p 47.

79   For a helpful summary, see Curran, J. and Seaton, J., 'Power without Responsibility: The Press, Broadcasting and the New Media in Britain, Chapter 20', *Sociology of the Mass Media* (6th edn, Routledge, London, 2003).

80   Haltom, W. and McCann, M., *Dis-torting the Law: Politics, Media and the Litigation Crisis* (University of Chicago Press, Chicago and London, 2004).

concluded that the power of the media to influence popular understanding of the law is immense, and using a single case[81] as the main focus for their argument, illustrated the way in which the media were able to use it as the symbol for all the shortcomings of the civil litigation system, and as a platform for tort reformers to advance their views concerning the restriction of access to the courts. The scope of their work is wider than clinical negligence and it is not necessarily helpful to compare the US position with that in the UK, though there are some similarities.

Counting the media involvement in the UK

The number of articles appearing in UK newspapers on subjects associated with medical or clinical negligence has shown a marked increase over the last two years.

A comparison made by the author, based on the number of articles appearing over the last two years and those published during preceding years on a variety of criteria around the clinical negligence theme, demonstrates that there have been consistently higher numbers in the two most recent years.

Methodology

Searches were undertaken for articles which appeared in UK newspapers, as recorded by LexisNexis Professional, which holds all UK Newspapers on its database. Using a variety of words and phrases, the number of hits was counted for the two years from April 2005 to April 2007, then over a varying number of preceding years. The analysis was undertaken on an approximate basis simply to provide a sketch of the rough extent of media interest in clinical negligence. It is recognised that the conclusions are impressionistic and that the subject is worthy of a much more detailed and scientific approach.

Articles which contain the words 'clinical negligence' published in all UK newspapers (national and local) show that over the two-year period there was a 79 per cent increase over the average for the preceding four years.

Articles which contain the words 'medical' and 'negligence' in UK national (exclusive of local) newspapers also increased during the two years in question, by 71 per cent over the average number containing the same words, which were published in the preceding 10 years.

Articles that contain the phrases 'medical negligence' or 'clinical negligence' or 'medical malpractice' in UK national newspapers show an increase of 87 per cent over the preceding four years.

81 Stella Liebeck's suit against McDonald's.

Research conclusions

Although this research was unsophisticated, it does demonstrate that there has been a considerable increase over the past two years in the number of articles about clinical negligence that find their way to the public through our newspapers. There are, of course, those who would argue that clinical negligence is simply a media obsession and that it is not a matter that interests the public to any great extent. This suggestion should be considered in the light of the different views of the role of the media in society. However, in a competitive market, it is likely that the media do play a key role in shaping public understanding and interest.[82] It is only possible to speculate as to the reasons for the increasing media interest in healthcare negligence, but it is ironic that this development has occurred since the speeches were made by Tony Blair[83] and Lord Falconer[84] denying that there is a compensation culture in the UK.

Conclusion

There is necessarily a strong focus in the media on compensation for claims. The higher the award, the more interesting the story and the higher the circulation of the newspaper. The role of the media in reporting clinical negligence and error in healthcare could mean that the overall status of claims and errors is possibly distorted, but nevertheless, there is a core of truth at the centre of media coverage. There is genuine public concern about the level of claims in healthcare, and there is a real problem identifying whether the media have simply reported accurately malpractice events and the rising level of claims, or whether the media are the cause of the malpractice crisis; whether this is a phenomenon that the media have generated and continue to feed upon. In any event, concerns may be misplaced, as the empirical evidence suggests that members of the public are not as gullible as may be imagined, and are as little inclined to believe journalists as they are to believe politicians.

Health reporting should, of course, be as accurate as possible, and accuracy requires adequate cooperation between the media and healthcare professionals. Willis expressed the position perfectly:[85]

> Journalists have as much power to do harm as any surgeon. The pen, indeed, is mightier than the scalpel.

---

82   Seaton, J., 'The Sociology of the Mass Media' in *Power without Responsibility*, Curran, J. and Seaton, J. (eds) (6th edn, Routledge, London, 2003).
83   Speech to the IPPR reported in the *Guardian*, 26 May 2005.
84   Speech on 10 November 2004 at the Insurance Times Conference.
85   http://www.friendsinlowplaces.co.uk/index.htm

References to the number of claims should be obtained easily from official sources such as the NHSLA and there should be no obfuscation, deliberate or otherwise, of the figures. Commentators[86] on Australia's media reporting of health and medical matters suggest the guidelines for the media should always be followed; press releases should include relevant explanations about the limitations of the research, funding and other financial matters. They continue:

> Essentially, the public places a great deal of trust in the health care system and in medical news, particularly if it is based on peer-reviewed data published by medical experts. It would be a pity to destroy such trust through substandard reporting.

The UK's Medical Journalists' Association (MJA) supports and encourages its members to enable them to work efficiently and at high levels of accuracy. There are more than 400 members of this organisation, which could play an essential part in ensuring that health journalists cover details of claims and errors with integrity.

---

86 Van Der Weyden, M.B. and Armstrong, R.M., 'Australia's Media Reporting of Health and Medical Matters: A Question of Quality' (2005) *MJA* 183(4): 188–89; see also The Association of Health Care Journalists (AHCJ) in the US guidance.

Chapter 5

Doctors

Over-paid, out of control, and under-regulated?

Introduction

There appears to be a general view that doctors are paid too much in comparison with the rest of the population,[1] with doctors in other jurisdictions, and with other professional people, for the work that they do, and following the Shipman case, that the medical profession is out of control and requires still more intensive monitoring and regulation. The question of doctors' salaries is one which must be considered in the light of the pressures they face in their work and the responsibilities they are required to bear. Whether they require further regulation is an interesting question in the light of the multiple layers of regulation imposed upon them in the past ten years or so.

Are doctors overpaid?

The question is 'Overpaid for what, and in comparison with whom?' Patricia Hewitt, Health Secretary, admitted that GPs might be overpaid, as they receive on average £107,000 per annum. Their income had risen by around 30 per cent in the first year of the new GP contract. She told a BBC interviewer that GPs had retained 45 per cent of their practice income as profit in the 2004–05 financial year, and that this was a rise of around 40 per cent over the preceding year according to the NHS Information Centre.[2] The view is that over-reliance on out-of-hours services is causing patients to suffer, while GPs are relaxing and enjoying their additional financial rewards. The Public Accounts Committee commented that the only people to benefit from the changes in the work patterns of GPs were the doctors themselves, giving the public the impression that not only are GPs overpaid, they are also under-worked. In one instance, a coroner criticised the out-of-hours system during

---

1   Comments such as that of Preston, P., 'Is one doctor worth three teachers?' *Guardian Unlimited*, 30 March 2006, abound in the media.
2   10 October 2005, reported by Reuters, 19 January 2007.

an inquest into the death of a woman who was misdiagnosed by eight doctors over a bank holiday weekend.[3] A study in 2005 by Stethos concluded that GPs in the UK earn on average twice as much as their equivalents in France and Spain, and found that doctors in Germany saw more patients than others in Europe, and GPs in France had longest average consultation times.[4]

Reported under the headline 'Salaries soaked up new funds, reveals damning report' in the *Observer*,[5] it was stated that:

> The King's Fund found that 34 per cent of the £ 19bn which the government has put directly into hospital and community health services in England since 2003 went on more pay for clinical staff. However, productivity levels among GPs, consultants and nurses have nowhere near matched the scale of the increase in the NHS's funding in England, which has gone up from £ 35bn in 1997 to £ 92bn in 2007–08.
>
> While consultants have seen their pay scales go up by 70 per cent under Labour, their productivity had actually fallen by 20 per cent over the same period, judged by the number of in-patients admitted per consultant ... the number of in-patient admissions per nurse fell by 15 per cent, and GPs are not markedly more productive than before they got hefty pay rises in 2004.[6]

John Appleby's analysis in the King's Fund Report indicated that of the £19 billion, £6.6 billion went on salaries; £2.2 billion on the rising cost of drugs, and implementing recommendations by the NICE; £1.6 billion on employing more doctors to comply with EU Working Time Directive; £1.1 billion on new buildings and equipment; £1 billion on medical equipment; and £600 million on negligence lawsuits.

Such accounts are obviously damaging to the NHS as whole, but also to doctors and other healthcare staff who appear to have been the beneficiaries of the latest cash injection.

There are even those in the medical profession who consider that doctors are paid too much. In a controversial comment published in the *New Statesman*,[7] Mark Joplin, a junior hospital doctor, stated that he thought he was being paid too much for the tasks that he was doing, writing:

---

3   *Daily Telegraph*, 6 October 2006.
4   'UK GPs top European pay league', BBC News, 2 September 2005, before the new GP contracts were operational.
5   10 April 2007.
6   Appleby, J., King's Fund 2007.
7   Cited by Britten, M., 'Trust Me. Doctors are paid too much', *Daily Telegraph*, 8 October 2005.

I am one of the least qualified, least skilled and lowliest paid doctors in my hospital,

and that he spent his time:

searching for missing heaps of patient notes, running errands and chasing up blood test results.

He also asserted that consultants earned too much, at up to £90,000 per annum. Figures released by the UK Treasury suggest that even three years ago, before the recent dramatic pay increases, doctors in the UK earned well above what their European counterparts were earning.[8] Blaming in part the medical press for pressing for higher medical salaries, he made the valuable point that as state-funded service providers, doctors should not expect to be highly paid, making the case that money saved from doctors' salaries could be redistributed elsewhere in the NHS for the benefit of patients, or dealing with the social deprivation that causes ill-health. The wages of care assistants, for example, are so low that it is impossible, even in the private sector, to attract larger numbers of dedicated and skilled staff to nursing homes to care for some of the most vulnerable people in society. The high turnover of staff and lack of proper supervision of carers, some of whom are very young and feel undervalued, can mean that there is a high incidence of patient abuse,[9] despite newly introduced regulations. Diversion of money from doctors' salaries to those of carers might go some way to remedying this situation.[10]

Needless to say, these comments caused a torrent of righteously indignant responses from doctors anxious to justify their positions. At the heart of this issue are questions about whether doctors, in whose hands we must be prepared to place our lives, deserve high salaries because of the heavy responsibilities that they bear. It is, of course, impossible to generalise, but there are undoubted anomalies within the NHS itself. Why, for example, are GPs paid relatively higher salaries than hospital doctors, whose salaries have again been kept at a lower level by a recent recommended increase of only around 2.2 per cent? How does the hourly rate commanded by a UK doctor differ from that which dentists, physiotherapists, senior stylists in hair salons, and footballers earn? Why, for so many years, have men been paid higher salaries than women?

8   Day, M., 'So How Much Do Doctors Really Earn?' (2007) *BMJ* 334: 236–37.
9   Lachs, M. S., Williams, C., O'Brien, S., Hurst, L. and Horowitz, 'Risk Factors for Reported Elder Abuse and Neglect: A Nine Year Observational Cohort Study', *The Gerontologist*, 1997.
10   See Pollock, A., *NHS plc: The Privatisation of our Healthcare* (Verso, London, 2004), p 192.

Some commentators argue that the NHS debt and the present financial crisis have been caused by the new contracts for consultants and GPs.[11] A report issued in 2007 by the National Audit Office blamed poor financial management, insufficient input from clinicians on financial matters, and underestimates by the Department of Health of the cost of doctors new contracts the financial difficulties in the NHS.

The BMA, in suitably defensive mode, placed the blame at the door of the Department of Health, which had assured it that the new consultant contracts had been properly costed, and that funds were available to meet them. Problems arose only because the Government had not been aware how hard consultants worked. The BMA pointed out that research indicates that the new contract yields health improvements for patients. For example, GP care under the new contract should, it is hoped, result in 8,700 patients in England avoiding cardiovascular problems, with equivalent benefits to patients in Scotland, Northern Ireland, and Wales.

One justification for the high level of income commanded by GPs is that this is necessary to maintain sufficient numbers of primary care practitioners in employment to service the needs of patients – a simple matter of market forces which require them to be highly paid.[12] As long ago as 1991, a national survey by the BMA of 42,360 GPs[13] before new targets and regulatory measures were introduced, showed that a quarter of GPs were seriously considering leaving the profession within the next five years, and 48 per cent intended to retire before the age of 60. Eighty per cent said they were suffering from excessive stress at work, and 93 per cent thought that the current times available to see patients were inadequate, suggesting that fewer patients and longer consultation times were necessary to provide proper care. Forty-six per cent expressed the view that they would not recommend to newly qualified doctors that they become GPs. By the year 2000 it was clear that there was a shortage of GPs throughout the country.

It has been pointed out that cuts in staff numbers are likely to result in more claims for negligence against the NHS.[14] Reports of a decrease in the number of nurses by 55,000 in 2007 from the previous year are particularly worrying.[15] Concerns have been voiced about changes in the training of consultants, which are likely to mean that early specialisation leaves them under-skilled, and campaigners have indicated that the pressure on staff will increase greatly if posts across the NHS for nurses and doctors are cut in order

11   Kmietowicz, Z., 'Doctors' Pay is One Reason for NHS Debt' (2007) *BMJ News* 334: 603 (24 March), doi:10.1136/bmj.39161.363102.
12   Young *et al.*, 'Imbalances in the GP Labour Market in the UK'.
13   Reported in The *Guardian*, 12 October 2001.
14   Sulis, S., 'NHS Cuts will cause rise in clinical negligence claims', *Hackney Gazette*, 2 February 2007.
15   BBC Television News, 15 April 2007.

to ensure that Trusts balance their books. The number of doctors and hospital beds per head of population in the UK was (and continues to be) well below that in France, Germany, and Italy in 1999, and it is not surprising that at the same time stress on hospital staff has been found to have increased.[16]

It is difficult to take a measured view on the justice of salaries earned as between public and independent sectors, and it is always necessary to compare like with like, which is very difficult to achieve when considering different professions and different countries, even within the EU. There is certainly no place in this book for an analysis of these complex social and economic questions. It is more useful to consider the responsibilities that doctors have to meet in the course of their careers, and the difficulties which they have to overcome, which might justify the high salaries that they earn.

Tasks and responsibilities

Doctors in the UK are now working in an environment that requires them to achieve goals and meet Government targets and standards in a way that is unprecedented in the rest of Europe. GPs are gate-keepers for access to other healthcare services, and are subjected to evaluation by their patients in regular surveys. They have become organisers, delegators, and administrators, often overseeing an impressive array of staff – including practice nurses, who take on more and more of the routine tasks originally undertaken by doctors – practice managers, receptionists, therapists, and in rural areas, dispensers. They have a legal obligation to deal with health and safety on their premises. They must implement clinical governance and risk management strategies. These responsibilities entail increasing requirements for documentation, regular reporting, and compulsory audit. GPs are responsible for seeing patients in nine out of ten of all consultations in the NHS, and following the recommendations of Dame Janet Smith who chaired the Shipman Inquiry, they will be monitored and regulated more closely than ever before. They must oversee complaints in their practices, and like all doctors, are obliged to attend regular training and updating sessions.

The emphasis on a patient-centred approach in healthcare, which was the theme that informed the analysis and recommendations of the Bristol Inquiry,[17] is not new, but it has been re-established since the Inquiry and has meant significant changes in the way healthcare professionals work. All doctors are required to assimilate information about new technologies and other developments connected with their practice. They also need to keep abreast of changes in the law. This is no easy task. For example, new rules of substantive law relating to consent to treatment are now explained in

16   Pollock, A., *NHS plc: The Privatisation of our Healthcare* (Verso, London, 2004, p 43).
17   'Learning from Bristol', Report of the Public Inquiry into Children's Heart Surgery at the Bristol Royal Infirmary 1984–95, p 272.

Government guidance,[18] but they became law as soon as the relevant cases on the subject were decided by the Courts,[19] at which time doctors could scarcely have been aware of them, as few doctors would have had the time or inclination to discover changes in the law.

Among the legislative reforms introduced in recent years which have a direct effect on medical practice are The NHS Redress Act 2006, The Compensation Act 2006, The Mental Capacity Act 2005, The Health Act 2006, The Health Service Commissioners Act 1996, the Data Protection Acts 1995 and 1998, the Freedom of Information Act 2000, the Health Act 1999, the Human Rights Act 1998, the Disability Discrimination Acts 1995 and 2005, the National Health Service Reform and Health Care Professions Act 2002, The Human Fertilisation and Embryology Act 1990, the Public Interest (Disclosure) Act 1998, the Health and Safety at Work etc Act 1974 and Regulations made under it, to name but a few. Healthcare professionals should ensure that they are aware of the many European Directives relevant to healthcare, and they have to cope with the implementation of new rules and regulatory frameworks, even though few receive training on new legislation.[20] They are flooded with documents explaining how proposed reforms are to be implemented, many of which contain civil service jargon, and are constantly reminded of the need to 'modernise' the NHS, such as 'standards', 'quality requirements', 'benchmarks', 'criteria', 'targets', 'guidelines', 'protocols', treatment plans', 'clinical networks', 'pathways of care', and 'quality assurance' to name but a few of the phrases listed in various glossaries to government documents.[21] The view of one writer[22] is that:

> New guidance appears to redefine the very nature of the NHS. ... Both within and without, observers may wonder whether the NHS is about to be reformed out of all recognition.

Common law is constantly developing complex concepts concerning, among other matters, end of life decisions, negligence and consent to treatment which doctors are obliged to apply. To take but one example, the intricate concept of 'best interests' now underpins medical decision-making in a range of situations (and has been added to by statute since the Mental Capacity Act 2005). Even lawyers have problems grappling with the minutiae of the law in

---

18   Department of Health, 'A Reference Guide to Consent'.
19   *Chester v Afshar* [2004] UKHL 41.
20   See Harpwood, V., 'In Defence of Doctors', in *First Do No Harm: Law Ethics and Healthcare* (2006) ed. McLean Ashgate, Aldershot.
21   See e.g. 'Healthcare Standards for Wales: Making the Connections Designed for Life', 2005, NHS Wales.
22   Lewis, R. and Gilliam, S., 'Back to the Market: Yet More Reform to the NHS', *International Journal of Health Services* 33(1): 77–84.

this respect, and judges can spend days considering the issue in court.[23] Yet there are many doctors who are expected to apply the legal rules relating to patients' best interests on a daily basis.

Healthcare professionals have numerous targets and can expect to see the results of their efforts and even their personal records publicised in national tables. The concept of targets can have a negative effect on clinical practice and there are numerous reports of manipulation or 'gaming' to give the appearance that targets are being met. Some of the ingenious devices that have been developed in this respect cannot be in the interests of patients and can be described at best as counter-productive. To take but one example, there are tales of seriously ill patients being kept waiting in ambulances outside Accident and Emergency Units so that others are pushed through the system within the target deadline.[24] Such a culture cannot be conducive to patients' well-being and is certainly not regarded as satisfactory by doctors. This matter is discussed further in Chapter 6.

The institutional and structural reforms that have been a feature of the NHS for almost two decades have added to the responsibilities which doctors are required to undertake. The NHS has been in a virtually perpetual state of reform and reorganisation for so long that there appears to be constant upheaval, and many reforms are simply thinly-disguised attempts to control finite resources within an ever-growing health service that aims to be free at the point of delivery. The Bristol Inquiry Final Report summed this up with the words:

> The fact that the NHS is, in essence, a value-driven, politically sensitive enterprise, means that it is always changing. It has never been free of the tinkering which shifting views on the proper role of the public and private sector and on levels of taxation inevitably bring to bear. But the 1980s and 1990s were somewhat special in both the pace and nature of the changes which took place.[25]

Ironically, one result of the Bristol Inquiry was a further acceleration in the pace of change through many of its recommendations for reform.

Another commentator noted of the changes:[26]

> The advocates of every new reform argue that it will make the NHS more efficient or effective, save money or produce more or better patient care ... By the time that the researchers have painstakingly documented and

23   *Wyatt v Portsmouth Hospital NHS Trust* [2006] EWCA Civ 52.
24   *Society Guardian*, 13 January 2003.
25   BRI Inquiry Report, supra cit, chapter 4, at p 50, para 2.
26   Walshe, K., 'Foundation Hospitals: A New Direction for NHS Reform', (2003) *Journal of the Royal Society of Medicine* 96: 106–10.

measured progress and assessed the impact of one set of reforms, the next wave of organisational change is already upon us.

Clinicians have worked under a range of different organisations – NHS Trusts, Health Authorities, and some now in Foundation Hospitals. They have adapted to new management structures which appear to owe more to industry and commerce than to healthcare, and have learned to cope with Non-Executive Directors, Chairmen, and Executive Boards. They argue that guidelines issued by successive organisations culminating in NICE have eroded their clinical autonomy, and are bewildered by conflicting guidance from their employers, Royal Colleges, the Courts and the Government concerning the treatment they can offer to patients. Drugs approved by NICE are funded by commissioners of healthcare, but it is generally recognised that NICE is working at a slower pace than cutting-edge researchers. This situation has led to ethical dilemmas for clinicians, who know that more effective treatments exist than those approved by NICE. Tensions between management and clinicians are heightened by the fact that Trust Boards have to bear the responsibility for financial overspend, and are reluctant to allow spending on high cost drugs which are not recommended by NICE.

Structural reforms have included increasingly devolved and fragmented healthcare systems within the UK, leading to a bewildering range of disparate regulation which directly contradicts the Government's commitment to 'end post-code prescribing'. NHS organisations with very similar functions are given different names in different regions. Doctors and patients in England, Wales, Scotland, and Northern Ireland, and even those responsible for the administration of healthcare within each region, are uncertain as to the legal framework elsewhere in the UK. This situation can lead to difficulties for doctors and patients who relocate within the UK, and for Trusts in the regions, whose staff are understandably confused over different approaches to healthcare provision. For example, some NHS Trusts in England commission services from NHS bodies in Wales. Confusion arises over differences in funding; differences in the year-on-year inflationary uplift; different approaches to waiting lists; differences in definitions of patient populations; differences in prescription charges (free prescriptions in Wales).

Devolution within the UK has led to fragmentation of healthcare systems and it can be difficult for doctors to adapt to regional variations. From the perspective of Central Government in Whitehall, devolved responsibility for healthcare allows a distancing from direct decision-making in some areas of the country and is seen as liberating bodies such as the Welsh Assembly to make local law in the field of healthcare for local people. However, it is becoming increasingly difficult for any individual to have an overview of the operation of the NHS in the UK as a whole, so creating further difficulties for movement of specialist staff within the UK. One thing that is clear, however, is that the UK has an ageing and more diverse society. In ten years' time there will be more people aged 65 and over than children under 16,[27] according to Social Trends published by the Office for National Statistics. Although life expectancy has increased, the number of years that we can expect to live in poor health or with a disability has increased accordingly, and it is the healthcare system that will bear the growing burden of caring for the elderly, creating still further responsibilities for doctors and others who work within that system.

Doctors have the responsibility for conducting clinical trials, without which medical science is unable to progress. However, the entire trial process, for several very good reasons, is hedged about with legal restrictions,[28] making procedures more complex and frustrating for all concerned.

Trends towards creating greater autonomy for patients have added to the pressure on doctors and other healthcare professionals and have increased the need to provide each patient with more information and therefore more time. The European Charter of Patients' Rights[29] sets out 14 rights of patients, including the right to information, the right to consent, the right to freedom of choice and the right to respect for patients' time. Although this has not as yet been incorporated into UK law, Government policy and trends in judicial decisions in the UK are clearly slanted towards the empowerment of patients. There have been numerous statements by people at the centre of policy-making about putting patients at the centre of healthcare.[30] This concept is not new, as it was a policy commitment at the inception of the NHS, but it is now being heavily promoted in Government literature. To take one of a number of recent examples, in *Creating a Patient-led NHS*,[31] the Government argues that:

> Wherever possible, the NHS should offer choices of services and treatment. Information services need to be supported by well-trained staff who can help people make more sense of the information, make choices and access the system.[32]

Initiatives are aimed at patient and public involvement in healthcare decision-making and the participation of patients in healthcare organisations. The public is consulted regularly on healthcare issues as a direct result of recommendations in the Bristol Inquiry Report. Although these initiatives are to be welcomed, they do place yet more pressure on doctors' time.

---

27   'Social Trends – 35 years of social change', Office for National Statistics 2007.
28   See Council Directive 200/20 on Clinical Trials.
29   Basis Document, Rome 2002, available at www.activecitizenship.net/health/European_
      Charter
30   E.g. Tony Blair's speech introducing the NHS Plan, 28 July 2000, reported in the *Guardian*.
31   NHS Confederation Briefing Paper, 2005 NHS Confederation.
32   Ibid., para 5.

Allowing for recognised cultural lag, the courts have now adopted policies that favour greater involvement of patients in decisions about their treatment. In *Chester v Afshar*[33] the House of Lords made inroads into medical paternalism, replacing older attitudes, including respect for physical causation, with recognition of the importance of the need to respect the autonomy of patients in the context of consent to treatment. Lord Hope examined the leading cases in the UK and other jurisdictions, and emphasised that the function of the law is to protect the patient's right to choose. Lord Walker took a similar stance, arguing that advice by the doctor is the very foundation of a patient's consent to treatment:

> In a decision which may have a profound effect on her health and well-being a patient is entitled to information and advice about possible alternatives or variant treatments.[34]

Lord Steyn said:

> A patient's right to an appropriate warning from a surgeon when faced with surgery ought normatively to be regarded as an important right which must be given effective protection whenever possible.[35]

Even the dissenting speeches were strongly in favour of autonomy. Bingham stated:

> The patient's right to be appropriately warned is an important right, which few doctors in the current legal and social climate would consciously or deliberately avoid.[36]

Lord Steyn's statement sums up the juridical basis of the approach:

> On a broader basis, I am glad to have arrived at the conclusion that the claimant is entitled in law to succeed. The result is in accord with one of the most basic aspirations of the law, namely to right wrongs. Moreover, the decision ... reflects the reasonable expectations of the public in contemporary society.[37]

There are long-term implications of this decision for the NHS as a whole, and for doctors in particular, since they are now obliged to spend time ensuring

33   [2004] 4 All E.R. 587.
34   Para 98.
35   Para 17.
36   Para 9.
37   Para 5.

that patients are provided with adequate information on which to base consent to treatment. The processes of clinical governance and risk management also need to embrace the principle established by this ruling, creating yet more paperwork and generating the need for further training of relevant staff.

The pressure placed by society on healthcare professionals led to the understandable question in a leading legal textbook:[38]

> Where then, does the doctor stand today in relation to society? To some extent, and perhaps increasingly, he is a servant of the public, a public which is, moreover, widely – though perhaps not always well – informed on medical matters. The competent patient's inalienable rights to understand his treatment and to accept or refuse it are now well established and society is conditioned to distrust professional paternalism. The talk today is of 'producers and consumers' and the ambience of the supermarket is one that introduces its own stresses and strains.

Stresses and pressures

There are many claims that clinicians are required to work under very stressful conditions and that this situation can adversely effect patients. It is not difficult to pinpoint a series of factors which have the potential to increase stress at work for doctors, including the pressures which can be attributed to the major NHS reforms outlined in the preceding paragraphs. Other pressures are the result of the attempts of successive governments to reduce funding costs, for example by requiring authorisation of the use of certain treatments through NICE. Regulatory frameworks have been designed with a view, at least in part, to reducing errors and consequently the cost of clinical negligence litigation.[39] There have been *ad hoc* responses to serious medical malpractice scandals and new initiatives to satisfy the demands of patients. Paradoxically, the result has been to increase stress on doctors, which can in its turn lead them to make mistakes.

Stress can be a difficult concept to define because of the subjective nature of individual responses. A satisfactory definition[40] is:

> Physical, emotional and mental strain resulting from the mismatch between an individual and his/her environment', which results from a 'three way relationship between demands on a person, that person's feelings about those demands and their ability to cope with those demands'.[41] Stress is

---

38   Mason, J.K., McCall Smith, R.A. and Laurie G.T., *Law and Medical Ethics* (6th edn, London, Butterworths, 2002).

39   E.g. The Health Act 1999.

40   As defined by Richards, C., 'The Health of Doctors', King's Fund 1989, at p 109.

41   Bynoe, G., 'Stress in Women Doctors' (1994) *British Journal of Hospital Medicine* 51(6): 267–78.

most likely to occur in situations where: demands are high; the amount of control an individual has is low; and, there is limited support or help available for the individual.

The Health and Safety Executive defines stress as:

The adverse reaction people have to excessive pressures or other types of demands placed upon them.

This definition was accepted by the Court of Appeal in the leading case on work stress.[42] Stress symptoms that occur when the factor which has the potential to cause stress (stressor) interacts with or affects an individual are anxiety, depression, restlessness and fatigue. Behavioural manifestations include heavy smoking, overindulgence in food or drink, and taking unnecessary risks. Physiological symptoms include raised blood pressure, increased or irregular heartbeat, muscular tension, pain and heartburn.

Doctors' representatives in the UK are quick to emphasise that members of the profession are working under considerable stress in the modern healthcare setting. The BMA has conducted several separate surveys of senior and junior doctors in the relatively recent past, and these have produced a substantial body of evidence that many senior doctors suffer high stress levels as a result of their work, which adversely affect their ability to provide the best quality of care to their patients. The BMA[43] has concluded that the chief cause of stress for consultants and GPs was volume of workload, and especially on personal life. Other sources of stress were identified as organisational changes, poor management, insufficient resources, dealing with the suffering of patients, and errors, complaints and litigation.

There are many recent examples of successful claims in the UK for psychiatric injury caused by stress or bullying at work,[44] and there is a fast-growing culture of stress awareness in all occupational settings. The first claim to be made by a doctor for work stress was *Johnstone v Bloomsbury Health Authority*.[45] This was a claim brought by a junior doctor for damages arising from psychiatric illness suffered as a result of working excessively long hours. Although the claim was settled out of court, it was soon followed by a large number of successful claims for work stress by employees of public bodies.[46] Claims for stress at work are not uncommon in the NHS, though not all are successful as each turns on its precise facts and it is necessary

---

42   *Sutherland v Hatton* [2002] EWCA (Civ) Part 2, para 7.
43   Work related stress among senior doctors, 2000; Work related stress among junior doctors, 1998.
44   *Majrowsky v Guys and St Thomas's NHS Hospital Trust* [2006] UKHL 34.
45   [1992] QB 333 (CA).
46   E.g. *Walker v Northumberland C C* [1995] IRLR 35.

to meet strict judicial criteria for establishing liability.[47] Nevertheless, for every claim there will be further pressures placed on staff who are accused of bullying or inadequate supervision, and on colleagues who are required to give evidence.[48]

A survey conducted for the BBC and Pulse by NOP found that virtually every one of the 569 GPs they questioned was suffering to varying degrees as a result of stress, attributing this to excessively high workloads, management pressures, and stress caused by the demands of patients. Five per cent of GPs claimed to be clinically depressed. This survey was carried out before the introduction of the new GP contract, and seven out of ten GPs stated that they expected their stress levels to increase once the new contract was introduced.[49] In an analysis of the 2003 NHS Staff survey in England, published by the Healthcare Commission, there were several references to work stress suffered by staff which could lead to errors being made. Doctors of all grades, including consultants, reported that they felt under pressure, with nurses also presenting a similar picture.[50] Levels of stress among NHS staff appeared to remain steady in 2005, according to a more recent Healthcare Commission Report. In the survey of 209,000 NHS employees, 36 per cent said they were suffering from work-related stress, the same percentage as 2004, but lower than the 39 per cent in 2003.[51] The Wales NHS Staff Survey in 2006 found that 39 per cent of NHS staff believed they were suffering from work-related stress. Those who felt under the most stress tended to be working in harrowing areas of healthcare such as cancer services. The majority of the 33,000 staff who participated in the survey complained that they do not have enough time to complete their work properly, and half said that they regularly work unpaid overtime. Sixteen per cent of staff who responded said that they had experienced physical violence in the workplace.[52] In the NHS there is a sickness rate of around 11.6 days per employee, higher than the 10.7 average for public sector employees.[53]

A survey carried out for the *Health Service Journal* in 2001 revealed that 62 per cent of consultant surgeons surveyed had plans to retire early, and 100 per cent of consultant paediatricians intended to seek early retirement

47   *Sutherland v Hatton* [2002] EWCA (Civ); *Walker v Northumberland C C* [1995] IRLR 35.
48   An example of just such a claim is *Merelie v Newcastle Primary Care Trust* [2006] EWHC 150 (QB).
49   Reported on BBC News 23 March 2004.
50   Commission for Healthcare Audit and Inspection 2004.
51   Results of Commission for Healthcare Audit and Inspection Summary of Staff Survey, March 2006, reported in Occupational Health Journal 5 June 2006.
52   NHS Wales Staff Survey Results 2006.
53   Chartered Institute of Personal and Development, 'Employee Absence 2204 – A Survey of Management Policy and Practice', July 2004.

from the NHS, in most cases blaming excessive stress.[54] There is also some evidence that 'high risk' specialties such as obstetrics and paediatrics are failing to attract doctors.[55]

A study conducted in 2004 revealed that of 2,727 who responded, of 1,047 junior doctors who were considering staying in medicine but practising outside the UK, 41 per cent gave the main reason as poor working conditions. A total of 279 doctors were seriously considering relinquishing medicine altogether, 75 per cent of whom gave working conditions as their reason. There are now more pressures than ever on junior doctors seeking employment in the NHS, despite the promise of better working conditions in accordance with the European Working Time Directive[56] and the 'New Deal' initiative,[57] as entry to the profession has been restructured, resulting in fewer job opportunities for those who are newly qualified.[58]

Violence exhibited against healthcare staff has been identified as a potential cause of stress, and although the results of the 2005 staff survey reported by the Healthcare Commission[59] suggest that violence against staff appeared to be on a downward trend, the rates reported are still unacceptable, since 28 per cent of staff who responded said they had experienced either violence or abuse in the previous 12 months, and there are many incidents of violence which go unreported, apparently because only half of the people questioned thought that their employer would take effective action. The BBC Television programme Panorama estimated that 75,000 NHS staff were attacked by patients in 2006, at a total cost to the taxpayer of at least £100 million. According to the same programme, that money could have paid for 4,500 more nurses or 800,000 paramedic call-outs. Under the NHS policy of zero tolerance, staff are encouraged to report any kind of violence or abuse, but fewer than 2 per cent of attacks on staff lead to prosecutions.[60]

Among the most prominent of stress factors in all the surveys of the NHS is the increased workload. This has been generated in part by demanding new structures and targets, by additional work as a result of the introduction of clinical governance and risk management, and by patient expectations. More time is required to comply with the new approach to obtaining consent to

54   Cited in Wyatt, J., 'Stress Management', *Institute of Health Management Journal*, June 2001, available at http://www.ihm.org.uk

55   See BMA Response to DoH Consultation 'Bearing Good Witness', BMA, London, March 2007.

56   Council Directive 93/104 and Department of Health, *Guidance on working patterns for junior doctors*, London 2002 available at http://www.dh.gov.uk/assetRoot/04/06/63/04066366

57   NHS Management Executive, *Junior Doctors: The New Deal*, London, Department of Health 1999.

58   Details of this, called the 'Modernising Medical Careers' programme, can be found on the Department of Health website.

59   Op. cit., fn 23.

60   BBC Panorama, 26 February 2007.

treatment established in the case of *Chester v Afshar*.[61] Other stressors in the workplace are poor communications between management and staff, strained work relationships, job insecurity, long working hours, role ambiguity, harassment, and bullying by seniors. Although a certain degree of pressure at work might be regarded as beneficial – by providing stimulus and the incentive to hard work – it is necessary for a proper balance to be struck, especially in an environment in which errors can result in death and injury.

The work ethos in the NHS, with added external factors such as those associated with increased patient and Government expectations, are potential causes of occupational stress in healthcare employment, and research has indicated that there workplace stress is regarded by managers as a low priority.[62] A survey conducted in 2002 by the Health and Safety Executive[63] together with the Royal College of Nursing (RCN) and the trade union UNISON, revealed that healthcare professionals were twice as likely to suffer occupational stress as people working in 2,000 other occupations.

In addition to the pressures experienced by clinical staff, managers have been adversely affected by the constant re-organisation and successive initiatives aimed at reducing errors, and this has resulted in poor morale and a confused workforce. A poll conducted by the *Health Service Journal* concluded that 69 per cent of Trust chief executives who participated thought that patient care would suffer as a result of short-term financial decisions. In the financial year 2006–07, 47 per cent of Trusts had declared redundancies and 78 per cent operated freezes on recruitment. Half of the Primary Care Trusts at that time were delaying funding for some surgery, and almost all were restricting patients' access to certain forms of treatment. Sixty-one per cent of the hospital chief executives said they had closed wards.[64] In more recent years, the implementation of initiatives such as 'Agenda for Change', 'Being Open', and emergency planning programmes have added to the financial and psychological pressures on healthcare organisations and their staff. Wyatt, who has carried out extensive work in this field, blames the professional, cultural, and psychological distances between NHS managers and clinicians, and serious weaknesses in the infrastructure of healthcare organisations for the rising levels of stress.[65]

---

61 *Pearce v United Bristol Healthcare NHS Trust* [1998] AC 48; *Chester v Afshar* [2004] UKHL 41. It is now necessary for doctors to provide more information to patients and to give them time to ask questions about their treatment which must be answered 'truthfully'.

62 Wyatt, J., 'Stress Management', (June 2001) *Institute of Health Management Journal*, p 4.

63 HSE, UNISON, and the RCN Survey, 'The Stress Research Project' 2002.

64 Carvel, J., 'NHS shake-ups hitting morale' *Guardian*, 1 March 2007.

65 Wyatt, J., 'Stress Management', (June 2001) *Institute of Health Management Journal*, p 6.

Despite many assertions by the medical profession and its supporters that occupational stress is a significant problem in the NHS, another study[66] based in University College London, and carried out over a 12-year period, investigated the extent to which individual approaches to work, workplace, stress, burnout and satisfaction with medical careers are the result of learning style and personality, measured five to 12 years earlier, when the same doctors were applicants to medical school or were medical students. The researchers concluded that approaches to work later in life could be predicted by study habits and learning styles at the point of application to medical school, and also in the final year of medical education. Differences of approach to work and individual perceptions of workplace ethos appeared to reflect stable, long-term differences in the personalities of the doctors themselves.

The obvious conclusion that will be seized upon by less sympathetic commentators is that doctors who claim to be overworked should not blame their jobs. However, the law would not accept such a view. Victims of psychiatric injury can succeed in obtaining compensation even if they have personalities that are vulnerable to stress, providing they can prove definite psychiatric illness and that management was aware that they were experiencing psychiatric problems as a result of pressure at work.[67]

The case of *Hiles v South Gloucestershire NHS Primary Care Trust*[68] is typical of many. The High Court ruled that the Trust was in breach of the duty owed to a health visitor to take reasonable care to avoid causing injury to her health, when a senior manager had become aware that difficulties she was experiencing at work were causing her to have psychiatric problems. The claimant had responsibility for children, and on commencing work for the defendants she was told by her then manager that her workload would not exceed responsibility for the cases of 200 children. When a new manager was appointed later, her workload increased to require her to take responsibility for the cases of 230–240 children. That increased workload was partly as the result of natural causes, and partly also the result of severe staff shortages. Her workload increased again, even after she had broken down in tears during an appraisal interview with her manager, and she felt under still more stress, eventually suffering a psychiatric breakdown.

Ironically, the EU legislation on health and safety at work that requires organisations to assess all the risks to employees' health posed by their work

66   McManus, I.C., Keeling, A., Paice, E., Department of Psychology, 'Stress, Burnout and Doctors' Attitudes to Work are Determined by Personality and Learning Style: A Twelve-year Longitudinal Study of UK Medical Graduates' (2004) *BMC Medicine* 2: 29.

67   *Walker v Northumberland CC* [1995] IRLR 35; *Sutherland v Hatton* [2002] EWCA (Civ); *Walker v Northumberland CC* [1995] IRLR 35; *Barber v Somerset CC* (2004) UKHL 13 (2004) 2 All ER 385.

68   QBD, 20 December 2006.

and to take reasonable and practicable steps to reduce the risks, if necessary, is itself placing greater pressures on the staff who are required to implement and monitor it.

The conclusion is that probably, on balance, doctors are being properly rewarded for the responsible and stressful work for which they undertake many years training. Other healthcare professionals working for the NHS do not appear to be over-rewarded for their work.

Are doctors out of control and under-regulated?

It seems that people in general may be dissatisfied with the service they receive from the medical profession, if the number of complaints to the GMC provides an accurate means of measuring public attitudes. Figures released by the GMC in 2006 showed a total of 4,980 complaints against doctors in 2005 – around 100 a week, as compared with 3,000 complaints in 1999 (58 a week) – and 1,000 in 1996 (19 a week).[69] This information was revealed at roughly the same time as the announcement that UK doctors are the highest paid in Europe, and did not create a good impression. Yet, despite the concerns of relatively few individuals that are reported to the GMC, as has been seen, members of the public in general continue to trust doctors more than any other group of professionals.[70] This was even after the lengthy Bristol Inquiry revealed serious shortcomings on the part of doctors, and Harold Shipman's murders passed undetected for many years, as well as numerous medical scandals, exposed after regulation of doctors had proved unsatisfactory.

It would be difficult to find another profession against which so many public criticisms have been levelled by so many official bodies in recent years, but perhaps the public as a whole is not as concerned as the Government about the apparent lack of control over healthcare professionals – with good reason, given the Government's role in funding claims. Countless comments in both the Bristol and Shipman Inquiry reports indicate a high level of dissatisfaction on the part of a senior legal academic and a highly respected member of the judiciary. It is possible to find numerous strongly worded criticisms of healthcare professionals in a host of other reports of official investigations into errors and malpractice incidents. In addition, in the course of judicial proceedings, including coroners' inquests and clinical negligence claims, judges make critical comments about the way in which healthcare professionals work and communicate with patients and with one another.

69   See *Independent*, 10 July 2006.
70   Renn, O. and Levene, D., 'Credibility and Trust in Risk Communication', in Pasperson, R.E. and Stallen, P.J.M. (eds), *Communicating Risks to the Public: International Perspectives* (Kluwer, Dordrecht, 2003).

If there is one single lesson to be learned from the Bristol and Shipman Inquiries and from numerous clinical negligence claims,[71] it is that even when individuals can be blamed – in the Shipman case to the point of criminality – the real fault lies in the complex systems that apply in the environments within which healthcare is delivered. The solution that immediately suggests itself to our political leaders is 'regulation, regulation, regulation'. The Government's response to the issues highlighted by the catalogue of errors and examples of malpractice has been to introduce ever more layers of regulation in healthcare to the extent that, far from being under-regulated, doctors, their employers, and their workplaces have become the most over-regulated sector of professional life.

The NHS has become the victim of initiativitis, which in some instances is counter-productive, stressful and wasteful of staff time. The NHS Confederation identified in its report on regulation at least 56 organisations in England that have a right to visit NHS hospitals and trusts, some without even being invited. The authors of the report[72] are unable to confirm that they have included all such bodies in their report, as there are so many. They include the Human Fertilisation & Embryology Authority, the Human Tissue Authority, the Medicines and Healthcare Products Regulatory Agency, Monitor, the Environment Agency, the fire authorities, the Health and Safety Executive, the Information Commissioner, the National Audit Office, local authority environmental health departments, the Audit Commission, the Commission for Social Care Inspection, the Healthcare Commission, the Mental Health Act Commission, overview and scrutiny committees of local authorities patient and public involvement (PPI) forums, and the Commission for Patient and Public Involvement in Health, the Council for Healthcare Regulatory Excellence, the various professional regulatory bodies such as the GMC and the GDC, the Health Protection Agency, the National Patient Safety Agency, the National Institute for Innovation and Improvement, the NHS Business Services Authority, the NHS Counter Fraud and Security Management, the NHS Litigation Authority, the 13 Royal Colleges, the Postgraduate Medical Education and Training Board, the Cancer Peer Review, various divisions of NHS Estates, the Health Information Accreditation Scheme, the Accreditation scheme for tissue banks, Investors in People, Clinical Pathology Accreditation Ltd, Health Quality Services, and the Hospital Accreditation Programme. The Government plans to rationalise the roles of many of these bodies, as the report claims:

> The sheer number of inspections, standards, and volume of information required to demonstrate compliance is making it difficult for NHS

---

71   E.g. the leading case of *Bolitho v City and Hackney Health Authority* [1997] 4 All ER 771 (HL).
72   NHS Confederation, 7 March 2007.

organisations to extract value from these various processes and use them to drive improvement in services for patients.

The position is further complicated by the existence of equivalent bodies with different names in Wales and Scotland. The annual check by the Healthcare Commission in England alone is described as 'overwhelming', since it requires 500 separate topics to be dealt with and overlaps in many respects with the requirements of the Clinical Negligence Scheme for Trusts. The same overlap occurs in Wales between the work of the HIW and the WRP. A concordat has been introduced between inspection bodies with a view to reducing the burden of inspection and regulation, but so great is the bulk of regulation that it will prove impossible to reduce the burden in a meaningful way without radical changes to the entire system.

In addition to the large number of external regulators, healthcare professionals have traditionally been self-regulating, though the end of this system is now in sight following the Shipman Inquiry recommendations. The Council for Healthcare Regulatory Excellence (CHRE) undertakes the role of assessing the decisions of the regulatory bodies in healthcare in order to decide whether certain decisions have been too lenient and need to be referred to the High Court under the National Health Service Reform and Healthcare Professions Act 2002 s 29. This organisation, which was set up in the wake of the Bristol Inquiry Report, offers a unique overview of the work of the healthcare regulators, logging cases on its database and maintaining virtually all its information

Distribution of Incoming Cases (Non-Erasure) By Regulator (Total 521)

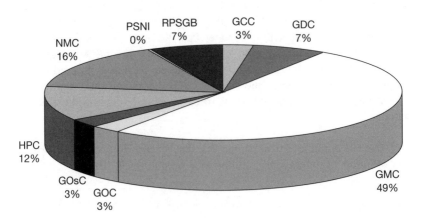

Figure 6 Number of written complaints by regulatory 2005–6

electronically, operating on the basis of a paperless office. The database of cases received and considered under s 29 is an invaluable tool for recording cases and for ensuring that they are considered by the surprisingly small staff of CHRE case officers within the prescribed 28 day limit. The electronic data base contains transcripts that have been requested, letters from complainants and regulators, details of learning points and other information relevant to each decision. It is possible to search the database by name of healthcare regulator, decision-maker, alleged offender, and offence.

As can be observed from Figure 6 on p 148, by far the most active of all the regulators during the year 1 June 2005 to 31 May 2006,[73] although it has been the most criticised, was the GMC, with almost 50 per cent of all cases going to the CHRE being referred by that organisation. The GMC deals expeditiously with the cases it is required to investigate. This is despite the fact that the GMC does not regulate the largest group of healthcare professionals; that role belongs to the NMC, which in fact refers only 16 per cent of the incoming cases. Delays by the NMC in hearing disciplinary cases as a result of financial problems were reported by the BBC,[74] which had obtained the relevant information under the Freedom of Information Act 2000. The response of the NMC to criticisms made of it by the BBC was that the 345 practitioners who are still waiting for a hearing represent less than 0.05 per cent of the 682,000 nurses, midwives, and specialist community public health nurses on its register. This situation is clearly unsatisfactory, and it is ironic that most of the headlines concerning professional incompetence are directed at doctors rather than nurses.

Part of the problem for the image of the medical profession lies in the fact that the media frequently give doctors a higher profile than other healthcare professionals, and should take responsibility for the shortcomings in care that are identified. However, the GMC has demonstrated its willingness to reform and had already made significant changes and improvements even before the fifth report of the Shipman Inquiry, dealing with professional regulation, was published. The concept of 'revalidation' of doctors had been proposed by the GMC in 1998, and has been adopted in a White Paper[75] published in 2007, and the re-licensing and re-certification processes are about to be implemented. The GMC had proposed earlier that the composition of its Council should be changed to ensure a more balanced membership with equal proportions of medical and lay members. It had agreed to introduce the civil standard of proof, to be applied flexibly, in its proceedings, and will implement this when

73　The author conducted a research study into the operation, during that year, of the National Health Service Reform and Healthcare Professions Act 2002 s 29.
74　BBC News, 28 November 2006.
75　'Trust, Assurance and Safety – The Regulation of Health Professionals', 21 February 2007.

the appropriate legislation has been passed. The White Paper on professional regulation sets out a comprehensive programme for reforming regulation of all healthcare professionals, based on the wide-ranging consultation on two reviews of professional regulation published in July 2006. The White Paper tolls the death-knell for self-regulation for doctors, and the role of the GMC will change radically, reducing the level of involvement of doctors in the regulation of their profession after more than 150 years. The result will be still greater scrutiny and increased pressure on healthcare professionals, which is the price that must be paid for ensuring patient safety.

There are numerous additional methods by which healthcare professionals are made accountable. Not least of these are the NHS Complaints System and the civil litigation system, both of which have been discussed earlier in this book. The coronial system also has a place in the intricate jigsaw of accountability, and coroners do not hesitate, in the course of inquests, to comment critically on the activities of healthcare professionals.[76] However, there has also been a trend in recent years, reflecting society's less tolerant attitude to doctors, towards criminalising medical errors[77] resulting in gross negligence manslaughter prosecutions in some instances where serious errors have caused the death of patients. In order to secure a conviction for gross negligence manslaughter, the prosecution must prove that the defendant owed the victim a duty of care (which is not usually difficult in the healthcare setting), that the act or omission of the defendant amounted to a breach of that duty; that the act or omission caused the death of the victim, and that the defendant's conduct was so bad in all the circumstances as to amount, in the eyes of the jury, to a criminal act or omission. Thus, for a doctor to be convicted, his or her conduct must be shown to have fallen far below the minimum acceptable standard where a risk of death was involved, to the extent that the conduct in question must have been so bad as to be characterised as 'gross negligence' and amount to a crime.[78] In the words of Lord Mackay:[79]

> The jury will have to consider whether the extent to which the defendant's conduct departed from the proper standard of care incumbent upon him, involving as it must have done a risk of death to the patient, was such that it should be judged criminal.

---

76 *R (Touche) v Inner North London Coroner* [2001] QB 1206.

77 See Ferner, R.E. and McDowell, S.E., 'Doctors Charged with Manslaughter in the Course of Medical Practice' (2006) *Journal of the Royal Society of Medicine* 99: 309–14.

78 *R v Adomako* [1994] UKHL 6 (30 June 1994); [1994] 3 All ER 79; *Attorney General's Reference No 2 of 1999* [2000] EWCA Crim 91 (15 February 2000) The court's opinion was sought in relation to two questions referred by the Attorney General under the Criminal Justice Act 1972 s 36.

79 *Brown v The Queen (Jamaica)* (2005) UKPC 18.

In the 1980s there were relatively few prosecutions of doctors for manslaughter. According to the leading research on this topic carried out by Ferner and McDowell, who analysed cases since 1795, the numbers increased over the next two decades until there were 17 such prosecutions in 2005. It has been argued[80] that this trend in relation to medical manslaughter reflects changing social attitudes towards the notion of gross negligence. Previous generations did not want to prosecute doctors for gross negligence manslaughter for making a mistake that a reasonably competent doctor could make simply through an error of judgment, or by some inadvertence or mischance. Of the 85 prosecutions identified in the study, 60 doctors were acquitted (71 per cent), 22 were convicted, and three pleaded guilty. Since 1990, it is noteworthy that 38 doctors have been charged with manslaughter. The reason for the low conviction rate is uncertain, possibly because prosecutions were pursued for reasons of vengeance or retribution – though this is unlikely, since the Crown Prosecution Service (CPS) takes the decision to prosecute and is unlikely to be influenced by personal motives. The CPS states of its own methods:[81]

> ... Crown Prosecutors must be satisfied that there is enough evidence to provide a 'realistic prospect of conviction' ... [that is] that a jury or a bench of magistrates, properly directed in accordance with the law, will be more likely than not to convict the defendant of the charge alleged.

The research by Ferner and McDowell identified gross negligence manslaughter cases according to the standard classification of human error, that or mistakes, slips or lapses, and violations, and concluded that the largest category of doctors were charged as a consequence of mistakes (37 in all) or slips (17), and only a minority as a consequence of alleged violations (16). The cases analysed excluded 47 people who were not medically qualified, three who were medical students and 31 practitioners who were accused of manslaughter in connection with abortion. The authors recognised that they may have failed to identify some relevant cases, and that the results were presented without looking at the broader context of the number of practising doctors or the number of interactions between doctor and patient.

In response to a Parliamentary question in 2002,[82] the Solicitor General commented that it is very difficult to give precise figures relating to the number of doctors who have been prosecuted for manslaughter since 1974, since before 1993 prosecutions were recorded only by the name of the defendant, with no mention of the defendant's occupation. However, in 1993 a new case-tracking system was introduced by the CPS, so prosecutions for manslaughter arising from gross medical negligence could be recorded, though these do

---

80 Holbrook, A., 'Criminalisation of Fatal Medical Mistakes' (2003) *BMJ* 327: 1118–19.
81 *About the CPS: The Principles We Follow*. http://www.cps.gov.uk/about/principles
82 Hansard, 19 Sept 2002 : Col 89W – Manslaughter (Doctors).

not distinguish between doctors and other medical staff. The CPS estimated, however, that between 1994 and 2002, 12 doctors had been prosecuted for 'medical' manslaughter. Of those, eight were acquitted of all charges and four were convicted of at least one count on the indictment. The costs of such prosecutions are an important factor, bearing in mind the already high cost of such incidents to the public purse, even when there is no prosecution.

Deaths, which have a high public profile, are more likely to result in a prosecution, however, as recent cases demonstrate. One of the best known cases in recent years is that concerning two doctors who were treating an 18-year-old who was suffering from leukaemia. He was due to receive cytosine, to be injected intrathecally on the first day of the particular treatment; and vincristine, which was to be injected intravenously the next day. The senior house officer correctly administered the cytosine. The registrar then handed the more junior doctor (an SHO) vincristine and instructed him to inject it into the patient's spine. Even though the SHO checked the instructions twice, he was told to go ahead with the injection. The patient died four weeks later, and the registrar, who was charged with manslaughter, pleaded guilty.[83] The NPSA has made a demonstration video based on this case to illustrate how systems can fail in a pressurised healthcare environment, and the Department of Health introduced guidelines with a view to preventing similar errors in the future.[84]

The low conviction rate and increasing number of prosecutions raise the question as to whether this is the most satisfactory way of dealing with clinical errors made by individual doctors resulting in death. The doctors involved in such cases will have had their lives and careers ruined and the relatives of the deceased will have been entitled to compensation through the civil courts. A further complication has been introduced by the Corporate Manslaughter and Homicide Act 2007. Surely a better approach is to consider how systems might be improved through lessons learned. A more recent approach to deaths caused by medical error has been to prosecute the hospital trust under the Health and Safety at Work legislation. The first example of this is the case in which Southampton University Hospitals Trust has been fined £100,000 for failing to supervise junior doctors with the result that a patient died following a routine operation. Senior House Officers at Southampton General Hospital had failed to diagnose toxic shock syndrome despite making eight assessments of his condition over two days. More recently, the Royal United Hospital (RUH) in Bath admitted two charges of failing to act on safety warnings, resulting in the death of patient from Legionnaires disease.[85] The patient

83   R v Mulhem [2001].
84   DoH: National Guidance on the Safe Administration of Intrathecal Chemotherapy 2001.
85   The Times, 22 March 2007.

in question contracted the illness from a hospital shower on the day that he was due to be discharged after successful treatment for leukaemia. Jennifer Gunning, chairwoman of the bench at Bath Magistrates Court, expressed her concern about the situation, and referred the case to Bristol Crown Court for sentencing, saying:

> Guidance was available for more than ten years, but this was blatantly not followed. The RUH management was inadequate. Mr Eyles died as a result of those failings and many other vulnerable patients were put at risk.

The consequences of over-regulation: demoralisation and defensive practice?[86]

Although it was apparent as a result of the Bristol and Shipman cases that there were definite problems inherent in self-regulation which meant that the medical profession had been under-regulated for many years, over-regulation can also present problems. Hyper-regulation, combined with fear of civil litigation, or even prosecution, could be contributing to the practice of defensive medicine. As Richard Smith, then editor of the *BMJ* pointed out:

> The dangers of over-regulation may be less obvious than those of under-regulation, but in the long run they may be just as damaging.[87]

The Government's solution for dealing with poor performance was finally set out in guidance issued in 1995,[88] but it has taken another ten years for the details of how the problem should be handled to be worked through. In his editorial, Richard Smith commented that the heavy regulatory burden on doctors has created a situation which highly confusing:

> Doctors now face revalidation, compulsory continuing medical education and audit, governance of their clinical activity by their trust or primary care group, peer review, and a possible visit from a hit squad from their college or from the Commission for Health Improvement. The dangers are that their internal motivation (the most important thing) is crushed,

---

86 This section is reproduced from a short article on defensive medicine published by the author in *Medical Law Monitor*, April 2007, Informa, by kind permission of the publishers.

87 Smith, R. 'Regulation of doctors and the Bristol Inquiry' (1998) *BMJ* 317: 1539–40.

88 Department of Health, 'Review of Guidance on Doctors' Performance. Maintaining Medical Excellence', London, DoH, 1995.

that their time is diverted into activities that are more bureaucratic than beneficial to patients, and that they resort to game playing to buck the system (something at which doctors are highly skilled).

A demoralised medical profession that believes that it is constantly under surveillance surely cannot be of any real benefit to patients. There is already a large body of literature supporting the view that doctors practise defensively, by which is meant that they carry out procedures and recommend treatments, which are designed not primarily because they are clinically necessary in the patient's best interests, but because such measures are likely to prevent the possibility of a legal claim. Another definition is:

> The alteration of Modes of Medical Practice, induced by the threat of liability, for the principal purposes of forestalling the possibility of law-suits by patients, as well as providing a good defence if such law suits are instituted.[89]

AvMA is on record as stating:[90]

> We are not aware of 'defensive medicine' being a significant issue in the NHS.

It is necessary at this point to consider the extent to which clinicians may be practising defensively in the UK. It is, of course, extremely difficult to identify whether doctors are making decisions defensively, because defensive practice might be one of several factors influencing a clinical decision.[91] A difficulty arising here is that, as Andrew Grubb suggests:[92]

> There is little clear understanding within the medical profession of what the term 'defensive medicine' means.

While there has been relatively little research in this area in the UK, more work has been undertaken on it in the US, where a variety of different methodologies have been employed, from surveys of clinicians to clinical scenario surveys and comparative hospital record analysis, each of which

---

89   Report of the Secretary's Commission on Medical Malpractice, Department of Health, Education and Welfare, Washington DC, 1973.
90   Evidence to the Select Committee on Constitutional Affairs, November 2005.
91   'Defensive Medicine: Is Legal Protection the Only Motive?' Editorial, *Modern Healthcare*, 14 September 1990, p 41.
92   Grubb, A., *Principles of Medical Law*, 2nd edn 2004, p 403.

has its own strengths and weaknesses.[93] The US research indicates that it is virtually impossible to measure precisely the amount of defensive medicine being practised and its cost.[94]

As far as the UK is concerned, there is evidence from several surveys that doctors themselves believe that they practise defensively, and as long as the threat of litigation remains, even the best doctors will feel uneasy and sense the infamous 'dagger at the doctor's back'.[95] One commentator, reviewing trends in general practice in the light of a survey conducted in 1999, which concluded that doctors were more likely to undertake diagnostic testing, refer patients, and avoid the treatment of certain conditions than they had been five years earlier, expressed the view that negative defensive practices have adverse consequences both for individual patients and for public health.[96]

A poll conducted in 2001[97] of over 700 doctors revealed that nine out of ten doctors surveyed were concerned about the growing complaints culture which they saw as threatening the future of the NHS. A large number of doctors (over two-thirds) who responded indicated that they had already adopted 'defensive' medical practices by requiring patients to undergo a large number of tests even for the most trivial conditions, merely in order to minimise the risk of litigation. Four out of ten of the respondents said they had received a complaint or a compensation claim had been brought against them by a patient in the preceding three years. The researchers concluded that the 'compensation culture' was contributing to low morale and the recruitment difficulties within the health service, and the vast majority thought patients had become more demanding in recent years.[98] A spokesperson[99] for the MDU said in response:

> There is no doubt that this climate is having an impact on the profession both in terms of clinical practice and morale. The strength of feeling among the profession about rising litigation is clearly evident in the number of doctors who have taken the time to reply to this survey.

In 2005, Dr Gerald Panting of the MPS re-echoed the same view when commenting on the reported rise in the number of caesarean section operations

---

93 See Baker, T., 'The Goods on Defensive Medicine' *The Medical Malpractice Myth* (University of Chicago Press, 2005, Chapter 6, p 119).

94 Ibid., p 133.

95 *Per* Lord Denning in *Hatcher v Black, The Times* 2 July 1954.

96 Summerton, N., 'Trends in Negative Defensive Medicine Within General Practice' (1 July 2000) *British Journal of General Practice* 50(456): 565–66(2).

97 Survey by the doctors-only website www.medix-uk.com 2001.

98 Reported on BBC News, 8 March 2001.

99 Dr Frances Szekely, senior medical claims handler, MDU.

in England from 22 per cent to 22.7 per cent.[100] The caesarean section rate has been used as an indicator of the rate of defensive medical practice for some time, though there are some who doubt the wisdom of this approach.[101] The view of lawyers and claims handlers is that the increase is linked to the cost of defending obstetric negligence claims, which has raised the level of 'defensive medicine' being practised. There is a strong opinion that 'defensive medicine is bad medicine' because it exposes patients to risks that are inherent in unnecessary procedures.

On the other hand, it can be argued that by taking extra precautions, doctors are achieving the goals of the law of tort,[102] and of the present clinical governance regime. Caesarean sections, in particular, are major surgical procedures carrying significant risks, and the Royal College of Obstetrics and Gynaecology considers that the correct rate, without defensive practice, should be between 10 per cent and 15 per cent.[103] However, taking an approach that accords with the climate of patient-centred care and current attitudes of the courts to consent to treatment, Dr Panting argued that defensive medicine may not be as bad a practice as many fear, commenting:

> If such cautious medicine has sparked a review, that must be a good thing. If it causes one clinician to seek the views of a second, that, too, is positive, and if in the end the decision is to intervene, rather than take a risk, I, as a patient, am all for that.

Some credence has been given to the notion that there are certain women who request caesarean section deliveries because they are 'too posh to push'.[104] The proportion of women in the UK who give birth by caesarean section has increased threefold over the past 30 years. The rate in England in 1970 was 4.5 per cent, but by 2005 the rate was closer to 16 per cent and still rising. However, research indicates that, far from this being the case, the majority of caesarean sections were carried out because doctors had advised this procedure. UK women are four times more likely to have a caesarean section than they were 50 years ago, but the 'too posh to push' idea has been

---

100   Bassett, K.L., Iyer, N. and Kazanjian, A., 'Defensive Medicine During Hospital Obstetrical Care: A By-Product of the Technological Age', Defensive medicine during hospital obstetrical care: a by-product of the technological age.
101   See Jones, M., *Medical Negligence* (3rd edn, 2003) 16–19; 252–58.
102   See Baker, T., 'The Goods on Defensive Medicine', *The Medical Malpractice Myth* (University of Chicago Press, Chicago, 2005, Chapter 6 passim).
103   'Doctors on the Defensive', *Society Guardian*, 1 April 2005.
104   Numerous newspaper articles have put this view, e.g. the *Guardian* 29 April 2004; the *Observer*, 4 September 2005; *Daily Telegraph*, 11 December 2006.

discounted as yet another myth perpetrated by the tabloid press.[105] Dr Helen Churchill's research showed that 44 per cent of obstetricians surveyed thought that the increase in caesarean section is because more women ask for the procedure, compared to 2 per cent in a similar survey 15 years ago. However, her team also found that only around 5 per cent of mothers had a preference for caesarean section deliveries. Of the 200 women in her survey, only six first-time mothers had requested a caesarean delivery, and that 70 per cent of women requesting the operation had had previous caesareans. Fifty-two per cent of consultants in the study blamed the inexperience of junior doctors and the practice of 'defensive medicine' for reasons for the rise. In fact, she concluded that there was virtually no difference between pre-planned preferences and on-the-day choices, finding:

> The ratio of planned to emergency Caesareans has remained constant over the past 20 years, further evidence that calls into question any argument suggesting that maternal request is driving the rate rise.

Dr Churchill calculated that the present rate of caesarean sections is both a financial and a medical problem, since if the rate were halved, the NHS could save £80 million per annum.

A further report from the Office of Health Economics[106] in February 2007 indicated that a quarter of all births in NHS hospitals are by caesarean section operation. The report covers figures from 2005 to 2007, and it supports the view that the current trend shows a steady growth in caesarean section deliveries. There is a suggestion that the use of emergency caesareans is more common because some women are delaying having their babies until later in life, and also because greater obesity in mothers leads to birth complications. The fear of litigation on the part of doctors is considered to be another factor. According to the same report, in 1995–96 one in six babies born in NHS hospitals were delivered by caesarean section; the figure increased in 2000–01 to one in five, and to almost one in four in 2004, despite the view of the WHO that the rate should be no higher than 10–15 per cent.[107] The rise cannot, according to the researchers, be the result of increasing elective caesareans, because these numbers have stabilised, and the growth is in fact attributable to increasing numbers of emergency caesareans.

---

105 Research presented by Dr Helen Churchill on 9 March 2007 at Lancaster University. Dr Churchill is a researcher at the Research Institute for Health and Social Change Manchester Metropolitan University.
106 *The Times*, 27 February 2007.
107 WHO Consensus Conference on Appropriate Technology for Birth, Fortaleza, Brazil, 22–26 April 1985, cited in the Report of the Office of Health Economics, February 2007.

The Courts have acknowledged on a number of occasions since the earliest days of the NHS that fear of litigation may lead doctors to practice defensively.[108] There are numerous references by judges to the potential danger of encouraging defensive medical practice. To take but a few examples: First at High Court level, *Per* Gross J:[109]

> I begin with the submission that, in all the circumstances (as they were perceived to be), the risk of cord prolapse was so slight that it could be ignored. I have given anxious consideration to this argument; in a fault based system, it is indeed necessary both (i) to exclude hindsight and (ii) to recognise the social costs of inadvertently encouraging 'defensive' medicine by setting unrealistic standards.

Then in the Court of Appeal, *Per* Lawton LJ:[110]

> If courts make findings of negligence on flimsy evidence or regard failure to produce an expected result as strong evidence of negligence, doctors are likely to protect themselves by what has become known as defensive medicine, that is to say, adopting procedures which are not for the benefit of the patient but safeguards against the possibility of the patient making a claim for negligence.

And in the House of Lords, on the basis of a number of assumptions, *Per* Scarman LJ in the Sidaway case:[111]

> There can be little doubt that policy explains the divergence of view. The proliferation of medical malpractice suits in the U.S.A. has led some courts and some legislatures to curtail or even to reject the operation of the doctrine in an endeavour to restrict the liability of the doctor and so discourage the practice of 'defensive medicine' – by which is meant the practice of doctors advising and undertaking the treatment which they think is legally safe even though they may believe that it is not the best for their patient.

The Government, while denying that a claims culture exists, nevertheless assumes that doctors are practising defensively because they fear litigation. Yet, ironically, policy makers and legislators, while criticising risk-averse

---

108   *Hatcher v Black, The Times* 2 July 1954.
109   *Reynolds v North Tyneside Health Authority* 30 May 2000, at para 43.
110   *Whitehouse v Jordan* [1980] 1 All ER 650, p 659.
111   *Sidaway v Board of Governors of Bethlem Royal Hospital* [1985] AC 871, at p 873.

behaviour, have taken rigorous steps to introduce strict regimes for ensuring safety in the healthcare areas. Lord Falconer has referred to defensive medicine on many occasions, for example in his speech at the Insurance Times Conference in 2004,[112] saying:

> Schools, hospitals, local authorities are beginning to feel they are more at risk from litigation than they really are. They have the impression that they are at risk from being sued for activities that, in a healthy society, we would want and expect them to carry out.

And again, in his famous 'Risk and Compensation Culture' speech to the IPPR in May 2005[113] and in his response to the Queen's Speech in the same month[114] he referred to defensive medicine:

> There are too many areas in life where productive activity is stifled and distorted by the fear of accidents and mistakes leading to disproportionate claims; for example, the school trip which does not go ahead, the leisure activities curtailed by the local authority, the voluntary sector bodies finding it difficult to recruit volunteers or run activities, the medical services practising defensive medicine.

Fenn *et al.*, in a well thought-out study, concluded that hospitals that expected a higher rate of claims were undertaking more diagnostic tests, and concluded that the threat of litigation has an impact on clinical discretion.[115]

It has also been claimed by the Chairman of the BMA that the proposals in the White Paper on professional regulation are likely to lead to further defensive medical practices,[116] and that would in turn add to the financial problems of the NHS:

> Sadly the White Paper proposals could lead to a climate of defensive medicine in which doctors are forever looking over their shoulders instead of concentrating on working in the best interest of their patients.

112 10 November 2004.
113 26 May 2005.
114 25 May 2005.
115 Fenn, P., Grey, A., Rickman, N., 'Enterprise Liability, Insurance and Defensive Medicine: UK Evidence'. Publication of work in progress, March 2004.
116 Johnson, J., Chairman BMA, Response to the White Paper proposals, BBC News, 21 February 2007.

Drawing the line between defensive medicine and risk management

The term 'defensive medicine' tends to be used pejoratively. It is considered to be a selfish activity on the part of doctors, and could even be regarded as potentially dangerous to patients. Yet there is a very fine distinction between defensive practice and risk management. While the latter appears to be based on highly organised pre-planned activities designed to ensure patient safety, with the primary aim of enhancing quality, it also has the effect, if properly carried out, of reducing the risk of litigation. The medical profession and indeed all NHS staff have, over the past decade or so, been learning to accept clinical governance, risk management and compulsory training in the form of continuous professional development. Clinical governance is defined as:

> A framework through which NHS bodies are accountable for continuously improving the quality of their services and safeguarding high standards of care, by creating an environment in which excellence in clinical care will flourish.[117]

Although expressed in terms of quality improvement, the hidden agenda in this process is clearly to introduce a system of identifying and managing risks in healthcare. NICE guidelines are a clear example of indirect defensiveness, as they are aimed at ensuring that certain standards are met which both reduce the risk of complications and also keep spending on drugs and other treatment within manageable bounds. The associated burdens of administration for doctors, and pressures from managers as a result of regular reporting, inspections, additional meetings and compulsory audit, have increased occupational stress on doctors. They are constantly receiving government documentation explaining how proposed reforms are to be 'delivered'. Many of the new developments are accompanied by a new vocabulary – that of civil servants – which regularly reminds healthcare professionals of the need to 'modernise.'[118]

Doctors are required to absorb information about new reporting systems for patient safety incidents and to understand requirements of the NPSA and other monitoring organisations. It has not been possible to discover how much is spent by the average NHS Trust on clinical governance and risk management,

117   'A first class service: Quality in the New NHS' Department of Health, 1998.
118   Listed in the randomly selected glossy brochure entitled: 'Healthcare Standards for Wales: Making the Connections Designed for Life', 2005 NHS Wales.

but an obvious question is whether this produces a real benefit in terms of patient care and reduced levels of claims.

Another area of potential defensive activity is the target setting in healthcare, which is a relatively new concept, emanating from initiatives introduced ostensibly to improve the quality of care that patients receive. There is some evidence that the requirement to meet targets is in itself likely to encourage defensive practices by institutions which, in a competitive market for healthcare, have an interest in appearing to achieve excellence. The end result can be counter-productive, as shown by tales of manipulated waiting lists[119] and other self-interested activities on the part of NHS Trusts.

It would appear that defensive medicine is a concept which is confined in some respects to the decisions of individual doctors, or groups of doctors within a particular setting, on an *ad hoc* basis when dealing with their particular patients. The level of defensiveness may vary from one patient to another. How many solicitors, for example, are under the impression that greater caution is exercised towards them when they are undergoing ante-natal care? It has been suggested that since the standard of care applicable to doctors requires them only to be 'reasonable' in the light of logic[120] and peer standards,[121] for a doctor to subject a patient to unnecessary but risky defensive procedures that cause harm to the patient, could in itself be negligence.[122]

Clinical governance and risk management, on the other hand, involve formal and uniform, usually externally imposed, systems applicable to healthcare institutions and their collective policies. Whatever the truth about defensive practice, it is at least heartening that the crisis in the level of claims has had the positive impact of greater care being taken to ensure that risks are identified and managed.

Baroness Hale, in *Gregg v Scott*,[123] took a view of doctors that is close to the truth when she said:

> But of course doctors and other health care professionals are not solely, or even mainly, motivated by the fear of adverse legal consequences. They are motivated by their natural desire and their professional duty to do their best for their patients.

---

119 Butler, P., 'Hospitals admit to waiting list manipulation', *Society Guardian*, 5 June 2001.
120 *Bolitho v City and Hackney Health Authority* [1998] AC 232.
121 *Bolam v Friern Hospital Management Committee* [1957] 1 WLR 582.
122 See Grubb, A., *Principles of Medical Law* (3rd edn 2003, Oxford University Press, p 403).
123 [2005] UKHL 2, para 217.

Conclusion

The working environment for healthcare professionals in the NHS today is complex and stressful. In a profession facing constant criticism by the media, inspections and monitoring by employers and external organisations, regular restructuring and a barrage of new legislation and evolving case law, as well as innovations technology and research finding, it is virtually impossible for even the most conscientious of doctors to keep abreast of developments. Further complications, and the potential for more claims, have been introduced by the development of 'nurse prescribing,' plans for which have been rigorously opposed by doctors who argue that while they spend years training and learning how to prescribe correctly, nurses are now able to prescribe a wide range of drugs after only a short training course. Pharmacists are also included in this plan, which doctors have described as irresponsible and dangerous.[124] Professional restructuring, targets, and changes in medical education necessarily create insecurity in a vocation which initially attracts idealistic and well-intentioned individuals. If a solution to the professional stresses does exist, it will inevitably be based on compromise to ensure that the balance is redressed in such a way as to enable doctors to work more effectively to meet the needs of patients in the 'modern and dependable' NHS. Any solution should include the fostering of a better understanding between doctors and patients through statements of the rights and responsibilities of both groups; better training for doctors in effective communication techniques; a reduction in the number of 'initiatives' in order to afford healthcare professionals a respite at least on a temporary basis; the support of management for clinicians in their working environments; and the introduction of a suitable balance between trust and accountability.[125] The introduction of a 'blame free culture' which was recommended by the Bristol Inquiry Report and is encouraged by the NPSA could go some way towards creating an NHS environment in which healthcare professionals can exercise discretion without fear. In any event, it is difficult to conclude that in the present climate, doctors are over-paid, under-regulated, and out of control.

124   Miller, P., BMA, BBC News, 10 November 2005.
125   As suggested in the Queen's Speech, May 2005.

Chapter 6

Treating the affliction
Are there any remedies?

Successive Governments have become increasingly aware of the problem of errors in healthcare, and the resulting demands for compensation from patients and families who are affected. This chapter charts the way in which the problem was first diagnosed when it was identified by the Courts, the defence organisations, the Government, and patients' representatives. The crisis in financing outstanding claims was recognised sooner than the need to monitor and control errors, and different mechanisms were introduced over the years, often on an *ad hoc* basis, for dealing with both problems. The final impetus for rigorous action arose around the time of the Bristol crisis, followed closely by the Shipman scandal and subsequent Inquiry. Richard Smith, then editor of the *BMJ*, explained the position perfectly when he said[1]:

> The Bristol case, ... will probably prove much more important to the future of health care in Britain than the reforms suggested in the white papers.

The recent reforms will be covered in the course of the ensuing discussion, though it is not possible to consider all of these, nor indeed to deal in depth with those that are discussed, so extensive and detailed have been the arrangements aimed at ensuring that the NHS offers a safer environment for patients. No doubt, by the time this book appears in print, many more changes will have been introduced. The remaining question for future consideration is whether the regime introduced in the opening years of the new millennium for dealing with the malaise afflicting healthcare is adequate.

Diagnosis and treatment

Since the founding of the NHS, clinical error and litigation problems have gradually come to light. The rate at which new problems were exposed increased

---

1   Smith, R., 'All Changed, Changed Utterly' (1998) *BMJ* 316: 1917–18.

rapidly towards the end of the twentieth century, until crisis point was reached at the time of the Bristol case and its coverage by the media. The Bristol Inquiry Report is an comprehensive document exposing a wide range of deeply rooted problems in the culture of healthcare, and is an education in itself. Long before it was written, the history of identifying and tackling the issues had begun in the courts, and it was not until relatively late in the day that there was a progression through Royal Commissions, Public Inquiries, Consultations and a series of reforming Acts, some of it obviously aimed at reducing the litigation and error levels, and some more obliquely.

The role of the courts

It goes without saying that the courts, as the public arena within which disputes are considered, were the first to observe problems arising from errors and subsequent claims.[2] There were very few claims against doctors[3] before public funding became available for claimants[4] as part of the post-war package of welfare reforms; ironically, at about the same time as the NHS was established. An early response of the courts to the problem of doctors being sued by their patients was the introduction of vicarious liability in *Cassidy v Minister of Health*,[5] so that while it continued to be necessary to identify the individuals involved, some of the focus of blame was removed from the individual doctor and responsibility for defending the claim was placed on the institution. While vicarious liability was based on a legal 'fiction', it was recognised in a limited number of later cases that in appropriate circumstances there may be primary liability on a hospital[6] – a concept that has the potential for further development in order to enhance the possibility of introducing a no-blame culture in healthcare.

Another swift reaction of the judiciary, it having already been settled that in most situations[7] doctors owed a duty of care to their patients,[8] was to establish a

---

2   *The Surgeon's Case* (Morton's Case) (1374) 48 Edw 11 is the earliest reported claim against a doctor.

3   The doctor's duty to patients was based on the concept of the 'common calling' within which professionals were required to exercise all due care and skill in connection with their calling. Following the decision in *Donoghue v Stevenson* [1932] AC 562, the case which established negligence as a separate tort independent of a contract between the parties, it was soon held that a doctor owes a duty of care to his or her patients.

4   Legal Aid and Advice Act 1949.

5   *Cassidy v Minister of Health* [1951] 1 All ER 575.

6   *Bull v Devon Area Health Authority* [1993] 4 Med LR 117 CA.

7   In marginal cases even the scope of the duty of care in clinical negligence has been restricted, e.g. *M (Minor) v Newham LBC* [1994] 2 WLR 554.

8   It was decided in some of the pre-1932 cases that doctors could be liable for both acts and omissions that injured their patients once a duty to act was established – *Pippin v Shepherd* (1882) 11 Price 400; *Edgar v Lamont* 1914 SC 277 cited in Lewis, C., *Clinical Negligence: A Practical Guide* (6th edn, Tottel Publishing, West Sussex, 2006), pp 184–85.

rule in English law, previously settled in the Scottish case of *Hunter v Hanley*,[9] that would provide an almost impenetrable defence for doctors in all but the most obvious instances of alleged negligence. The *Bolam*[10] defence, by which a doctor could escape liability for negligence by establishing that he or she 'acted in accordance with a practice accepted as proper by a responsible body of medical opinion',[11] remained water tight, despite numerous criticisms, for 40 years: The formula was stated by McNair J, in a direction to the jury,[12] as:

> A doctor is not guilty of negligence if he acted in accordance with a practice accepted as proper by a responsible body of medical men skilled in that particular art. Putting it another way round, a doctor is not negligent if he is acting in accordance with such a practice merely because there is a body of opinion that takes a contrary view.

This formula was soon extended, and eventually underpinned medical decision-making in other fields, such as consideration of patients' best interests,[13] and the law of consent to treatment, in so far as it concerned negligence.

There were many criticisms of the *Bolam* defence. As well as being considered unreasonably protective of doctors, early in its history the test was thought to be unacceptable because it was sociological in nature (based on what is done) rather than normative (based on what ought to be done).[14] It was considered to be objectionable in that it allowed treatments, which were only marginally acceptable, to meet the required standard of care simply because there was a body of opinion to support them. However, in accordance with the system of judicial precedent applicable in the UK, as the *Bolam* test had been approved by the House of Lords in two instances in the 1980s,[15] it could not be modified until a suitable case was put before the same court, and that did not happen until 1997 in *Bolitho v City and Hackney Health Authority*.[16]

---

9   [1955] SLT 213. In that case Lord Clyde explained that there is ample scope for differences of opinion in the medical context, and that a doctor is not negligent merely because his view differs from that of others in the profession.

10 *Bolam v Friern Hospital Management Committee* (1957) 1 BMLR 1.

11 *Per* McNair, J in *Bolam* – a view later approved by the House of Lords in *Whitehouse v Jordan* [1981] 1 All ER 267.

12 Since 1963 juries have not been used in clinical negligence and other personal injury cases.

13 *Re F (Mental Patient: Sterilisation)* [1990] 2 AC 1 – later extended to a two stage test in *Re A (Male Sterilisation)* [2000] 1 FLR 549, *Per* Thorpe, LJ at 560.

14 See Montrose 'Is Negligence an ethical or sociological concept?' (1958) 21 MLR 259.

15 *Whitehouse v Jordan* [1980] 1 All ER 267; *Maynard v West Midlands Regional Health Authority* [1984] 1 WLR 634 (HL).

16 *Bolitho v City and Hackney Health Authority* [1998] AC 232 (HL).

Even under the modified approach expressed by the House of Lords in the Bolitho case, if there are two or more different opinions as to the appropriate medical practice, a judge is only able to rule that the doctor under consideration has been negligent if there is evidence that one of those opinions is not 'logically defensible.' This is very extreme and has made little visible difference,[17] though in practice more cases may now be settling out of court as a result of the *Bolitho* approach.

There are judicial pronouncements with a very clear policy basis which indicate recognition by the judges from an early stage that bringing claims against the NHS was not a desirable activity and should not be encouraged. The frequently cited view of Lord Denning in *Hatcher v Black*[18] that the negligence action represented a dagger at the doctors' back was symptomatic of the prevailing policy in the courts in the years following the founding of the NHS. Apart from the obvious motivation connected with the need to protect fellow professionals from anxiety about claims, concerns on the part of the judiciary about the possibility of defensive medicine may have formed the basis of this approach. Even though judges did not necessarily always take the view that doctors should be exonerated easily from liability,[19] in practice the operation of the *Bolam* defence meant that relatively few clinical negligence claims reached the courts, and of those, few were successful in comparison with other varieties of claim for negligence.[20] Lord Nicholls was clearly aware of the effect of the Bolam test when he said:[21]

> Any fear of a flood of claims may be countered by the consideration that in order to get off the ground the claimant must be able to demonstrate that the standard of care fell short of that set by the Bolam v Friern Hospital Management Committee [1957] 2 All ER 118, [1957] 1 WLR 582 test. That is deliberately and properly a high standard in recognition of the difficult nature of some decisions which those to whom the test applies are required to make, and of the room for genuine differences of view on the propriety of one course of action as against another.

17   E.g. *Swift v South Manchester Health Authority* (2001); *Reynolds v North Tyneside Health Authority* [2002] Lloyds Rep Med 459.

18   *The Times*, 2 July 1954.

19   In *Barker v Nugent* [1987] (QBD) cited in Grubb, A., 'Principles of Medical Law', op. cit., p 403, fn 152, e.g., Rougier, J. was highly critical of defensive practices in *Barker v Nugent* but still took the view that it would be inappropriate for doctors to be able to rely on the general principle that they might be exonerated for certain acts or omissions which would otherwise be classed as negligence.

20   See Pearson Commission Report, Royal Commission on Civil Liability and Compensation for Personal Injury Cmnd 7054, 1978, London, HMSO.

21   *Phelps v London Borough of Hillingdon; Anderton v Clwyd CC; Jarvis v Hampshire CC; Re G (A minor)*, [2001] 2 AC 619, [2000] 4 All ER 504, [2000] 3 WLR 776, [2000] 3 FCR 102, [2000] ELR 499, 56 BMLR 1.

The same very senior member of the judiciary commented on the problems for the NHS involved in the ever-increasing volume of claims, but policy arguments seeking to restrict the development of the law are often considered best left to open debate in Parliament. In *Gregg v Scott*[22] Lord Nicholls (dissenting) made the following points:

> More fundamentally, if a claim is well-founded in law as a matter of principle ... the duty of the courts is to recognise and give effect to the claim. If the government considers that some or all of the adverse consequences of medical negligence should be borne by patients themselves, no doubt it will consider introducing appropriate legislation in Parliament.
>
> Nor can I accept a further submission to the effect that the approach set out above will encourage wasteful defensive practices. ... Every doctor is fully aware he may be sued if he is negligent.

There are some areas of clinical negligence litigation in which the courts have been openly restrictive. In *McFarlane v Tayside Health Board*[23] the House of Lords, overruling a long line of established cases, held that it would no longer be possible to claim damages for the upbringing of a healthy child following a failed sterilisation operation. The opinion of each of the judges was based on difference policy considerations. In *Gregg v Scott*[24] the House of Lords held that damages for loss of a chance will not be available in clinical negligence claims.

Yet in *Chester v Afshar*[25] the scope of liability in the field of consent to treatment was extended, demonstrating a major difficulty in relying on the common law to control the litigation problem, which is that it is vulnerable to the vagaries of judicial policy. While the courts remain protective of the medical professions in some respects, they have been prepared to expand the scope of liability in others, and have reached the point when deference to doctors is no longer a driving force behind some of the decisions. The question of the standard of care and the role of Parliament will be given further consideration in this chapter in the context of the Compensation Act 2006.

Government intervention

Although the judiciary played a significant role from the 1950s in limiting the number of successful clinical negligence cases and a consequential rise in claims, this was insufficient to prevent claims rising to a virtually unmanageable level, and it became apparent by around 1989 that some further remedial action might be necessary.

22 [2005] UKHL 2 paras 54–56.
23 [2002] 2 AC 59.
24 [2005] 2 WLR 268.
25 *Chester v Afshar* [2005] 1 AC 134.

Claims management

The first measure to be introduced became operational in 1990 when NHS indemnity was established in order to assist the doctors' defence organisations, which had insufficient funds to meet the compensation payments required for successful claimants in the immediate future years. In November 1989, Virginia Bottomley announced in the House of Commons[26] that health authorities would take financial responsibility for the negligent acts of their medical and dental staff in the course of their NHS employment, and that new arrangements would apply to claims initiated in earlier years as well as to new claims arising from 1 January 1990. The result was that although the number of claims was not contained, at least claimants would receive the compensation which was due to them. As the system was formalised, various official bodies were created for managing claims and developing incentives for safer medical practice.

In 1995 the NHSLA was established, initially to indemnify NHS organisations in England against claims for clinical negligence and administer the Clinical Negligence Scheme for Trusts from 1 April 1995. Shortly afterwards, its remit was extended to include claims arising before that date. From 1999 the NHSLA was also given the tasks of handling non-clinical and property claims. This organisation is part of the NHSLA, as it is a special health authority, and its framework document sets out still more functions which it has acquired, embracing, for example, risk management, human rights advice and certain disputes between NHS bodies.[27] As has already been explained, roughly equivalent organisations have been established for the devolved regions of the UK. These arrangements ensure greater uniformity in the management of claims and linked activities of risk management and learning from mistakes.

A new NHS complaints system to stem the tide of litigation?

When the new NHS complaints system was introduced in 1996 it was hoped that this would ensure that fewer claims reached the courts. Data relating to the number of written complaints is dealt with in Chapter 2. After an initial gradual rise in the number of NHS complaints the level stabilised, as is shown in the table below.

However, in 2006, the number rose sharply, and there were 95,047 written complaints about hospital and community health services. There was very little change in the number of written complaints about family health services,

---

26   House of Commons, *Hansard Debates*, 2 November 1989, col 314.
27   See NHSLA Framework Document Fact Sheet 1 NHSLA for further details.

Table 13 Number of written complaints in England 1999–2005

1999–2000	2000–2001	2001–2002	2002–2003	2003–2004	2004–2005
86,536	95,734	93,020	91,023	90,156	90,066

Source: Taken from Hansard, 11th October 2006, column 771W.

though, with 43,349 in 2005–06 compared to 43,407 in 2004–05.[28] It is very difficult to assess the effect of the NHS complaints system on the level of claims, but the picture presented by the statistics does not suggest that it has been of great significance in containing the rise in claims. It is only very recently that NHS Trusts, in Wales at least, have been asked to record the number of complaints which develop into claims, despite a long-standing need for such data to be available.[29]

On major advantage in having a uniform NHS complaints system throughout the entire UK is that patients are able to access it easily wherever in the UK they happen to be treated. Unfortunately, as healthcare systems are becoming increasingly devolved, so are complaints systems and the result is fragmentation of information and statistics. Nevertheless, the complaints system does allow healthcare organisations to learn from their mistakes and implement improvements through clinical governance, which might prevent further complaints and claims.

Although many complaints do not concern matters which are actionable as claims, and despite the fact that complaints managers have been able to refuse to investigate complaints where there is evidence of an intention to bring a claim, the number of claims has inevitably continued to rise in a culture in which awareness has been raised of shortcomings in healthcare performance. NHS organisations have always been able to offer to satisfy a complainant by making an ex-gratia payment up to a fixed limit without official Treasury approval. Unfortunately, some patients are less than honest about their intentions, and use the system for 'fishing expeditions' in order to gather sufficient information to assist a decision as to whether it would be advisable to make or abandon a claim. This artificial situation has led some to suggest that it would be sensible to combine the complaints system with some form of system for dealing with lower value claims. It was perhaps to that end that the 2004 Complaints Regulations require healthcare organisations to offer appropriate conciliation or mediation services to assist the resolution of complaints.

28   Data supplied by the NHS Information Centre, September 2006.
29   See Harpwood, V., 'The NHS Complaints System' in Powers, M. and Harris, N., *Clinical Negligence* (ed.) Lockhart-Mirrams, A. (Lexis Nexis, London, 1999).

Information issued by the Department of Health about the reforms to the complaints system stated that the intention was to deliver a programme of 'complaints and clinical negligence reform' as an 'essential and integral element of the Department's programme for improving patients' overall experience of health care'.[30] This bracketing together of complaints and claims suggests an agenda for reform which is more radical than is generally realised. Whether it will result in more efficient complaints handling and fewer claims remains to be seen. This matter is discussed further later in this chapter in the light of the NHS Redress Act 2006.

Audit, clinical governance, and risk management

The idea of reviewing an area of medical practice in order to identify potential pitfalls and learn from mistakes, with a view to enhancing the quality of care, is not new. Clinicians were familiar with the Confidential Inquiries, which had been conducted into pressing matters such as maternal deaths, for many years. The first triennial Confidential Inquiry into maternal deaths was conducted in 1952, and the object of such exercises was to prevent similar deaths in the future by learning about causes and past mistakes.[31] It had become apparent to the Government by the late 1980s that one approach to the problem of errors would be to introduce standards and monitoring systems that should ensure that uniform care was taken in the course of medical practice. This approach was initially introduced gradually, but was later "sold" to the profession as an attempt to introduce high-quality care for all patients wherever they were treated, and was closely bound up with the structural reforms that were being phased in at the same time.

The White Paper 'Working for Patients,' published by the Department of Health in 1989,[32] explained plans for creating an internal market in the NHS. Another White Paper, 'Working for Patients: Medical Audit Working Paper No. 6',[33] gave comprehensive information about the Government's plans for a system of what was then called 'medical' audit (later to become 'clinical' audit), intended to operate within the internal market. Extensive ring-fenced funding was made available to support the new concepts and ensure that they were realised, and the regional and district health authorities which were in existence at the time were encouraged to develop strategies, establish audit committees and to publish reports annually on the progress of audit activity.

---

30   Policy and Guidance, Department of Health, 'Reforming the Complaints Procedure', 8 February 2007.
31   Arthure, H., 'Confidential Inquiries into Maternal Deaths' (1975) *BMJ* 1: 322–23.
32   HAA 0165 0145; DoH, 'Working for Patients', London, HMSO, 1989 (Cm 555).
33   DoH, 'Working for Patients: Medical Audit Working Paper No. 6', London, HMSO, 1989.

Introduced formally into the NHS in 1993, and rapidly becoming a growth area, Clinical Audit was defined as:

> A quality improvement process that seeks to improve patient care and outcomes through systematic review of care against explicit criteria and the implementation of change.[34]

The process involved setting standards (preferably evidence-based), measuring current practice and comparing it with those standards, changing practice where necessary and re-auditing to ensure that practice and outcomes had improved (often referred to as 'closing the loop'). When first introduced, clinical audit was not compulsory, and it usually involved peer review, but later practices did not necessarily include this. Eventually, clinical audit was linked with research, but it still tended to be confined to particular areas of practice, sometimes involving multi-disciplinary teams, and the ultimate product might well be guidelines which would be applied to that specialty. It was distinguishable from financial and managerial audit, but in reality it could be applied to resource allocation and management as well as to the quality of care, and it became a tool that was used as a fundamental principle in Western medical systems such as those pertaining to the US and Sweden.[35]

When it was first developed in the UK, there were several drawbacks inherent in the system of clinical audit. For example, audit was not compulsory and it was agreed that the results would not be published outside the immediate group of professionals. Nor was audit systematic, since it was carried out only in certain services which were selected by participating clinicians, and sometimes by an audit committee in a hospital. There was little consistency in the bases upon which a view could be formed as to the adequacy of clinical performance nationally or locally. Clinicians and others who had been subject to audit were anxious to prevent sensitive information from reaching management, so clinical audit was directed by doctors and treated, as the Bristol Inquiry concluded, as an educational tool, rather than a mechanism for ensuring accountability to the profession as a whole, the NHS or the public.[36] However, by 1994–95, clinical audit, through funding arrangements, had become part of the contract between the purchaser and the provider.

The Bristol Report found[37] that during the 1990s:

> Healthcare professionals remained sceptical about the benefits of the audit process, and concerned both about the practical problems of undertaking

---

34   'Principles of Best Practice in Clinical Audit', NICE/CHI 2002.
35   Frostick, S., Radford, P. and Wallace, W. (eds) *Medical Audit: Rationale and Practicalities* (Cambridge University Press, 1993).
36   Bristol Royal Infirmary Inquiry, Chapter 6, para 12.
37   Bristol Royal Infirmary Report, Chapter 6, para 13.

effective clinical audit and the use to which information might be put by management.

Closely connected with clinical audit is the concept and process of clinical governance, another initiative of the 1998 consultation document, 'A First Class Service: Quality in the New NHS'.[38] Indeed, audit was subsumed into Clinical Governance and later became compulsory, as it was apparent that the more conscientious clinicians were self-selecting and enthusiastic about reviewing their practice, while those who most needed to be self-critical were less than keen to participate. Clinical governance was introduced as central to the 'new' approach towards a patient-led health service, and became, along with 'modernisation', part of the rhetoric of the 1990 reforms. However, it does have the potential for ensuring real accountability for the safe delivery of health services, and has been defined as:

> A framework through which NHS organisations are accountable for continuously improving the quality of their services and safeguarding high standards of care by creating an environment in which excellence in clinical care will flourish.[39]

That definition led to numerous interpretations and misunderstandings as to what clinical governance meant. In fact, it is an umbrella term covering a range of themes, including patient–public involvement; risk management, which involves incident reporting, infection control, prevention and control of risk; staff management and performance, involving education and Continuous Professional Development; re-validation; management development; confidentiality and data protection; clinical effectiveness which involves clinical audit, planning, monitoring, learning through research and audit; information management; communication and leadership.[40]

The clinical governance programme demanded that there should be clear lines of accountability, that comprehensive programmes should be introduced to improve the quality of care by means of evidence-based guidelines, compulsory audit and monitoring, and that risk management policies should be established in healthcare organisations to identify and remedy poor performance.

NHS Trusts and other organisations are now required to implement clinical governance and have done so according to their own individual approaches, so that several models now exist, but every model should involve the entire

---

38   HSC 1998 113, p 33.
39   Ibid., and see also Scally, G. and Donaldson, L., 'Clinical Governance and the Drive for Quality Improvement in the New NHS in England' (1998) *BMJ* 317: 61–65 for an appraisal of its implementation.
40   NHS Clinical Governance Support Team 2007.

organisation. Clinical governance has progressed significantly since the days when it was simply one of many new initiatives. It is now a statutory duty for all NHS Trusts, and should be part of the process of reducing errors and therefore the risk of litigation. As Dame Janet Smith said in the Shipman Report in relation to primary care:

> In my view, if properly developed and well resourced, clinical governance could provide the most effective means of achieving two important aims. First, it could enable PCTs to detect poorly performing or dysfunctional GPs on their lists. It could also help practices to discover any problems or weaknesses among their own number. Second, it could have the beneficial effect of helping doctors who are performing satisfactorily to do even better.

Part of the process of clinical governance is identifying and managing risks in healthcare, a practice which had already been recognised as important by the courts. When *Bolitho v City and Hackney Health Authority*[41] was considered by the House of Lords, Lord Browne-Wilkinson, who gave the opinion of the Court, indicated that risk management was an important feature of the decision:

> In particular, where there are questions of assessment of the relative risks and benefits of adopting a particular medical practice, a reasonable view necessarily presupposes that the relative risks and benefits have been weighed by the experts in forming their opinions. But if, in a rare case, it can be demonstrated that the professional opinion is not capable of withstanding logical analysis, the judge is entitled to hold that the body of opinion is not reasonable or responsible.

Significant progress has been made in risk management procedures through the requirements of the NHSLA, the Healthcare Commission, HIW and similar organisations. One definition of risk management refers solely to financial risks:[42]

> The activities required to minimise financial loss for hospitals and the doctors who work in them.

This would appear to be too narrow an approach in the present NHS climate, though it seems that there is still confusion between risk management

---

41   [1997] 39 BMLR 1 (HL).
42   Wilson, L.L., Goldschmidt, P.G., *Quality Management in Healthcare* (Sydney, McGraw-Hill, 1995).

and quality management,[43] and the Government prefers to place the emphasis on quality and safety for obvious reasons. However, for many purposes, risk management is only concerned with avoiding patient harm in order to minimise financial loss and not as an end in itself – unlike the quality agenda. Whatever its purpose, risk management is now deeply entrenched in the agenda for managing NHS Trusts and it does have a place in limiting litigation costs as well as improving safety.[44]

Targets and tables

The elements of marketisation and competition which had crept into the healthcare arena since the 1990s were the product of the Government's ambition to inject efficiency into the system. However, as Allyson Pollock aptly says:[45]

> It was soon evident that these targets were corrupting the purposes of care. Chief executives were resorting to fiddling the figures, as the Audit Commission discovered.

There were targets relating to waiting lists, ambulance arrival times, Accident and Emergency efficiency, financial management, operating successes and so on. There were some enthusiasts for the advent of a system of performance management in the NHS,[46] and the ensuing league tables published in the press gives the system credibility, even though it is in many respects statistically flawed.[47] Once it was realised that this approach was counter-productive, the Government announced in 2004[48] its intention to reduce the number of targets from 62 to 20, but at the same time new categories of targets were introduced relating to hospital infection rates, and John Reid, Health Secretary at the time, announced that targets would still have a role in the NHS. In some instances the nomenclature changed from 'targets' to 'core standards' and the hotel-style star rating system administered by the Healthcare Commission was allowed

---

43   'Quality and Outcomes Branch, Commonwealth Department of Health and Aged Care. Clinical Risk Management in Rural Victoria. Better Health Outcomes (A newsletter for the Health Service)' 1998, 16 December, cited in Wilson, L. and Fulton, M. below.

44   Wilson, L. and Fulton, M., 'Risk Management: How Doctors, Hospitals and MDOs can Limit the Costs of Malpractice Litigation' (2000) *MJA* 172: 77–80.

45   Pollock, A., *NHS plc* (Verso, London, 2004), p 133.

46   Smith, P., 'Performance Management in British Healthcare: Will it Deliver?' (2002) *Health Affairs*.

47   McLellan, A., 'Milburn Secured Three Stars for PM's Trust', *Health Service Journal* 18 December 2003; cited Pollock, A., op. cit., p 123; see also Timmins, N., 'NHS Quality Drive Most Ambitious in the World', *Financial Times*, 27 November 2003, p 7.

48   Reported in *The Times*, 21 July 2004.

to continue in order to assess whether certain organisations could move to 'foundation' status. The result was that the names of Trusts which were zero-rated were emblazoned across the newspapers, with much less attention being focused on those with top ratings. There were even 'death charts' compiled and published in national newspapers. These developments may well have provided obsessive reading for the prurient public, but they have done little for the morale of healthcare professionals, many of whom are aware of the ability of ingenious managers and clinicians to manipulate the figures and of the inherent unfairness in a system that does not compare like with like in a meaningful way.

Paradoxically, while introducing targets with a view to improving safety, the Government has announced measures to enhance patient choice which are not easily reconciled with the safety agenda, such as an NHS guarantee to give women in England the full range of choices relating to the birth of their babies, including home births and ongoing care from a midwife they know, by the end of 2009.[49] This commitment has been made despite the fact that there is known to be a shortage of midwives.[50]

Plans for a new set of targets, also called standards, were announced in 2005, following the publication of 'Standards for Better Health',[51] covering safety, clinical cost effectiveness, governance, patient focus, local priorities, accessible and responsive care, healthcare environment and amenities, and public health. These proposals have been adopted and are being supported by an organisation called the Healthcare Standards Unit, working closely with the Department of Health. Similar developments are taking place in Wales.[52] Whether this approach to managing healthcare will reduce the levels of litigation is difficult to predict. It does not appear to have had a significant effect to date, and once patients and carers are made aware of targets, and discover that they are not being achieved, there is the potential for litigation. Failing to meet a target would not necessarily amount to negligence, but claims can be brought on related matters, such as demands for certain forms of treatment, or treatment in other EU countries, as happened in the case of *R(on the application of Watts) v Bedford Primary Care Trust*,[53] which went as far as the ECJ. The Court held that patients should not have to wait longer for treatment than is clinically advised, and if, because of waiting lists, a

---

49   NHS Maternity Strategy, April 2007.
50   See Mayor, S., 'More funding for maternity services is needed if women are to get choice over place of birth' (2007) *BMJ* 334: 768 (14 April).
51   Department of Health 2004.
52   See Healthcare Standards for Wales; Making Connections. Designed for Life. Welsh Assembly Government, Welsh Health Standards May 2005 and progress statement 11 August 2006.
53   Case C-372/04.

procedure which is clinically necessary cannot be performed within the time considered advisable by the treating clinician, the patient is entitled to seek treatment abroad, the cost of which should be covered by the NHS.

Involving patients

Since the Bristol Inquiry Report, the Government has pressed forward with plans that it had been developing for some time to ensure greater involvement of patients and the public in healthcare planning on a local and national basis. There had previously been a certain amount of patient involvement in healthcare over many years, and the Government rhetoric had proclaimed the need to 'put patients at the centre' in a variety of ways for decades. This process is continuing. The NHS Plan had made a commitment to developing the involvement of patients, carers and the public in health decision-making as part of the 'modernisation' (a word much favoured by those wishing to introduce change in healthcare) programme.

'A Stronger Local Voice'[54] is just one of the recent documents, setting the Government's plans for the future of patient and public involvement in health and also in social care in England. The initiative includes the establishment of Local Involvement Networks (LINks) to replace the older patient forum system. These organisations will work with existing voluntary and community sector groups and individuals to promote public and community influence in health and social care. There is a package of plans designed to promote the importance of user and public involvement, and the Government claims that this will create a system which enables more people to express their views. Local people are also able to become involved in Foundation Trusts. These apparently inclusive plans do not always generate the same enthusiasm as pressing local issues, such as the proposed closure of small hospitals. In Wales, Community Health Councils have been retained to promote local involvement in healthcare.

Carrots and sticks: foundation hospitals

In the process of reinforcing the incentives it has introduced into the NHS, the Government has created a new and more independent status for certain high-achieving institutions – that of the Foundation Trust.[55] The first ten NHS hospitals to achieve Foundation status were identified in 2004, and the Government aimed to give all trusts in England Foundation status within five years. Ostensibly, Foundation Trusts resemble old-style co-ops, and local people, staff, patients, and carers will be able to become 'members'. The

---

54   'A stronger local voice: A framework for creating a stronger local voice in the development of health and social care services', 13 June 2006.
55   Health and Social Care (Community Health and Standards) Act 2003, P 1.

members elect a board of governors who choose the hospital's non-executive directors. However, operational control will remain in the hands of the board of directors, not the governors. Theoretically, this system allows managers to have greater autonomy as they will not be line-managed by the Department of Health. Although they are less rigorously monitored, they are still subject to some inspection by a body called Monitor. They can borrow money from banks to finance capital programmes and can retain the proceeds of land sales for reinvestment in local services. They have access to central development budgets, and can establish private companies. Although the Government insists that Foundation Trusts are part of the NHS family, they are highly controversial. Numerous opponents of Foundation Trusts, including labour back benchers, claim that they are divisive because they create a two-tier system, having access to more resources at the expense of failing hospitals, so widening health inequalities. They are perceived to be the first step towards privatisation, or at least towards denationalisation of healthcare within a mixed health economy.[56] The distancing of the Government from direct involvement with healthcare decision-making will in some respects allow it ostensibly to remain free of blame for shortcomings and failures.

Inspection and monitoring

Concerns of the Government and patients' organisations focused on the limitations of clinical audit in detecting clinical failures and bringing about improvements. The Government therefore decided to establish two new organisations, ostensibly external to the NHS, to reinforce the duty of quality. These were given the titles of the National Institute for Clinical Excellence (NICE)[57], and the Commission for Health Improvement (CHI)[58], and each of these bodies has evolved considerably since they were established. CHI has now become the Healthcare Commission, taking over an important audit function, and NICE has the title of the National Institute for Health and Clinical Excellence. When first established in 1999, NICE had three main functions: to appraise and develop new and existing technologies; to commission and disseminate clinical guidelines, also taking over guidelines previously commissioned by the Department of Health; and to promote clinical audit and the Confidential Inquiries.

The original functions of the CHI were set out in s 20 of the Health Act 1999 as follows:

---

56   Pollock, A., *NHS plc* (Verso 2004) p 129 et seq.
57   Set up by the National Institute for Clinical Excellence (Establishment and Constitution) Amendment Order 1999; and the National Institute for Clinical Excellence (Amendment) Regulations 1999.
58   Health Act 1999, s 19.

(a) the function of providing advice or information with respect to arrangements by Primary Care Trusts or NHS trusts for the purpose of monitoring and improving the quality of health care for which they have responsibility,

(b) the function of conducting reviews of, and making reports on, arrangements by Primary Care Trusts or NHS trusts for the purpose of monitoring and improving the quality of health care for which they have responsibility,

(c) the function of carrying out investigations into, and making reports on, the management, provision or quality of health care for which Health Authorities, Primary Care Trusts, or NHS trusts have responsibility,

(d) the function of conducting reviews of, and making reports on, the management, provision or quality of, or access to or availability of, particular types of health care for which NHS bodies or service providers have responsibility, and

(e) such functions as may be prescribed relating to the management, provision or quality of, or access to or availability of, health care for which prescribed NHS bodies or prescribed service providers have responsibility.

This wide remit, and the broad powers of the Secretary of State in this connection, meant that as well as carrying out routine inspections, the CHI could swoop on poorly performing Trusts, interview staff and seize documents in the course of its investigations. As time passed, the Government realised the advantages of an organisation such as the CHI and broadened its statutory functions,[59] so that its title has become the Commission for Health-care Audit and Inspection, though it is popularly known as the Healthcare Commission. It is responsible for assessing the management, provision and quality of NHS healthcare and public health services; for reviewing the performance of each NHS Trust in England and awarding annual performance ratings; for regulating the independent healthcare sector through registration, annual inspection, monitoring complaints and enforcement; for publishing information about healthcare; for dealing with the Independent Review stage of complaints about NHS organisations; for promoting the coordination of reviews and assessments; and for investigating serious failures in the provision of healthcare. Although there are now different arrangements for these matters in Wales, the Healthcare Commission retains certain duties in Wales,[60] mainly involving national reviews and the annual 'State of Healthcare' report. The Healthcare Commission also works with the Mental Health Act Commission

59   Health and Social Care (Community Health and Standards) Act 2003, launched on April 1 2004.

60   Local inspection and investigation of NHS bodies in Wales is carried out by Healthcare Inspectorate Wales, and the Care Standards Inspectorate Wales inspects organisations providing independent healthcare in the Principality.

(MHAC), whose function is to ensure that there is effective protection of patients detained under the Mental Health Act 1983. Under the Government's review of legislation on mental health, it is expected that most of the functions of MHAC will be transferred to the Healthcare Commission in the very near future.

Other organisations have a role in monitoring and inspecting healthcare organisations. The NPSA plays an important part in this process, as do the NHSLA and the WRP. The overload of inspection agencies (56 in total) has already been discussed in Chapter 5, and the importance of a Concordat to reduce the burden on doctors and managers cannot be over-emphasised. However, it is also necessary to ensure that patients are as safe as possible when they receive treatment, and some form of compromise will no doubt be necessary to maintain a sensible balance between patient safety and clinical freedom.

Following a review of so-called 'arms-length' bodies, the remit of NICE was extended in 2005 to incorporate the work of the Health Development Agency, so creating a single Special Health Authority which is described as an 'excellence-into-practice organisation' covering both the prevention and treatment of ill health. The management of the Confidential Inquiries was transferred at the same time to the NPSA.[61]

One crucial aspect of the role of NICE, detailed discussion of which is in some respects beyond the scope of this book, is the formulation of guidelines for the treatment of patients following the appraisal of new drugs and technologies. This function enables NICE to ration scarce resources and to control the drug budget. NICE takes into account both cost effectiveness and clinical effectiveness when assessing treatment and drafting guidelines. NICE has found itself at the centre of controversy over the guidance it is providing on certain high cost drugs,[62] and its decisions in this respect are subject to judicial review. At the time of writing, Eisai, a Japanese pharmaceutical company, which holds the licence to Alzheimer's disease drug Aricept (donepezil), has been granted permission by the High Court for it to proceed to a judicial review to challenge the process by which NICE arrived at its decision to ban anti-dementia medicines for patients newly diagnosed with mild Alzheimer's disease. This development suggests that NICE might face further reform over the next few years.

In tandem with its role as gatekeeper of the drugs budget, NICE has the potential for making some progress towards dealing with the clinical negligence problem by setting standards for treating patients through NICE guidelines which could be regarded as 'logical' and 'responsible' within the scope of the *Bolam/Bolitho* tests for the standard of care.

---

61   Special Health Authorities Abolition Order 2005, No. 502.
62   *Rogers v Swindon Primary Care Trust & Secretary of State for Health* [2006] EWCA Civ 392.

These machinations are yet another example of the complexity of the structure and organisation of healthcare in England alone (in some respects different structures apply in Wales and Scotland). While progressing the safety and monitoring agenda, the added complexity enables Central Government to distance itself still further from decision-making and therefore from blame. If difficult decisions about the funding of treatment for life-threatening diseases are made by NICE, the Government can remain outside the battle field.

Removing clinical autonomy from doctors

By the Health Act 1999 s 18, the Government introduced a statutory duty to promote quality, giving chief executives the ultimate responsibility for monitoring quality within their organisations, and consequently control over the way in which clinical resources are allocated. This development, according to Allyson Pollock,[63] meant that:

> The line between clinical decision-making and general management was formally breached.

The same author argues that this development, introduced at the time of the Bristol Inquiry, promoted the views of its chairman, Sir Ian Kennedy[64], which he had expressed in 'The Unmasking of Medicine' and would later express in the Report of the Bristol Inquiry. He had been highly critical of doctors and had recommended shifting the balance of power from clinicians, many of whom were considered arrogant and paternalistic, to managers. There is more than a grain of truth in the view that some doctors are arrogant and have been content to foster a culture that may be damaging to patients, as events in Bristol Royal Infirmary clearly demonstrated. However, there are also problems in promoting changes which could lead to gagging doctors who wish to speak out in support of their patients, which is what happened in the Consultants' Contracts introduced in 2003, which prevent them from disclosing information of a confidential nature about patients, contractors, employees or the business of the organisation employing them. Allyson Pollock contends that this clause could, as in a private healthcare setting, place the interests of profit in direct conflict with those of patients.[65]

It might be considered that the controls imposed by the Health Act 1999 will also have an impact on clinical discretion. The role of NICE in developing and disseminating guidelines has the potential for setting the standard of care and at the same time removing from doctors the freedom of decision-making that they previously enjoyed. It has been argued that to demand that

---

63   Pollock, A., *NHS plc* (Verso, London, 2004) p 121.
64   Now Chairman of the Healthcare Commission.
65   Ibid., at p 122.

doctors adhere rigidly to clinical guidelines will discourage research and stifle innovation in medical practice. Doctors are unhappy about being subjected to 'cookbook medicine' in order to avoid being sued, and in any event, there is the danger that claimants might use guidelines in order to bring claims. Against that view, however, is the real possibility that carefully drafted guidelines, even for the purpose of avoiding liability, can and do allow for appropriate deviations and exceptions in order to preserve the physician's right to provide appropriate care in the best interests of the patient.

Could guidelines provide a solution to the litigation problem?

The potential for using guidelines to define the standard of care and reduce the number of claims coming before the courts has been recognised for many years.[66] There are numerous organisations which issue guidelines to doctors and other healthcare professionals, and it is important to establish which are likely to have priority. This in itself could create problems.[67] Guidelines are referred to frequently in the course of litigation, and Sir Michael Rawlins, Chairman of NICE, has stated:[68]

> NICE guidelines are likely to constitute a responsible body of medical opinion for the purposes of litigation ... Doctors are advised to record their reasons for deviating from guidelines.

While the Bolam *Bolitho* test will still apply as a first indication of what would be expected of the reasonable and responsible doctor, guidelines issued by NICE are likely to form a normative basis assessing the standard of care to be met by doctors in place of the 'sociological' approach (based on what is done rather than what ought to be done), implicit in the *Bolam* test. Guidelines

---

66 For extensive discussion on the potential of guidelines to determine the standard of care in clinical negligence litigation, see Harpwood, V., 'NHS Reform Audit Protocols and Standard of Care' (1994) 1 *Medical Law International* 241; Harpwood, V., 'Medical Negligence: A Chink in the Armour of Bolam' (1996) *Medical Law Journal* 64; Harpwood, V., *Medical Negligence and Clinical Risk: Trends and Developments 1998*, IBC Publications, London, May 1998; Harpwood, V., *Legal Issues in Obstetrics* (Ashgate Publishing, Aldershot, 1996); Harpwood, V., 'Guidelines In Medical Practice: The Legal Issues', Cephalalgia, Supp 21, 1998; 53–62; Harpwood, V., *Negligence in Healthcare: Clinical Claims and Risk in Context* (Informa Publishing, Colchester, 2002); Harpwood, V., Clinical Governance, Litigation and Human Rights', *Journal of Management in Medicine* (2001) Special issue on Clinical Governance, 15(3): 227–41; Harpwood, V., 'The Manipulation of Medical Practice', Current Legal Issues (2000) vol 3, *Law and Medicine*, Freeman and Lewis (eds), pp 47–66; Harpwood, V., in 'Law of Tort', Butterworths Common Law Series, Grubb (ed), chapter 13, 2002.

67 See Harpwood, V., 'The Manipulation of Medical Practice', *Current Legal Issues* (2000) vol 3, *Law and Medicine*, Freeman and Lewis (eds), pp 47–66.

68 Taylor, J. 'Tough Talk from the NICE man', *Medeconomics*, November 2003.

accepted and adopted by the profession would satisfy the *Bolitho* 'logic' test and doctors who do not follow them could well be required to explain why they have not done so. There are several examples of courts having been strongly persuaded by evidence of official standards of professional conduct as constituting strong evidence of the standard of practice required of the medical profession.[69]

One of the earliest indicators of this approach in the UK was *Thomson v James,*[9] where it was held at first instance that a GP who had not followed guidelines issued by the DoH about infant vaccinations for measles, mumps and rubella had been negligent. The child in question had not been vaccinated, and later contracted measles, as a result of which she suffered permanent brain damage following serious complications. The Court of Appeal decided the matter on the issue of causation, concluding that even if the parents had been told of the Government's advice, they would have chosen not to follow it. More recently, there have been further decisions indicating that the courts are prepared to accept that failure to follow guidelines can amount to negligence.[70] Conversely, it has been held that a doctor who had acted fully in accordance with the policy laid down by the hospital where she was employed was not in breach of her duty of care when she failed to administer steroids to a mother.[71]

It is impossible to ascertain how many cases are settled out of court because healthcare professionals have not adhered to guidance issued by NICE, a professional body, or an organisation such as the NPSA which issues detailed guidelines on matters concerning cleanliness and safety. This position was anticipated by the Scottish Office in its advice in 1994:

> With the increasing use of guidelines in clinical practice, they will be used to an increasing extent to resolve questions of liability. Those who draft, use and monitor guidelines should be aware of these legal implications.

If there is uniform acceptance of guidelines as establishing the standard of care, more cases will be settled out of court and fewer hopeless claims will be pursued. This theory has been borne out to some extent by experiences in the US. In the state of Maine[72] in the US, a five-year experiment[73] was introduced by statute, aimed at reducing the cost of clinical negligence litigation.[74] Legally

---

69   *Re C (A Minor)* (1997) 40 BMLR 31; *W v Egdell* [1990] Ch 359, [1989] 1 All ER 1089.
70   *Richards v Swansea NHS Trust* [2007] EWHC 487 (QB); *Antoniades v East Sussex Hospitals NHS Trust* [2007] EWHC 517 (QB).
71   *Cowley v Cheshire & Merseyside Strategic Health Authority* [2007] EWHC 48 (QB).
72   Florida, Maine, Minnesota and Vermont have also used guidelines in attempts to define the standard of care.
73   The Medical Liability Information Project.
74   USGAO, 'Medical Malpractice: Maine's Use of Practice Guidelines to Reduce Costs', October 1993.

validated guidelines developed by the Maine Licensing and Registration Boards for high risk specialties, such as obstetrics and radiology, became the legal standard of care. From 1 January 1992, 20 practice guidelines created by advisory committees had the full force of state law and could be cited in a doctor's defence in the event of a malpractice suit, but could not be relied upon by claimants as presumptive of negligence, and could not be introduced by them in argument unless the defendant doctor had already put them in evidence. By September 1993, the United States General Accounting Office (GAO) could find no instances in which the Maine guidelines had affected malpractice litigation, though defence attorneys suggested that the guidelines would have affected the state's pre-trial screening process. In particular, if the independent panel (required in Maine to initially review all malpractice claims) decided that the defendant doctor had followed the practice guidelines, this plaintiff's (claimant's) attorney would advise not taking the case to trial. Indeed, in the six-year history of over 400 claims, there was not one single successful attempt by a claimant to introduce a guideline during a malpractice trial. The project encountered predictable difficulties in involving the doctors concerned, and obtaining their support.

The *Bolam* test and the approach taken in *Maynard v West Midlands Regional Health Authority*[75] do at least have the merit of respecting professional decision-making and recognising that medicine is as much an art as a science. As Lord Scarman[76] said in Maynard:

> It is not enough to show that there is a body of competent professional opinion which considers that theirs [the defendants'] was a wrong decision, if there also exists a body of professional opinion, equally competent, which supports the decision as reasonable in the circumstances.

However, times have changed since those cases held sway, and the modified approach introduced by the House of Lords in the *Bolitho* case will permit judges to decide whether the conduct of a doctor is logically defensible, even when there are several expert opinions. Carefully developed, logical, evidence-based guidelines, drafted by NICE with the co-operation of the medical profession, do have the potential to assist healthcare professionals in defending claims and may also reduce certain common errors and concomitantly reduce the number of medical experts who profit from litigation. Little empirical research had been conducted into the practicalities of this theory in the UK until very recently. Then an important survey, the results of which were published in the *Medical Law Journal* in 2006,[77] revealed that a high

75   [1984] 1 WLR 643 (HL).
76   P 647.
77   Ash, S., 'The Role Of Clinical Guidelines In Medical Negligence Litigation: A Shift From The Bolam Standard?' (2006) *Med LR* 14(321).

proportion of barristers and solicitors who had participated in the research were familiar with guidelines and had used them in the course of litigation. They also expressed the view that guidelines would play a more important role in clinical negligence litigation in the years to come. The authors argued that guidelines might well be used more proactively in the future to establish the standard of care. They concluded, convincingly, that it might be possible to use a four-stage conceptual model by which guidelines could inform the standard of care in clinical negligence litigation.

Controlling the wider arena

A duty of partnership between local authorities and health bodies has been established in the National Health Service Act 1977, and was extended by the Health Act 1999, when a duty of co-operation between Health Authorities, NHS Trusts and Primary Care Trusts was introduced. The partnership concept was extended to a duty to secure and advance the health and welfare of the population, and co-operation was made the primary focus on commissioning and delivering healthcare, and in strategic planning. This encompassed housing, education, environment and social services. The 1999 Act stipulates that all Health Authorities should plan to improve health and healthcare provision for people living in their areas, and there is a duty on Primary Care Trusts, NHS Trusts and local authorities to participate in this planning exercise. Since that time further measures[78] have been introduced to ensure not only co-operation between sectors, but also greater uniformity in standards, with monitoring and a quality agenda in the private sector as well as in local authority institutions. This development was essential in the light of new partnerships between social and health care introduced under the Health Act 1999. The result of the legislative activity has been the bringing of large areas of public service provision, more comprehensively than ever before, within the control of government.

Ensuring safety: the role of the NPSA

The Department of Health publication 'Making Amends'[79] contained the following statement:

> Until recently, relatively little attention had been given in any country to trying to identify the sources of risk in health care and to finding ways to reduce it in a planned and organised way. A much higher level of error has been tolerated in health care than has been acceptable in other sectors. This

---

78   Care Standards Act 1999; Health and Social Care (Community Health and Standards) Act 2003 which contained arrangements for establishing Foundation hospitals.
79   Department of Health, 'Making Amends – Clinical Negligence Reform', 2003.

is now changing and the NHS is one of the first health care systems in the world to give high priority to enhancing patient safety by systematically learning from what goes wrong.

The report 'Building a Safer NHS for Patients'[80] which formed the basis for the present system for identifying errors recognised that:

> In the past, most health services around the world have underestimated the scale of unintended harm or injury experienced by patients as a result of medical error and adverse events in hospitals and other health care settings. There has been no real understanding of the approach necessary to reduce risk to patients based on analysing and learning from error and adverse events.

The precise number of incidents, either harming patients or with the potential to harm them, is not known. However there are estimated to be around 900,000 such incidents relating to NHS hospital inpatients in the UK every year. It follows that it is essential to reduce medical errors and improve patient safety, measures which would also reduce the number of claims in healthcare. The Government accepted all the recommendations made in the report of an expert group in June 2000. Entitled 'An Organisation with a Memory',[81] the report identified that there has been insufficient effort to learn in a systematic way from patient safety incidents.[82] The authors drew attention to the scale of the problem, and proposed solutions based on developing a culture of openness, reporting and safety awareness in NHS organisations.

A new national system for reporting and identifying patient safety incidents was recommended, in order to collect information on the causes of adverse incidents and learn from them so that action could be taken to reduce risk and prevent similar events occurring in future. Not all healthcare organisations systematically report incidents as yet, and it will be necessary to introduce vital measures to ensure that staff report all incidents in future years.

The NPSA, a Special Health Authority, was created to co-ordinate the work of identifying and recording patient safety incidents occurring in the NHS, so that lessons could be learned from them. Guidance is drafted on specific issues, especially those arising from particular incidents, and is disseminated throughout the NHS. From 1 April 2005, the NPSA has an extended remit covering safety aspects of hospital design, cleanliness and food, safety

---

80   'Building a Safer NHS for Patients: Implementing An Organisation with a Memory', DoH.

81   DoH Expert Group, 13 June 2000.

82   'Building A Safer NHS For Patients', April 2002, sets out the Government's plans for promoting patient safety following the publication of the report 'An Organisation with a Memory' and the commitment to implement it in the NHS Plan.

of research, and the support of local organisations, by dealing with their concerns about the performance of individual doctors and dentists, through its responsibility for the National Clinical Assessment Service (NCAS), formerly known as the National Clinical Assessment Authority. It now manages the contracts with the Confidential Enquiries.

A particularly important function of the NPSA is that of ensuring that incidents are reported, by promoting a culture of openness and fairness in healthcare settings, encouraging staff to report incidents and 'near misses' without fear of personal reprimand. If this can be achieved, and there are those who doubt that it is possible, staff will be urged to share their experiences so that others can learn from them and patient safety will be improved. A national reporting and learning system is being developed. One of the problems with the present incident reporting requirements identified by the National Audit Office is that too many agencies are involved in the process. It recommends that if possible incidents should be reported only once, and that there should be a single point of entry to the system, or at the very least the number of entry points should be rationalised by means of the concordat currently being developed.[83]

The Final Report of the Bristol Inquiry also referred to the 'defensive and secretive culture' which was then prevalent in the NHS and for the need for better communication, openness and honesty. One recommendation was that there should be reports about the outcomes of particular treatments at particular hospitals, and acceptance of responsibility for errors. The recommendations continued:

> For a culture of openness to succeed, those who work in the NHS must be confident that they will be supported by the organisation at all levels. Openness must be valued and rewarded. Otherwise, healthcare professionals will understandably be reluctant to embrace it. What this means, crucially, is that blame and stigma should not be the response of managers or colleagues.

If it is indeed possible for such a culture to be introduced, it will assist greatly with the collection of data concerning errors, and with the development of educational programmes which should ensure that healthcare is a safer environment in the future. As will be seen, the concept of openness and honesty underpins the thinking that led to the NHS Redress Bill being introduced. The NPSA has developed a 'Being Open' programme, based on its views concerning the need for a radically new approach to the culture

---

83   National Audit Office Report, 'A Safer Place for Patients: Learning to Improve Patient Safety' 2005.

of safety in healthcare, as set out in its publications, 'Seven Steps to Patient Safety'[84] and 'Seven Steps to Patient Safety in Primary Care'.[85] This involved communicating with patients honestly and sympathetically when things go wrong in order to deal effectively with errors in their care. The 'Being Open' policy is stated by the NPSA to apply to errors that lead to moderate or severe harm or death. Trusts are advised to promote the programme among staff in their organisations, and to provide them with support and training to put the ideas into practice. The concept of 'Being Open' involves not only incident reporting, but also learning and sharing safety lessons and implementing them within a safety culture that focuses strongly on involvement with patients and the public. The NPSA considers that this policy will reduce the levels of litigation involving the NHS, and its approach has been linked with developments such as the NHS Redress Act 2006. Some of the solutions suggested by the NPSA are straightforward and based on common sense. One such proposal is for all hospitals in England and Wales to have the same 'crash' telephone number for staff to dial in the event of cardiac arrest. That may appear to be common sense, but it required a survey by the NPSA and further consideration and guidance for such a simple idea to be implemented.[86]

The NPSA has not been without its critics, including the National Audit Office, and following the publication of the National Audit Office report 'A Safer Place for Patients: Learning to Improve Patient Safety in November 2005', a review was ordered by the Chief Medical Officer of arrangements to support patient safety.

A report entitled 'Safety First: A Report for Patients, Clinicians and Healthcare Managers'[87] was subsequently published, which makes fourteen recommendations, including the following:

> The role of the NPSA should be refocused on its core objective of collecting and analysing patient safety data to inform rapid patient safety learning, priority setting and coordinated activity across the NHS. A number of current functions, for example the development of technical solutions to improve patient safety, presently delivered by the organisation, should in future be commissioned from other expert organisations with the requisite expertise.

The result is that yet another set of organisational reforms will be on the political agenda.

---

84   NPSA, November 2003.
85   NPSA 2005.
86   'Establishing a standard crash call number in hospitals in England and Wales', NPSA 2004.
87   December 2006.

Evidence-based medicine

Evidence-based medicine has become central to the quality and monitoring agenda in the NHS. Clinical decisions and wider health policies are increasingly less dependent on individual opinions, and are rooted instead on evidence gathered from clinical trials and other research. 'Evidence-based medicine' has been defined as:

> The conscientious, explicit, and judicious use of current best evidence in making decisions about the care of individual patients. The practice of evidence based medicine means integrating individual clinical expertise with the best available external clinical evidence from systematic research.[88]

The seminal work entitled 'Effectiveness and Efficiency: Random Reflections on Health Services' by Cochrane,[89] was first published in 1972, and forms the basis for the extensive development of evidence-based medicine in the UK. Cochrane was the first writer to emphasise the importance of randomised controlled trials in assessing the effectiveness of medical treatment. Through his work the Cochrane Collaboration was established, which led to an international effort to evaluate and synthesise randomised controlled trials across the whole spectrum of medicine. The work goes beyond the healthcare professions, as it has enabled consumers of healthcare to take greater responsibility for their own healthcare decisions. Within the NHS there is an active research and development programme which continues to assist the discovery and analysis of evidence underpinning clinical decisions and the broader context of service planning. The concept has found its way into clinical governance, which is evidence-based. The results of this process have been far-reaching, from the drafting of guidelines for the individual treatment of specific conditions, to major decisions relating to public health and service provision that affect entire populations.

It is through the careful and systematic application of evidence-based medicine that some of the problems giving rise to litigation can be cured.

Dealing with poor performance

The pervasive problem of poorly performing healthcare staff is of course of serious significance in the context of errors, and the Bristol and Shipman cases highlighted the need to tackle it urgently. A series of reforms was implemented in the early years of the new millennium, some by the professions themselves and some following intervention by the Government. This ongoing

88   Sackett,D.L.,Rosenberg,W.M.,Gray,J.A.M.,Haynes,R.B.andRichardson,W.S.,'Evidence-based Medicine: What It Is and What It Isn't' (1996) *BMJ* 312(7023), 13 January, 71–72.
89   Royal Society of Medicine Press, 1972.

process was discussed in Chapter 5, and in addition to more independent and rigorous professional regulation, there is to be an emphasis on continuing education, appraisal and revalidation as a means of ensuring that healthcare professionals who are unable to cope with their work are identified and dealt with effectively. Clinical governance will be one of the mechanisms in this process, and will complement the work of the professional organisations as they are reconstituted.[90]

The Department of Health published a review of non-medical healthcare professional regulation in July 2006, and a report on the reform of medical regulation by the Chief Medical Officer, 'Good Doctors, Safer Patients'. It was the GMC itself which identified several crucial issues arising during the course of the Bristol Inquiry concerning the practice of medicine which demanded the urgent attention of the profession. However, the Bristol Inquiry Report highlighted numerous additional areas in need of urgent attention, too detailed to evaluate here. Among them were the need for clearly understood clinical standards; for proper assessment of clinical competence and technical expertise are assessed and evaluated; for the need to identify the individual with responsibility in team-based care; for better training of doctors in advanced procedures; for more effective use of medical and clinical audit; for consultants to take appropriate actions in response to concerns about their performance; for better communication between healthcare professionals and with patients, especially about the risks involved in treatment; for more effective ways in which people concerned about patients' safety can make their concerns known.

Some of the suggestions made by the GMC for reforming its own practices had already been put in place when the Government published a White Paper entitled 'Trust, Assurance and Safety – The Regulation of Health Professionals' on 21 February 2007, setting out a programme for reforming the system for regulation of health professionals. It is based on the wide-ranging consultation on two reviews of professional regulation published in July 2006. The White Paper is complemented by the Government's response to the recommendations of the Fifth Report of the Shipman Inquiry, which sets out proposals designed to improve and enhance clinical governance within the NHS.

It is hoped that the proposed reforms will ensure that confidence will be restored to patients, the public and professionals in the various regulatory mechanisms for improving patient safety. The new proposals have at their heart the protection of patients and the public as a priority, and favour the approach represented by Hobbes, of tight external control and regulation of professionals, as opposed to that preferred by Locke, of trust, respect and self-regulation – as so ably explained by Richard Smith in his much quoted *BMJ* editorial.[91]

---

90   'Reform of professional regulation and clinical governance', DoH, February 2007.
91   Smith, R. (1998) *BMJ* 316: 1917–18 (27 June).

The main developments include measures to ensure that the regulators are more independent; that members of the healthcare professions will no longer form the majority of council members and there will be an independent adjudicator for doctors; that healthcare professionals are objectively revalidated throughout their careers, and that they remain up to date with current clinical best practice; and more controversially, a change in the standard of proof used in fitness to practise cases from the criminal standard to the civil standard with a sliding scale.

In future there will be a move towards a more rehabilitative approach to regulation, and a comprehensive strategy for prevention, treatment and rehabilitation services for all health professionals. Many of these, and the proposals made in response to the Shipman Inquiry recommendations, should have the effect of ensuring that there is a safer environment for patients, and that if errors are made there will be accountability without the need to resort to litigation. There are plans to establish new safeguards for the public by building on and strengthening existing clinical governance processes. Thus, if the proposals are implemented, there will be better support for patients wishing to register concerns about doctors, and measures to ensure they are taken seriously; more systematic use of information about clinical outcomes of individual practitioners and teams; measures to ensure that information from different sources is coordinated to provide a fuller picture about professionals; and a requirement for all primary care organisations to adopt best practice in investigating and acting on concerns.

In addition to the proposed changes, better recruitment, retention, and staff development should contribute to safety in healthcare, and there are plans to support staff to facilitate better practice through skills training, modern information technology and access to evidence. Staff will be encouraged to participate in developing strategies for improving quality, and for looking critically at existing processes of care and ways of improving them. The Public Interest (Protection) Act 1998 had been introduced long before the Bristol Inquiry produced its final report. This Act enables healthcare professionals to report concerns about the performance of their colleagues without the fear of repercussions in the employment setting.

Improving the quality of patient records

There have been concerns for some time about the quality of clinical record keeping.[92] The collection and analysis of data concerning patients has been an important part of planning and administration since the founding of the NHS. Data analysis enables planning on a number of fronts, such as the targeting of waiting lists and identifying of priorities for patients on a macro level in

---

92   To take but one example, Dion, X., *British Journal of Community Nursing* (9 April 2001) 6(4): 193–98.

terms of public health, and a micro level in the interests of individual patients. Unfortunately, this is one particular area in which problems are frequently encountered. Delays in obtaining patients' records can protract the litigation process, and lost records are a regular source of concern in clinical governance terms. An ambitious project to establish a central electronic database holding the records of all NHS patients has been put in place. This has yet to come to fruition, having encountered numerous technical and financial difficulties and ethical problems involving confidentiality[93] – to add to the legal maze which doctors are required to negotiate. Finally, in March 2007, the first test of the system in England was launched, involving two GP practices.[94] Meanwhile, Connecting for Health, the IT agency of the NHS, will inform 50 million patients in England about a procedure to notify their GP if they do not want their records to be held on the system. There are complications with compatibility between the systems in England and Wales, which might mean that for some time it will be difficult for patients whose records are held in Wales to access them in the course of treatment in England, and vice versa. There has not been great enthusiasm among doctors for the project, which has already cost far more than was originally anticipated, and a poll of more than 1,000 GPs by the *Guardian* in November 2006 revealed that half would consider refusing to put patient records automatically onto a new national database. One of the main reasons given was doubt about the security of the new system.

Further fears have been expressed by doctors about the changes that they will need to introduce into their practice once patient records are more completely automated for recording notes and storing results and correspondence. The new system will need to be risk-managed effectively, and doctors will be required to implement a new set of targets and standards in connection with the new system. There is also the potential for negligence and Data Protection Act claims if information is incorrectly recorded. While there are advantages in a system aimed at safer prescribing, better legibility and simpler presentation of information, there will inevitably be risks for both doctors and patients.[95]

Public health reforms

All the strategies designed to improve patient safety and reduce litigation in healthcare are complemented by a comprehensive public health agenda aimed at keeping people out of hospital. Measures aimed at reducing tobacco smoking and alcohol consumption, and campaigns to persuade people to eat

---

93 See Thornton, P., 'Why Might NHS Database Proposals be Unlawful', January 2006, http://www.ardenhoe.demon.co.uk/privacy/NHS
94 Carvel, J., *Guardian Unlimited*, 15 March 2007.
95 See Rogers, A., 'Clinical Negligence & the Electronic Patient Record', *Medical Litigation*, April 2001.

healthy food, should have some effect on the overall health of the population and prevent early deaths from lung disorders and cardio-vascular disease. However, in the longer term, people who live longer will require healthcare to deal with the diseases of ageing, and as the population increases, so does the number of people requiring healthcare, with resulting potential for litigation if mistakes are made.

Legal procedural reforms

While the Government was deeply engaged in plans for making healthcare safer for patients, radical changes in legal procedures for handling clinical negligence claims were introduced in the hope that, along with other areas of civil litigation, there might be more effective ways of managing cases and reaching just solutions. The Civil Procedure Rules 1998 (CPR) were the product of Lord Woolf's survey and evaluation of the civil justice system and proposed reforms. The new system was implemented in April 1999, and was aimed at reducing cost, delay and complexity in the handling of personal injury claims, and at preventing litigation wherever possible. The fundamental underlying objective is to achieve justice for the parties. In the latest version of the rules, the Lord Chancellor makes the following comment, which is a testament to the success of the new procedures:

> The title of Lord Woolf's report, 'Access to Justice', became the phrase that marked a paradigm shift in the administration of civil justice. That every citizen and business in England and Wales now has the ability to approach our legal system and ask for justice without always needing expert knowledge and aware of the continuing drive to control costs is something we should be proud of, and we must ensure that these ideals are never lost in the business of reviewing, changing and implementing these rules.

A vital feature of the CPR is the use of pre-action protocols. The protocol relating to clinical negligence claims[96] is described in Chapter 2.

The Protocol, which was developed by a working party of the Clinical Disputes Forum, had the support of the Lord Chancellor's Department, the Department of Health and NHS Executive, the Law Society, the Legal Aid Board, and other organisations, and incorporates many of the messages used in the clinical governance area, such as a recommendation that healthcare providers:

> Develop an approach to clinical governance which ensures that clinical practice is delivered to commonly accepted standards and is routinely monitored.

96   Pre-action Protocol for the Resolution of Clinical Negligence Disputes.

As regards the management of claims, the protocol encourages early communication between both sides of any dispute, prompt investigation, and timely handing over of relevant documents. It emphasises the need for effective clinical risk management strategies, adverse incident reporting, and instructions from professional organisations such as the GMC to their members on the importance of this matter. It contains detailed guidance on the preparation and defending of claims, and on the use of alterative dispute resolution, as well as guidance on the use of expert witnesses.

Research[97] carried out into the operation of the CPR and the use of the protocol indicates that the system has been a success in many respects. There has been an overall drop in the number of personal injury claims issued, in particular in the types of claim where the CPR has been introduced. There was found to be anecdotal evidence that the pre-action protocols were promoting settlement before issue of proceedings, and to reducing the number of ill-founded claims. The use of Alternative Dispute Resolution (ADR) was found to be helpful in certain instances, and more offers to settle were being made.[98] Although mediation was considered to be helpful in some instances,[99] it has not been taken up as widely as was hoped in the healthcare context.[100]

While there is some evidence that claims are being managed more efficiently under the new procedural framework, there is little evidence that this has had an effect on the number of claims being initiated. In 2002, after the CPR had been given time to take effect, a National Audit Office Report concluded that the clinical negligence litigation system was still failing patients and needed to be reformed. A Commons Public Accounts Committee Report criticised the system for failing to deal with patients with speed and compassion, and its research revealed that many cases were taking more than five years to be resolved, with 8 per cent of cases taking more than ten years. It found that in six out of ten cases the legal bill frequently far exceeded the award of damages or settlement, and that people felt that they had been cornered into pursuing litigation, commenting that a more intelligent approach to claims was required.[101]

The Government was at that time in the process of considering how it might build on the reforms introduced by the CPR and was also taking soundings about a far more radical approach to the litigation problem.

97   Goriely, T., Moorhead, R. and Abrams, P., 'More Civil Justice? The Impact of the Woolf Reforms on Pre-action Behaviour' (2002) p 462.
98   CPR P 36.
99   Mulcahy, L., Selwood, M., Summerfield, L. and Netten A. (2000): Mediating Medical Negligence Claims: An Option for the Future? HMSO, London, p 11.
100 See e.g. Liverpool County Court Mediation Scheme Report 2005–06; and Allen, T., 'Increasing the use of mediation in clinical negligence disputes', CEDR, August 2002.
101 *Daily Telegraph* report, 13 June 2002.

In Wales, a confidential report which had been leaked to the press indicated that there were many problems in the principality and that Winston Roddick, Counsel General, thought the system needed to be given a radical overhaul if it was to become 'fairer, swifter and less expensive'. The same report recommended that a fast track scheme for dealing with clinical disputes worth between £10,000 and £25,000 should be piloted, and a 'Speedy Resolution' scheme was established, which has yet to be evaluated.

Making amends and statutory intervention

The most crucial influence on the agenda for reform of clinical negligence claims was the Bristol Report, as it highlighted so many shortcomings in the system of medical practice and professional regulation, error detection and management, communications between staff and patients and the entire culture within which medicine was practised, which would undoubtedly have led to a lack of trust on the part of patients who were driven as a last resort to litigation. The Chief Medical Officer produced a consultation paper entitled 'Making Amends'[102] shortly after Sir Ian Kennedy had published his final report on events at Bristol. It contained 19 suggestions, some of them radical, for reform of the clinical negligence litigation system, and provides an excellent summary of the tort system and its shortcomings.

Many of the criticisms of the present compensation system expressed in 'Making Amends' had already been well-rehearsed over many years.[103] The system for claiming compensation is complex, slow and often unfair, and it encourages defensiveness. The fault principle as a basis for compensation has numerous drawbacks, and in the healthcare context it is particularly unhelpful. Legal proceedings are frequently acrimonious, and by their very nature confrontational, even since the implementation of the CPR, and changes in the way damages are paid. Delays involved in litigation can leave claimants and doctors demoralised and are counter-productive; staff are diverted from patient care; and medical expert witness work has developed into an industry. The system is unwieldy and expensive to administer. In clinical negligence claims, the legal administrative costs exceeded the amount paid in damages in most claims below £45,000, and the cost of the entire system is a very heavy burden on the NHS.[104]

The vision for the future stated in 'Making Amends' was ambitious. It envisaged effective reporting and efficient correction of errors; a remedial system offering rehabilitation of injured patients; a fair, practical and affordable system of financial compensation; strengthening of relationships between

---

102   'Making Amends': a consultation paper setting out proposals for reforming the approach to clinical negligence in the NHS, A report by the Chief Medical Officer.
103   See Cane, P., *Atiyah's Accidents Compensation and the Law* (7th edn, Cambridge University Press, Cambridge, 2006) passim, and in particular Chapter 7, p 1.
104   'Making Amends', p 26.

doctors and patients; and a range of different entry points for complaints. The Government hoped that the Act would reform the handling of lower value clinical negligence claims in order to provide appropriate redress, which should go beyond financial redress to include investigations, explanations and apologies, without going to court.

There are some eminently sensible proposals in 'Making Amends', for example, that judges should receive special training in dealing with clinical negligence cases[105] (as has already happened in some areas of the country). Also, recommendation 14:

> Mediation should be seriously considered before litigation for the majority of claims which do not fall within the proposed NHS Redress Scheme.
> The successor body to the NHSLA should require their panel solicitor firms to consider every case for mediation and to offer mediation where appropriate.

And again:[106]

> Claimants [can be offered] the package of measures they say they seek: apologies, explanations, an opportunity to discuss the issues with the healthcare providers face to face and to explore issues other than financial compensation. It can also be followed by an out-of-court settlement in a large claim.

Some of the more radical proposals in 'Making Amends' proved to be unpopular and did not find their way into the NHS Redress Act. Among these was the so-called 'duty of candour'. The desirability of being honest about mistakes and providing patients with an explanation at the earliest opportunity had been emphasised in the Bristol Report,[107] in which it was stated:

> Healthcare professionals should have a duty of candour to patients.

However, the idea had been canvassed long before that in the UK.[108] In 1987, in *Naylor v Preston Area Health Authority*,[109] Lord Donaldson MR had said:

> I personally think that in professional negligence cases, and in particular in medical negligence cases, there is a duty of candour resting on the professional man.

The UK Defence Organisations had for many years advised their members to offer an explanation and apology to injured patients at an early stage:[110]

---

105   Recommendation 18.
106   Recommendation 15.
107   Final Report Synopsis, para 14.
108   *Lee v South West Regional Health Authority* [1985] 2 All ER 385.
109   *Naylor v Preston Area Health Authority* [1987] 2 All ER 353, [1987] 1 WLR 958.
110   The Medical Protection Society Advice to Members 2006.

The MPS advises doctors to investigate complaints thoroughly and give patients an honest, comprehensive response. If something has gone wrong, then an apology is appropriate. Contrary to popular belief this does not encourage patients to sue or claim compensation.

In some common law jurisdictions the concept has been developed further, into something close to a fiduciary duty,[111] or at least to a recognition that the doctor-patient relationship has some fiduciary elements.[112]

In a paper published in 1999[113] Kraman and Hamm reviewed the effects in the US of a policy of proactive disclosure to patients injured as a result of accidents or negligence, coupled with fair compensation for injuries. They concluded that in the Veteran Affairs Medical environment where the policy had been tried and tested over several years, there were substantial benefits in financial terms, and in diminishing anger and the desire for revenge on the part of patients. The authors argued that an honest and forthright so-called 'humanistic' risk management policy, placing patients at the centre:

> May be relatively inexpensive because it allows avoidance of lawsuit preparation, litigation, court judgments, and settlements at trial. Although goodwill and the maintenance of the caregiver role are less tangible benefits, they are also important advantages of such a policy.

The sample of patients in the study may well not be truly representative of the patient population in the US as a whole, and may not easily be transferred to the UK. However, there could be lessons in it for healthcare professionals in the UK, and in the longer term, coupled with a strengthening of the safety culture and reporting programme, there is a possibility that such a policy might have some effect on our litigation levels. There is evidently a need for more empirical research in order to ascertain whether patients want to be given the option of being told about errors made in the course of their treatment and care. Research studies to date in the UK indicate that despite the GMC's statement of the professional duty set out in 'Good Medical Practice', few who admit to making errors take the further step of disclosing them to the patient or the family.

---

111   A concept that belongs to the law of trusts and certain areas of the law of contract.

112   See e.g., *Norberg v Wynrib* [1992] 2 S.C.R. 226 and *Breen v Williams* (1996) 186 CLR 71, for dicta on this point, and Faunce, T.A., and Bolsin, S.N., 'Fiduciary Disclosure of Medical Mistakes: The duty to promptly notify patients of adverse healthcare events' (2005) 12 *JML* 478.

113   Kraman, S. and Hamm, G., 'Risk Management: Extreme Honesty May be the Best Policy', Medicine and Public Issues, Annals Internal Medicine, 21 December 1999.

The GMC guidance sets out a professional duty which must be distinguished from a legal rule. It states that:

> If a patient under your care has suffered harm or distress, you must act immediately to put matters right, if that is possible. You should offer an apology and explain fully and promptly to the patient what has happened, and the likely short-term and long-term effects.[114]
>
> Patients who complain about the care or treatment they have received have a right to expect a prompt, open, constructive and honest response including an explanation and, if appropriate, an apology. You must not allow a patient's complaint to affect adversely the care or treatment you provide or arrange.[115]

Wu's research results, published in 1991,[116] indicate that although 90 per cent of House Officers in a survey admitted making an error with a serious adverse outcome, only 24 per cent discussed this with the patient or the patient's family – even though patients had died in up to 31 per cent of the incidents. What is still more worrying, though it is not surprising, is that as few as 54 per cent of the House Officers discussed the mistakes they had made with other doctors in attendance at the time. Eighty-eight per cent said that they had discussed them with another doctor who was not in a supervisory position. Again, after researching the reporting levels in an obstetric ward on which more than 75 per cent of reportable events went unreported, Vincent and colleagues[117] discovered that the reasons for not reporting included fear of litigation, pressure of work (being 'too busy'), ignorance about whose responsibility it was to make the report or which incidents needed to be reported, and the belief that once errors had been rectified they did not need to be reported.

Following this theme, recommendation 12 of 'Making Amends' states:

> A duty of candour should be introduced together with exemption from disciplinary action when reporting incidents with a view to improving patient safety.

114 GMC Guidance 'Good Medical Practice', 2006, para 30.
115 GMC Guidance 'Good Medical Practice', 2006, para 31.
116 Wu, A.W., Folkman, S., and Lo, B., 'Do House Officers Learn from their Mistakes?' (1991) *JAMA* 265: 2089–94.
117 Vincent, C., Stanhope, N. and Crowley-Murphy, M., 'Reasons for Not Reporting Adverse Incidents in an Empirical Study' (1999) *Journal of Evaluation in Clinical Practice* 5(1): 13–21.

It continued:

> The concomitant of the duty of candour should be provisions providing for exemption from disciplinary action by employers or professional regulatory bodies for those reporting adverse events except where the healthcare professional has committed a criminal offence or it would not be safe for the professional to continue to treat patients.

Strangely, in view of the commitment to openness, Recommendation 13 stated:

> Documents and information collected for identifying adverse events should be protected from disclosure in court.

The Bristol Report demanded practical changes aimed at greater openness about errors, and at removing the fear of clinical negligence litigation, which is an obvious barrier to openness in healthcare. The Report called for a change in culture, both internally within the NHS and externally in its relationships with patients. Richard Smith, in his *BMJ* editorial,[118] said:

> We need a culture that allows doctors to express fears, doubts and vulnerabilities; identifies and helps those in difficulties; refuses to condone inappropriate delegation; values teamwork and continuous learning and improvement; and genuinely puts the interests of the patients first.

Although there is some evidence that progress has been made towards implementing a duty of disclosure in other jurisdictions,[119] in the event, the notion of a duty of candour was dropped from the UK legislation, amid considerable controversy during the House of Lords debates on the NHS Redress Bill.[120] However, a voluntary duty of candour continues to be promoted under the 'Being Open' initiative of the NPSA.[121]

There was a large number of responses to the consultation from members of the public and professional bodies, and the result was a Bill, which after a stormy passage through Parliament, became law in November 2006: the NHS Redress Act. As the Bill passed through such protracted debates and amendments in both Houses of Parliament, there was doubt for some time whether it would become law at all, as it narrowly escaped being lost altogether because of lack of Parliamentary time.

---

118   Smith, R., 'British Medical Journal' (1998) *BMJ* 316: 1917–18.
119   Krala, J., Massey, K.L. and Mulla, A., 'Disclosure of Medical Error: Policy and Practice' (2005) *JR Soc Med* 98: 307–09.
120   E.g. Baroness Neuberger, House of Lords Hansard, 2 November 2005, col 213–14.
121   'Being Open when Patients are Harmed', NPSA London, 2005.

The NHS Redress Act 2006 is, in effect, the implementation of Recommendation 1 of 'Making Amends', together with a range of reforms based on some of the other recommendations. Recommendation 2 (the extension of the scheme proposed by Recommendation 1 to severely brain-damaged babies), appears to have been abandoned. Most of the future arrangements will be introduced in the regulations introducing separate schemes for dealing with claims in England and Wales.

Briefly, the Act covers NHS liability to compensate patients up to £20,000:

> in respect of or consequent upon personal injury or loss arising out of or in connection with breach of a duty of care owed to any person in connection with the diagnosis of illness, or the care or treatment of any patient, and in consequence of any act or omission by a health care professional.

This is confined to care provided in hospitals, and does not cover GPs, dentists working outside hospitals, ophthalmic or pharmaceutical services. Thus, if a patient is injured in the hospital setting through some error and the Trust admits negligence, the patient may be entitled to compensation up to a set limit of £20,000.

Compensation appears to be payable under the schemes only if liability could have been established under the common law rules of negligence. It would not cover, for example, non-negligent incidents such as deliberate abuse or Consumer Protection Act 1987 claims. The new rules are intended to apply only to lower value claims, and secondary legislation will either specify an upper limit of compensation or set a limit on the maximum that can be paid for pain, suffering and loss of amenity, with no limit on other heads of damage. The period during which an investigation takes place under the scheme is to be disregarded for the purposes of any other limitation period in a subsequent civil claim.[122] Redress may be an offer of compensation, an explanation, an apology and the making of a report on the action which has been or will be taken to prevent similar cases arising in the future. The compensation offered to the injured party might take the form of a contract to provide care or treatment. Legal advice will be provided to individuals under the scheme without charge, but only once the offer has been made.[123] There is no provision mentioned in the Act for further independent legal advice.

122   NHS Redress Act 2006, s 7.
123   NHS Redress Act 2006, s 8.

Under s 9(4) of the Act arrangements:

> should, so far as practicable, be independent of any person to whose conduct the case relates or who is involved in dealing with the case.

This would enable any rehabilitation or care to be given by some person other than the potential 'defendant' or in a different institution, so avoiding any embarrassment for any of the individuals concerned.

Several problems arose during the passage of the Bill through Parliament, and patients' organisations lobbied very hard to change certain sections. They were successful on some points. One such victory is the option of joint instruction of independent medical experts to report on the merits of cases in which the NHS has not already offered redress. However, patients will still encounter some dilemmas in certain instances. If an offer of compensation is accepted under the redress scheme, the right to bring legal proceedings is waived – but access to independent legal advice is not available until after compensation under the scheme has been offered. As AvMA pointed out,[124] the scheme:

> would not enjoy public confidence and would lead either to people litigating as an alternative to using the scheme, or at the end of the scheme, thereby costing the NHS more than would otherwise be the case.

A number of criticisms of the Act can be made even at this early stage. The Act was originally to be implemented after a three-month consultation on the regulations, but the redress schemes are still under discussion by teams of experts. These will be implemented through regulations, as secondary legislation, free from Parliamentary scrutiny, and cynics would argue against this approach to legal change:[125]

> The success of this behind doors process is to be seen in the Conditional Fee Agreement Regulations 2000; recently abolished in infamy.

Further comment in the same vein was made by Baroness Barker during the second reading debate on the Bill in the House of Lords:[126]

> ... I wondered aloud whether the day would come when this House would consider a Bill that stated, 'There is the Secretary of State and here is a list of regulatory powers.' To my horror, I think that day has come.

Among the interested parties to express reservations about the Act was Citizens' Advice, which was of the view that the absence of detail about how

---

124   Peter Walsh, Chief Executive 'Action against Medical Accidents', November 2005.
125   Bevan, N. and James, E., Butterworths Personal Injury Litigation Service, March 2007, PILS 2007.86.
126   Hansard, 2 November 2005, col 229, cited by Gooderham, P., 'The NHS Redress Bill – Implementing Making Amends' (March 2006) *Medical Law Monitor*, p 6.

the scheme was likely to operate was a worrying feature, since much of the essential detail and design would be left to the DoH, albeit on the advice of an expert panel.

Another complication lies in the fact that the Act does not apply to Scotland, and that Wales is to have its own scheme under the Act.[127] There has been a 'Speedy Resolution Scheme' in place in Wales for dealing with lower cost healthcare claims since February 2005, which aims to provide a fast, proportionate and fair way of resolving clinical negligence claims. One particular comment made in the protocol sums up the difficulties faced by those involved in clinical negligence litigation:

> It is clearly in the interests of patients, healthcare professionals and providers that patients' concerns, complaints and claims arising from their treatment are resolved as quickly, efficiently and professionally as possible. A climate of mistrust and lack of openness can seriously damage the patient/clinician relationship.

The project was devised by a working group and a pilot project was established, which is due for evaluation at the time of writing. To date approximately 60 cases have been dealt with under this experiment, which has used joint experts, fixed timetables, and fixed fees, covering claims valued at between £5,000 and £15,000. The policy objectives of the Speedy Resolution Scheme were a reduction in the time taken to resolve claims, and in the cost of settling claims, improved lessons learned from each case and more explanations provided to patients about what had happened to them in the course of their treatment. If the evaluation concludes that the scheme was a success, it is possible that it could form the basis of the Welsh scheme to be put in place under the NHS Redress Act, though with certain modifications in the light of the Act, and this might differ in a number of respects from the scheme that will apply in England, which had its own pilot scheme (RESOLVE).

One major problem with implementing the Act in England is that several commentators[128] and patients' groups are unhappy with the lack of independence and the involvement of the 'Special Health Authority,'[129] likely to be the NHSLA, which will be the administrator of any scheme to be devised. As has been pointed out,[130] the astonishing response to the many concerns about lack of independence raised in the debate across all parties by Burnham was

---

127 NHS Redress Act 2006, s 11.
128 Hunjan, S. and Fox, S. 'Defeating itself', barristers practising from No.5 Chambers – Birmingham, Bristol and London; *Solicitors' Journal*, 30 March 2007; Conservative MP Andrew Lansley; Conservative MP Graham Stuart, during debates on the Bill.
129 NHS Redress Act 2006, s 10.
130 Ibid.

... it must be right that the NHS can make its own response to take ownership of the situation. It must be right for the NHS to understand what is going on. The service is perfectly capable of establishing and presenting the facts ... patients will retain the ability to take their claims to the Courts through an independent legal process.

Thus the NHS will be investigator, judge, and jury in its own cause,[131] (which could lead to a challenge under Art 6 of the European Convention on Human Rights if the result were to be that a fair trial was denied to a potential claimant), and the Act will have achieved little to inspire the confidence of patients and the public.

The pilot schemes carried out separately in England and Wales had both afforded patients the advantage of using independent experts, and decisions on eligibility were made by an independent medical expert on the basis of information provided by the NHS trust and a solicitor with specialist experience. It would appear that the schemes to be drafted under the Act would not be able to offer this independent support to patients.

Those who had hoped for a more radical approach were disappointed that redress is to be triggered by a qualifying liability, namely liability in tort arising from personal injury caused by breach of duty of care owed in connection with diagnosis of illness, care or treatment of any patient. Thus the common law will apply and the test will be equivalent, therefore, to *Bolam v Friern Hospital Management Committee*[132] as modified by *Bolitho v City and Hackney Health Authority*.[133] Implicit in this is that any developments in the common law would also be applicable to the scheme. Any developments arising from the new statutory provision relating to the standard of care set out in the Compensation Act 2006 s 1 would also be applicable.

Yet another drawback of the Act which will still be present in any scheme made under the NHS Redress Act concerns proof of causation. It will be necessary to consider the question of causation when dealing with complaints under the scheme. This can be a difficult and intricate process and it is one of the more complex areas of litigation. The Independent Complaints Advocacy Service (ICAS),[134] has recently been awarded by the DoH in England the contract to support patients and their carers wishing to pursue a complaint about their NHS treatment or care. The statutory service, which was launched on 1 September 2003, provides a national service delivered to agreed quality standards. However, few of its advisors are sufficiently well qualified to give

131   See Earl Howe's comments as opposition spokesman during the second reading debate, 2 November 2005.
132   [1957] 1 WLR 582.
133   [1997] All ER 771.
134   DoH announcement 6 March 2007.

advice about complex areas of the law of tort, and patients are disadvantaged by not having legal advice other than that which concerns any offer made to them. That advice will be given on the basis of a flat fee, so there will be little space for a detailed legal investigation of causation and the balance of litigation risk in addition to the valuation of the offer.

Since there is no appeals process within the scheme itself, if a patient is not content with what is being offered under the scheme and wishes to enter the litigation process, further time-consuming and stressful procedures will be invoked. In any event, as the scheme will only be applicable to claims of a low value, it is likely to be of limited use to the NHS in the longer term.

The question whether the Legal Services Commission will refuse to fund claimants who were eligible to apply under the redress scheme has not yet been decided, but if this transpires, it will reduce the options available to potential claimants.

As investigations under the scheme will be carried out by the NHS, it is not very different from the existing complaints procedures, except that compensation can be paid up to £20,000. As Hunjan and Fox explain,[135] both the complaints procedure and the proposed scheme provide for investigations which are carried out by the organisation about which complaint is made; neither allow access to legal advice during the investigation; both have the aim of learning from mistakes; both allow for a clinician who is independent from the treating team to consider the circumstances of the treatment; and both allow the ultimate the right to a civil claim. In a considered analysis, they conclude that the Act simply adds another layer of bureaucracy, at considerable expense for the NHS. It is likely that the same people will be dealing with investigations and offers under the scheme as deal with complaints and claims. Since few people who are injured as a result of negligence have any confidence in the complaints system as a vehicle for obtaining compensation, it is unlikely that the Act will make a significant difference in practice.

There are the usual resourcing issues connected with the implementation of the schemes. It seems that no new resources will be allocated to Trusts, nor to the NHSLA to deal with investigation, and it is therefore unlikely that any more offers of settlement will be made than are already possible outside the scheme. The only change will be that patients will have to bear the risk of not recovering the cost of legal advice on claims under the schemes.

Questions that still need to be answered concern the way in which the value of compensation will be calculated and by whom, the timeframe for the drafting and implementation of schemes in England and Wales, the precise nature of the assistance which may be provided for users of the scheme by way

135   Op. cit., supra.

or advice and/or representation,[136] and the effectiveness of the schemes, over and above existing mechanisms,[137] for admitting and learning from mistakes and eliminating mistrust between doctors and patients.

It appears that an important opportunity to implement rigorous measures for deflecting claims from the litigation system has been lost, at great financial expense and the immeasurable cost in terms of wasted time and energy. It appears that once the schemes have been implemented in England and Wales, what we will have is what Lord Howe, Conservative peer, speaking in the House of Lords debate, described as 'a repackaging exercise; the same system with a few knobs on'. We should not, as he said in the same debate:

> allow ourselves to be seduced by the idea that the goal provides a genuinely novel alternative to litigation.[138]

The Compensation Act 2006: varying the standard of care

One further means by which the Government hopes to deal with the so-called 'compensation culture' problem is through the creation of a statutory approach to the standard of care to be applied by judges in determining negligence cases. The Act states:

1. Deterrent effect of potential liability

A court considering a claim in negligence or breach of statutory duty may, in determining whether the defendant should have taken particular steps to meet a standard of care (whether by taking precautions against a risk or otherwise), have regard to whether a requirement to take those steps might:

(a) prevent a desirable activity from being undertaken at all, to a particular extent or in a particular way, or

(b) discourage persons from undertaking functions in connection with a desirable activity.

This appears to do little more than re-state the common law standard of care in negligence, and the *Bolam* formula, discussed elsewhere in this book, is testimony to the existing variants to the standard of care which have been

---

136   NHR Redress Act 2006, s 9.
137   E.g. 'The Being Open' policy; the NHS Complaints System; Clinical Governance and so on.
138   House of Lords, Hansard, 15 February 2006, col 1208.

developed by the judiciary. The explanatory notes to the Act attempt to clarify what is involved, stating that the Act does not alter the standard of care or the circumstances in which a duty of care will be owed. Instead, we are advised, it reflects the existing law and the approach taken by the courts as indicated in recent judgments.

The section is an attempt to codify the approach taken in some of the recent judgments in the higher courts in the UK, and especially relevant is the reasoning and policy underlying the House of Lords ruling in *Tomlinson v Congleton Borough Council* in 2003.[139] It was held in that case that a local authority could not be expected to protect a man from injuries sustained when, in a drunken state, he dived into a shallow lake. The House of Lords took the view that:

> It is not, and should never be, the policy of the law to require the protection of the foolhardy or reckless few to deprive, or interfere with, the enjoyment by the remainder of society of the liberties and amenities to which they are rightly entitled ... The pursuit of an unrestrained culture of blame and compensation has many evil consequences and one is certainly the interference with the liberty of the citizen.

Under the Act, courts will be encouraged to consider the wider social implications of their judgments. However, one of the problems has been the absence of a clear definition of 'desirable activity' while the Bill was proceeding through Parliament. The Government's response was that the courts had not defined the concept, and that the objective of the provision was to simply to restate the need for the proper assessment of risk, in the context of potential benefit and effect on society.

The statute means that courts will be able to take into account whether taking certain steps would prevent or interfere with a 'desirable activity' from taking place, though since the application of the section can only ever relate to past behaviour its influence has yet to be observed. It should ensure that risk-averse behaviour and fear of litigation do not lead to excessive caution, and this is as relevant in the field of healthcare as it is on the football pitch, although the section was intended to be most relevant in spheres outside healthcare.

In the field of clinical negligence, when, for example, a surgeon would like to carry out a new type of treatment, it might be possible to argue that the scientific development of science justifies protection of the surgeon from spurious claims if the treatment is not successful. In the passage of the Compensation Bill through Parliament, reference was made to the work

139   [2003] UKHL 47.

of emergency services, and to the social utility of such activities, which do of course have a place in healthcare.[140]

When Tony Blair introduced the Compensation Bill in Parliament he explained the provision in this way:

> The Bill will also clarify the existing common law on negligence to make clear that there is no liability in negligence for untoward incidents that could not be avoided by taking reasonable care or exercising reasonable skill. Simple guidelines should be issued. Compliance should avoid legal action. This will send a strong signal and it will also reduce risk-averse behaviour by providing reassurance to those who may be concerned about possible litigation.[141]

What remains to be seen is whether this heralds further recognition of the value of guidelines in establishing the standard of care in healthcare and other settings.

S 2 of the same Act deals with apologies:

> An apology, an offer of treatment or other redress, shall not of itself amount to an admission of negligence or breach of statutory duty.

This is also a restatement of the common law, with the added words 'other redress' reflecting the approach taken in the NHS Redress Act, which was debated the week before the Compensation Act.

Is no-fault compensation the solution?

One conclusion of the Bristol Inquiry was that 'Clinical negligence litigation, as a barrier to openness, should be abolished'.[142] What was intended was not simply the introduction of some form of strict liability, which was at one time contemplated by the Government, but a far more radical system, by which people who are in need as a consequence of an incident which has occurred in the course of care or treatment could be compensated without the need to enter the litigation arena or use the courts at all 'a system where that person will be provided for in terms of compensation needs or whatever else'.[143]

---

140 House of Commons Hansard Debate on the Compensation Bill, 2nd reading, 6 June 2006, col 421.
141 Referred to by Lord Elton in The Grand Committee, 15 December 2005, Hansard, col GC184.
142 Bristol Inquiry synopsis, para 14.
143 Professor Sir Ian Kennedy in a BBC interview, 19 July 2001.

There have been numerous suggestions[144] that this would offer the only sensible long-term solution to the clinical negligence problem,[145] bearing in mind the cost to the public purse of compensating injured patients through the tort system. Careful consideration of the no-fault question in relation to the UK can be found in the work of several writers.[146] In the conclusion to 'Errors, Medicine and the Law', Merry and McCall Smith argue:

> If a way could be found for compensation to be paid without any finding of negligence with all that entails in terms of blame and moral censure, this would be highly desirable.[147]

Whether a no-fault compensation system would be cost-effective and offer practical alternative to the present tinkering with the tort system remains to be researched, and can only be considered in the light of lessons learned in jurisdictions where such a system has been tried and tested. The New Zealand system, introduced in the 1970s, offers many salutary lessons to UK policy makers, demonstrating many difficulties, obvious in retrospect, in a pure no-fault system, with no concomitant safety and quality commitment. That system has been subject to several amendments, including a definition of medical misadventure. The Swedish no-fault system is based on the 'avoidable injury' principle, and under it, if an injury is 'avoidable' or is the result of treatment that is medically unjustifiable and causes an individual to spend at least ten days in hospital, or to miss at least 30 days of work, the injury is compensated. One of the attractions of the Swedish system is that doctors are prepared to confess to errors, and they help patients to obtain the support that they need to apply for compensation. The result it is that healthcare workers are actively involved in 60 per cent to 80 per cent of claims under the system, even informing patients that they could be eligible for compensation and assisting them with the paperwork.

It is still arguable that such a system would be a viable alternative, as it would be unlikely to be less efficient than the tort system as a compensator, and with the spectre of litigation removed from medical practice healthcare professionals would be more likely to confess to mistakes and participate in the much-desired culture of openness.[148]

---

144 E.g. the BMA at its conference in Belfast, 6 July 1999.
145 See Cane, P., *Atiyah's Accidents Compensation and the Law* (7th edn, Cambridge University Press, Cambridge, 488).
146 McLean, S., 'No fault Liability and Medical Responsibility', in Freeman, M.D.A. (ed.) *Medicine, Ethics and the Law* (Stevens & Sons, London 1988), p 147–61.
147 Merry, A. and McCall Smith, A., *Errors, Medicine and the Law* (2001) Cambridge University Press, Cambridge, at p 247.
148 For a discussion of the possibilities or lack of them in the US, see Wiess, G., 'Malpractice: Can No-Fault Work?' (4 June 2005) *Medical Economics*.

It would take a courageous and radical step to introduce a no-fault scheme in the UK, and such an option was rejected after consideration by Lord Woolf in 1996[149] and more recently by the Chief Medical Officer in 'Making Amends'.[150] There is little point in devoting more time to consideration of this matter until the political will exists to promote it.

Concluding recommendations

In the years to come, the Bristol and Shipman Reports will stand as extremely valuable records of the state of healthcare in the UK at the end of the twentieth century. Future generations will no doubt consider whether the many short-comings revealed in these excellent documents have been alleviated, and the proposals heeded and acted upon. Yet despite many responses, *ad hoc* reforms and new initiatives, some still in the process of implementation, the countless complex problems involved in assessing, regulating and compensating for medical error are still largely unsolved. The same is true of the procedures for introducing an effective quality and safety agenda. Given that any progress towards reform will inevitably be slow, and that no-fault compensation, which might cure many of the ills in the present system, is not envisaged by the present Government, some tentative suggestions for improvement follow.

Improving the statistical evidence

One of the first priorities, before decisions can be made about how the present position might be improved, must surely be to establish an over-arching body to collect and analyse data about errors, complaints and litigation in healthcare. There is currently little uniformity in the way that data is currently collected, handled and presented.

The relatively small number of defence organisations, and other bodies that have responsibility for handling claims, produce information in a variety of ways. Indeed, each organisation can present figures in a different format from one year to the next. This situation has arisen because of the absence of a single regulatory organisation to which each of the relevant organisations is required to submit figures. The Audit Commission does undertake some valuable work, but there is no comprehensive overview available of all relevant statistical information covering healthcare in England and Wales. The result is that an industry-wide picture of the entire medical error and litigation picture is not available. Statistical research in this area appears to be unco-ordinated, and the truth about the number of errors and whether malpractice and claims

149   Access to Justice 1996.
150   'Making Amends', 2003.

are increasing, decreasing or stable is impossible to ascertain as long as this situation continues, as was seen in Chapter 1.

Policy initiatives are difficult to justify unless they are evidence-based, and any system requires monitoring in order to assess not only where change might be necessary, but also to quantify what difference, if any, previous reforms have achieved. At present, much of the evidence which is necessary for the formulation of policy is unavailable or inconsistent. Policies which have already been introduced in an attempt to control the litigation and error problems need to be adequately analysed, and without reliable statistical evidence this is difficult. For example, how can the philosophy of centring excellence in a smaller number of large hospitals be justified, if there is inadequate information available in advance to indicate whether errors are more likely to occur in smaller centres or larger hospitals? On another level, if claims are indeed rising, more specialised training of healthcare staff may be required. However, since it is impossible to be certain whether the trend is towards an increase or decrease in the number of incoming claims, it is difficult to assess the precise need for training programmes.

A review of the Government's progress in implementing improvements in the quality of care since 1997 concluded that there are serious weaknesses in data collected about the NHS, which means that it is impossible to carry out any robust, definitive, transparent assessment of progress. The reviewers suggested that to solve this problem it would be necessary to create a national quality information centre under the supervision of the Healthcare Commission.[151]

Admittedly the Government is in the process of attempting to improve matters as far as errors are concerned, through the work of the NPSA, but this initiative does not cover claims. In the healthcare arena, one of the main organisations in possession of evidence about the number of claims is the NHSLA. Unfortunately, that organisation may be too close to the heart of Government to command confidence from the media and the public. Earl Howe said as much when the NHS Redress Bill was debated in the House of Lords:[152]

> The Minister will no doubt tell me that the NHSLA operates at arm's length from the NHS proper. I can accept that only up to a point. Its remit is clearly bound up with the day-to-day work of the NHS, and it is not a body that one could call detached in that sense. The Minister may also say that there are professional standards to which NHSLA employees must work. I certainly do not wish to cast aspersions on the integrity and capabilities of those who work for the authority. I have nothing against them at all. But there is the clearest possible conflict of interest here.

---

151   Leatherman, S. and Sutherland, K., 'The Quest For Quality In The NHS', Nuffield Trust, 2003.
152   House of Lords, Hansard, 21 November 2005, GC 278 debate on NHS Redress Bill.

The public needs to be informed accurately about the level of claims, and the media, in order to report events accurately, require reliable statistics. The Office of National Statistics and the Statistics Commission, in their joint research report on Public Confidence in British Official Statistics,[153] acknowledged that the public believe that the Government manipulates official figures, that the media misrepresent official statistics and that selective reporting was widespread. The research results indicate that there is a need for a single organisation, independent of Government, to collect statistics and communicate them to the public.

One solution to this pressing problem could lie in The Statistics and Registration Service Act 2007, which was introduced in the House of Commons on 21 November 2006. The present problem is that the statistical system in the UK has always been decentralised. Although the Office for National Statistics (ONS) is the main central repository for statistics, a large proportion of the data collected, analysed, published and managed in the UK is the responsibility of Government departments, arms' length bodies and other organisations and agencies outside the remit of the ONS. At present, the ONS is the body responsible for the maintenance of the NHS Central Register.

The Bill followed a consultation entitled 'Independence in Statistics' launched in March 2006, and it provides for the creation of a new body, to be called 'The Statistics Board' which is to have statutory responsibility for ensuring quality and comprehensiveness throughout all official statistics. It will have a Board of Directors with non-executive members and will be a Non-Ministerial Department at arms' length from Government. The responsibilities of the Board will cover the entire UK statistical system encompassing England, Wales, Scotland, and Northern Ireland, and will have power not only to collect statistics but also to produce statistics, provide statistical services and commission research. The overall objective of the Board will be to promote and safeguard the quality and comprehensiveness of national statistics.

The proposed Statistics and Monitoring Board may provide the mechanism by which healthcare statistics relating to errors and claims can be standardised, in order to provide figures which can easily be analysed. This is necessary for directing future policy and quantifying the effect of existing measures. If and when the new statistical body comes into existence, the task of producing meaningful sets of statistics for claims will continue to be beset with problems. Perhaps the most obvious complication is that it may take a very long time for all claims relating to incidents that occurred in a particular year to be received. For example, the NHSLA reports that of all claims received in 2005–06, one related to an incident that occurred in 1961–62, and 2 per cent of claims

153   Kelly, M., 'Public Confidence in British Official Statistics', *National Statistics*, 28 February 2004.

related to incidents which had occurred more than 20 years ago. In fact, only 80 per cent of the total claims can be expected to be received four years after the year of incident.

It will take a considerable number of years before meaningful statistics can be generated. Given the nature of litigation and the current law on limitation periods, that situation will not change. The final tally for every incident in any given year cannot become available until many years later. This delay in the availability of information means that any system which relies solely on *actual* figures is incapable of being sufficiently responsive to identify problems as soon as they occur. It would be capable of providing accurate historical comparisons – but only for years that are too far distant to make a difference to 'corrective' policy. The stable door would then have closed after the proverbial horse had bolted.

The only way in which the responsiveness of 'long delay' systems can be improved is to use such information as is available as a basis for making forecasts, calculated on past figures. A simple example might help to explain this approach. If each organisation concerned with claims were to supply standard information on the total number of claims it received in each financial year, after two years it would be possible to calculate a very basic trend. Thus, if the number of claims rose by 1 per cent in the second year, it could be assumed that the claims in year three would also rise. This would be in line with the trend suggested by the totals for the last two years. However, any prediction based on such a small history would almost inevitably be highly inaccurate – for example, if the figures for the ten years preceding the two years in the above example had each shown a 10 per cent year on year fall in the number claims, and this was also taken into account, it would follow that the trend from all twelve years would not suggest that the claims received in year three would also rise – quite the reverse. Clearly, the longer the history, the more accurate any forecast is likely to be.

In summary, the problem is this – if standard information is only made available from today, the historical data will take many years to accumulate before reasonable forecasts can be made. One solution might be to require each organisation dealing with claims to provide data from all past years (which they must possess) in a standard form. This might be a very daunting task, but it is the only way in which any system could provide accurate predictions and timely indications of potential problems.

Changing the culture

The Bristol Inquiry Report recommended that there should be a change of culture in the NHS. Organisational culture is a complex concept, falling within the domain of social scientists. It involves the shared beliefs and values of individuals within an organisation, and includes behavioural norms, working routines, and even traditions and ceremonies.[154] There are many facets to the culture of an organisation, and even within healthcare, different institutions have different cultures operating at different levels within the working environment. As one writer explained:

> The most superficial are the visible manifestations (sometimes called cultural artefacts) – the doctor's white coat; the surgeon's list; the use of professional titles, and the commonly accepted reward structures. At a deeper level are those espoused values that are said to influence standard practice – a belief in evidence, for example, or a commitment to patient-centred care. Deeper still, and much harder to access, are the hidden assumptions that underpin day-to-day choices.[155]

Any attempt to change the culture throughout the NHS would be a formidable task, yet the intention of the Government is that this should happen immediately by the introduction of numerous new concepts – clinical governance, no-blame, monitoring, public-patient involvement, root cause analysis, and so on. Scholarly discussion of how a cultural change might be achieved, in order to encourage openness and willingness to admit mistakes, is far beyond the scope of this book. Much has been written on the topic and some progress has been made in the NHS to date. It appears that people working in organisations are less resistant to change if systems rather than individuals are blamed for mistakes. This can be developed by means of root-cause analysis – identifying what was responsible, rather than who should be blamed. The patient safety agenda and the role of the NPSA through its 'Being Open' policy are important in this respect, and with perseverance it might be possible to achieve a culture change in years to come.[156]

Developing the concept of primary liability

The common law might be of assistance in promoting openness and cultural change by encouraging wider use of the concept of primary liability. In practice, as has been seen, it is most usual for claims to be brought against healthcare organisations such as hospital Trusts, under the doctrine of vicarious liability, when patients suffer injury as a result of alleged negligence. One or more individuals are identified as responsible, and the Trust, as employer, accepts that if the claim is proved, it will be vicariously liable for the wrongs

---

154 Davies, H.T.O., Nutley, S.M. and Mannion, R., 'Organisational Culture and Health Care Quality' (2000) *Quality Health Care* 9: 111–19.
155 Davies, H.T.O., 'Understanding Organisational Culture in Reforming the National Health Service' (March 2002) *R Soc Med.* 95(3): 140–42.
156 See Magill, G., 'Ethical and Policy Issues Related to Medical Error and Patient Safety', in *First Do No Harm: Law Ethics and Healthcare*, S.A.M. McLean (ed.) (Ashgate, 2006).

of its employees. This tradition stems from the tort system itself, which has traditionally requires that someone be blamed, but is prepared to accept the legal fiction that employers as 'masters' have control over their employees and should accept legal responsibility for civil wrongs committed by them.

However, as root-cause analysis frequently demonstrates, it is often not an individual, but an entire system that has failed the patient, even though, at the end of the chain, it might have been a single individual who delivered the error which resulted in the claimant's injury. Clinical governance and risk management place emphasis on systems rather than individuals, and these concepts have already thrown into focus the need for the entire organisation to become involved in the safety agenda.

Although there are strenuous efforts underway to introduce a no-blame culture in healthcare, its realisation seems to be little more than an aspiration at present. A practical solution to developing this concept would be for claimants' solicitors to bear in mind that there may well be more cases in which it is suitable to bring a primary liability claim against an institution for organisational failure,[157] rather then automatically treating the institution as vicariously liable for the negligence of individual employees. It is possible to identify cases in which this approach has been applied. For example, in *Bull v Devon Health Authority*[158] the claimant sought damages on behalf of herself and her son who was disabled, alleging that he had been born with brain damage as a result of the negligence of the Health Authority. The hospital maintained services on two separate sites, and the system it had put in place for summoning doctors from one site to the other had broken down. As a result there was a delay in delivering her baby because there was no doctor available at a crucial time in her labour. Her claim, brought on the basis of primary liability, was successful, and Dillon LJ said:

> The failure to supply Mrs Bull the prompt attendance she needed was attributable to the negligence of the defendants in implementing an unreliable and essentially unsatisfactory system for calling the registrar.

In *Robertson v Nottingham Health Authority*[159] Brooke LJ recognised that there may be situations in which there is a non-delegable duty on the part of a hospital:

> to set up a safe system of operation in relation to what are essentially management as opposed to clinical matters.

157   *Robertson v Nottingham Health Authority* [1997] 8 Med LR 1; *Bull v Devon Health Authority* [1993] 4 Med LR 117 CA.
158   [1993] 4 Med LR 117 CA.
159   [1997] 8 Med LR 1, at p 13, cited by Jones, M., in Grubb, A. (ed.) *Principles of Medical Law* (Oxford University Press, Oxford, 2001), p 416, fn 215.

If an organisation does not have a satisfactory system for treating or communicating with patients, it is clear from the above authorities that there will be primary liability. However, if there is a system in place and the organisation fails to ensure that it is properly implemented to treat patients safely, it has been argued that this would fall within the ambit of vicarious liability – lest, by requiring them to take wider responsibility, too heavy a burden be imposed on NHS organisations.[160]

Despite this view, if it is the fault of an organisation that a system has not been adequately followed, there is an argument, given the approach under the Health and Safety regime and by analogy with developing case law on breach of statutory duty, that the organisation ought to accept legal responsibility for the operation of a safe system of work. Should Doctor Horn, for example, have been treated as solely to blame in the *Bolitho*[161] case when the hospital did not have a suitable system for managing bleeps, nor a paediatric intensive care ward? In any event, simply because no individual can be found to blame does not preclude a claim on the grounds of organisational failure.

In the context of primary care there have been some developments in this direction. The case of *M v Calderdale and Kirklees Health Authority*,[162] unfortunately decided only at County Court level, offered an opportunity for the concept of primary liability to be taken a stage further. The claimant had received negligent treatment in a private hospital as an NHS patient, and the judge held that the Primary Care Trust which had arranged for her operation owed her a primary non-delegable duty of care and was liable for her injuries. This approach has serious implications for Primary Care Trusts, which might, on the same basis, have a non-delegable organisational duty to patients entering secondary care.[163] However, the same principle was not extended by the Court of Appeal[164] to negligent treatment provided during the birth of a baby in Germany, the son of a British soldier stationed in that country, though that case was confined to its own facts and would probably not have more general application.

It might be extending the legal responsibilities of Primary Care Trusts (Local Health Boards in Wales) too far by imposing on them a non-delegable duty to ensure that their patients are treated with due care and skill wherever that treatment takes place. However, it is certainly arguable that the same approach might not be unreasonable within secondary care, where a hospital ought to take responsibility for having safe systems in place. A movement towards more general application of the principle of primary liability is already

---

160   See Grubb, A. and Kennedy, I., *Medical Law* (3rd edn, Butterworths) p 113.
161   *Bolitho v City and Hackney Health Authority* [1998] AC 232.
162   [1998] Lloyd's Rep Med 157.
163   See Brazier, M. and Beswick, J., 'Who's Caring For Me?' (2006) *Medical Law International* 7: 183–99.
164   *A (Child) v Ministry of Defence* [2004] EWCA Civ 641.

beginning to develop in relation to claims for breach of statutory duty (under the COSHH Regulations) when injuries are caused by hospital infections, in which it is possible to bring a claim directly against a Trust. In such cases it is often impossible to find a particular individual to blame, and under that area of law it is not necessary to do so.[165] Further developments along these lines would be desirable to expand the principle into cases of negligence more generally. The result would be that patients would be treated more justly and healthcare professionals might be more ready to admit their mistakes without fear of being blamed. There would, however, be problems if there continued to be an obligation to report the offender to his or her professional disciplinary organisation, or where staff could face disciplinary action from their employers, as is frequently the case at present.

Modifying the burden of proof

AvMA argued for a change in the burden of proof in clinical negligence, in its response to 'Making Amends'. Such a development might well increase the number of successful claims and redress the balance in favour of claimants if one accepts that too few claims are brought, in the light of the number of avoidable errors:

> We believe there is a strong argument for creating a lesser burden of proof. We have suggested an 'avoidability test' or 'reversing the burden of proof' as an alternative methodology for this type of scheme.

The Pearson Commission[166] had considered, and rejected, the notion of reversing the burden of proof in medical cases on the grounds that it would lead to defensive practices. Such a development would, of course, prove to be unpopular with those who seek to reduce the number of claims and especially the number of successful claims, and The Compensation Act 2006, which has already been applied in a case outside the healthcare setting in favour of a defendant, might counter the approach recommended by AvMa. However, the wider use of guidelines to determine the standard of proof may yet alter the picture and lead to more cases being settled out of court or withdrawn, depending on the circumstances.

Dealing with the claims farmers

One of the major causes of the rise in claims in recent years seems to have been the aggressive marketing techniques of claims farmers. This is apparent

---

165 See Chapter 3 supra.
166 Royal Commission on Civil Liability and Compensation for Personal Injury, Cmnd 7054, 1978, London: HMSO.

from the time-line in Chapter 2, which charts the rising levels of claims against events and developments in the legal arena. The Government has recognised this problem and is taking steps to control it by means of the framework established by the Compensation Act 2006. It is to be hoped that this will break the relentless cycle of advertising, which leads to a rising numbers of claims, leading to further media coverage, which in turn feeds the culture of claiming, and the ever-rising level of financial investment required to pay compensation. Taking appropriate control of the claims market is likely to have a more significant effect on clinical negligence litigation than any reforms achieved by the NHS Redress Act 2006, which does little more than create an enhanced complaints system.

Improving communications

Communication problems have been identified as a serious source of errors in healthcare, and there is a pressing need for further training of staff in order to overcome this difficulty. Not only are there numerous cases in which patients are injured because staff fail to communicate with one another, but there are also many cases in which a breakdown in communication between staff and patients leads to claims which might otherwise have been avoided. Training programmes are in place to develop communication skills. For example, in Wales, hospital Registrars are expected to participate in communications training as part of their Continuing Professional Development requirement, and in England, distance learning programmes are provided in some hospitals to enable a wide range of healthcare staff to improve communication skills.[167] A cultural change could be achieved by this means, as long as there are adequate means to support such programmes.

Maintaining the momentum

This book has considered a selection of myths and misapprehensions about the state of the NHS in modern times. There are popular misconceptions about a number of issues, but there is more than a grain of truth underlying many of them. The picture is so complex that it is impossible to achieve straightforward clarification of many of the myths surrounding the so-called claims culture in healthcare, and the final misapprehension is that it is possible to find a panacea for the problems surrounding errors and litigation across the entire health and social care system. Progress is being made in a number of ways to tackle the almost intractable problems of errors and claims in healthcare. The bombardment of the already highly complex system with a series of initiatives and reforms may not be the solution, but solid progress may be possible

---

167   For example, the EIDO course on Consent to Treatment.

towards the creation of an environment in which people trust one another, in which medicine can be practised freely and safely, and justice can be achieved for those who are unfortunate enough to be injured as a result of error. What is important is that all those involved in the practice, management, delivery and receipt of healthcare continue to work together to contemplate how real improvements can be achieved.

Index

'A First Class Service: Quality in the New NHS' 172
'A Stronger Local Voice' 176
accidents 39; road traffic 43
Action Against Medical Accidents 30, 59, 66, 94
Action for Victims of Medical Accidents (AvMA) 30–1, 58, 66, 84, 154, 200, 215; and compensation culture 94–5
'The Actuary' 80–1
'adverse event' 30, 37, 39, 198; definition 32, 33, 35
advertising: lawyers 54–9; media 119–21
ageing population 22, 138
Agenda for Change 98
Alder Hey 116–17, 124; Inquiry 50
Alternative Dispute Resolution (ADR) 193
Aon 88–9
Appleby, John 131
Aricept 179
asbestosis 14
Association on Infection Control Nurses 75
Audit Commission 208
Australia 35–6; compensation culture 104; media 129
awards: levels of 24–9

Baker, Tom 34, 104
Barker, Baroness 200
'Being Open' programme 186–7, 198
'best interests' 135
Better Regulation Task Force 55–6, 57, 99, 100, 101–2, 118, 119, 120; Report (2004) 55–6, 62, 83

'Better Routes to Redress' 81–2, 86
Bevan, Aneurin 60
Bingham, Lord 103
Blair, Tony 57, 82–3, 99, 100–1, 111, 206
BMJ 116
Bolam v Friern Hospital Management Committee 72, 165, 166, 179, 181, 202
Bolitho v City and Hackney Health Authority 72, 73, 165–6, 173, 179, 182, 183, 202, 214
Booth, Cherie 99
Bostock, Lloyd 75
Bottomley, Virginia 168
brain damage 26
breach of duty 44
Bristol heart babies *see* Bristol Inquiry
Bristol Inquiry 50, 114, 123, 146–7, 180, 189, 206; Final Report 136–7, 164, 172, 186, 194, 195, 198, 211
British Medical Association (BMA) 133; on stress 141
British Official Statistics 47
Brooke LJ 213
Browne-Wilkinson, Lord 173
'Building a Safer NHS for Patients' 185
Bull v Devon Health Authority 213
burden of proof 202–3, 215
Burnham, A. 201
Byers, Stephen 97

caesarean sections 156–60
Cane, Peter 2, 120
Care Standards Act (2000) 71
Cassidy v Minister of Health 164
causation, proof of 202–3

Chester v Afshar 42, 73, 85, 139, 144,
    167
Churchill, Helen 157
Citizens Advice Bureaux (CAB) 7,
    200–1
Civil Procedure Rules (1998) 45, 51–2,
    54, 56, 58–9, 192–3
claims: and complaints 42–3; and errors
    41–2; increases in 75–6, 77; legal
    costs 22–4; levels of awards 24–9;
    management 168; statistics 1–3, 8–14;
    time line 76–7, trends 10–11, 59–62
claims farmers 55, 57–8, 83, 92–4,
    101, 215–16
Clarke, Sally 119
cleanliness 75
Clinical Audit 171, 177–80
Clinical Disputes Forum 52
Clinical Negligence Scheme for Trusts
    (CNST) 5; awards statistics 25
clinical trials 138
Clostridium difficile 39, 87, 98
Cochrane Collaboration 188
Collins, Anthony 54
Commission for Healthcare Audit and
    Inspection 178
Commission for Health Improvement
    (CHI) 71, 72, 177–8
'common calling' 164
Commons Public Accounts Committee
    Report 193
communications 216
Community Health Councils 66
compensation: no-fault 206–8
Compensation Act (2006) 58, 62, 80,
    100, 204–6, 215
compensation culture 52–3, 57, 80–5,
    103–5; Action Against Medical
    Accidents (AvMA) 94–5; advantages
    of 103; Australia 104; changing
    211–12; and employment 92;
    evidence for 84–7; and healthcare
    professionals 96; and insurance
    companies 88–91; and lawyers
    92–4; and the media 95–6; and
    New Labour Government 97–102;
    USA 83, 89, 104, 119–20
Compensation Recovery Unit (CRU) 5,
    8, 14, 42, 43, 45
complaints: against doctors 146; awards
    for 25–7; and claims 42–3
complaints systems *see* NHS Complaints
    System

Conditional Fee Arrangements (CFAs) 9,
    56–7, 75, 76
Confidential Inquiries 170
Connecting for Health 191
consumerism 64–7, 69–71
Consumer Protection Act (1987) 12, 19,
    199
Consumer Protection Charter of the
    Council of Europe 69
Consumers Association 64
Continuous Professional Development
    172, 216
coroners 150
COSSH Regulations 54
Council for Healthcare Regulatory
    Excellence (CHRE) 148
courts 72–4, 164–7
Cranston, Ross 69
Crown Prosecution Service 151–2

Daily Mail 112
Daily Telegraph 107
data: reliability of 46–7
David, David 93
defence cover 3
defensive medicine 154–8; and risk
    management 160–1
dementia 22
Denning, Lord 65, 72, 166
dental treatment 26
Department for Work and Pensions
    (DWP) 15
devolution 137
Dillon LJ 213
discount rate 28; *see also* liabilities
Dobson, Frank 23, 97
doctor-patient relationship 67–9
doctors: clinical autonomy 180–1;
    complains against 146; over-
    regulation of 153–60; regulation of
    146–53; relationship with patients
    67–9 *see also* healthcare professionals
Donoghue v Stevenson 86
Donaldson, Liam 38–9, 195
drugs 137
Duncan, Nigel 124

'Effectiveness and Efficiency: Random
    Reflections on Health Services' 188
Eisai 179
elderly people 22, 138
employment and compensation culture
    91

errors: and claims 41–2; identification
   of 33–4; rates of 29–33
European Charter of Patients' Rights
   66, 138
European Convention on Human Rights
   (1950) 53, 70, 202
European Court of Justice (ECJ) 21–2
European Union health and safety
   legislation 145–6
evidence-based medicine 188
Existing Liabilities Scheme 5–6, 11
Ex-Regional Health Authorities Scheme
   (Ex-RHAs) 6, 11

Falconer, Lord 55–6, 83, 84–5, 99–100,
   102, 106, 111–12
Fenn, P. 102
Fenn, Paul 41
Ferner, R.E. 151
Ferudi, F. 53, 80
Final Report of the Bristol Inquiry 95
Finnemore, J. 65
Foundation Trusts 176–7
Fox, S. 203
France 131
Frankel, Maurice 112
Freedom of Information Act (2000) 106,
   111–12

Gaskin v United Kingdom 70
General Medical Council (GMC)
   149–50, 189, 196–7
Genn, Hazel 43
Germany 131
Goldacre, Ben 117
'Good doctors, safer patients' 189
Gorringe v Calderdale MBC 93
Gregg v Scott 161, 167
Gross, J. 158
group actions 14–15
Grubb, Andrew 154
guidelines: and litigation 181–4; NICE
   181, 182
Gunning, Jennifer 153

Hale, Baroness 52–3, 57, 73, 74, 81,
   161
Haltom, W. 15, 102, 103, 107, 126–7
Ham, C. et al. 63
Hamm, G. 196
Hammond, Phil 113
Harvard Medical Practice Study 34–5
Hatcher v Black 166

'Headline Figures' 8–9, 17
Health Act (1999) 71, 180, 184
Healthcare Commission 6–7, 42, 148,
   178–9
healthcare professionals: and
   compensations culture 96; increased
   workload 143–4; and the media
   116–17; pay 130–4; stress 140–6;
   tasks and responsibilities 134–40;
   and violence 143
Healthcare Standards Unit 175
Health Development Agency 179
Health Protection Agency (HPA) 40, 75
Health and Safety Executive 85
Health and Safety legislation 51,
   145–6
Health and Safety at Work 152
Health Service Journal 142–3, 144
Heil v Rankin 26, 76
Hewitt, Patricia 130
Hiles v South Gloucestershire NHS
   Primary Care Trust 145
Hobhouse, Lord 93
hospital acquired infections 39;
   Scotland 40
House of Commons Constitutional
   Affairs Committee Report 117–18
Howe, Earl 204, 209
Human Fertilisation and Embryology
   Authority (HFEA) 101
Human Rights Act (1998) 67, 68, 70,
   73–4
Hunjan, S. 203
Hunter v Hanley 165

Incurred But Not Reported (IBNR) 12
'Independence in Statistics' 210
Independent 109, 111–12
Independent Complaints Advocacy
   Service (ICAS) 202–3
information and patient choice 69–71
injuries 29
Institute of Actuaries 89–90
Institute of Medicine (US) 32, 35
insurance companies and compensation
   culture 88–91
international patient safety incidents 36
internet 74

James, Hugh 54
Johnson v Bloomsbury Health Authority
   141
Joplin, Mark 131–2

Kemp, Vincent 80
Kennedy, Ian 49, 50, 180, 194
King's Fund Report 110, 131
Kraman, S. 196

Lawton, L.J. 158
lawyers: advertising 54–9; and
    compensation culture 92–4;
    competence 54–5; cost of 22–3; and
    the media 118–19; role of 53–4
Ledward, Rodney 113–14, 119
legal advertising 54–9
legal aid 56, 57
legal procedure: changes in 51–3
Legal Services Commission 9, 43,
    56, 203
legislation: health and safety 51,
    145–6; reforms 135
Levine, Lord 88
Lewis, Charles 65
Lewis, R. *et al.* 86–7
liabilities 12–13
life expectancy 28
Limitation Act (1980) 19
limitation period 19–20
litigation 150; changes in 48–9; and
    guidelines 181–4; process 44–5,
    192–4
Local Health Boards 6
Lowe, J. *et al.* 84

*M v Calderdale and Kirklees Health
    Authority* 214
McCall Smith, A. 30, 50, 207
McCann, M. 15, 102, 103, 107,
    126–7
McDowell, S.E. 151
McFarlane v Tayside Health Board
    86, 167
Mackay, Lord 150
McNair, J. 165
Major, John 62
'Making Amends' 4, 16, 23, 29, 33,
    184–5, 194–5, 197–8, 199
manslaughter 150–3
Maynard v West Midlands 183
Meadow, Roy 119
media: and advertising 119–21;
    analysis 121–4; Australia 129;
    and compensation culture 95–6;
    confidence in 124–6; and healthcare
    professionals 116–17; involvement
    126–8; and lawyers 118–19; and

politicians 117–18; responsible
    reporting 111–15; and rises in claims
    46–51; and sensationalist reporting
    106–10
Medical Defence Union (MDU) 7
Medical Journalists' Association (MJA)
    129
Medical Law Journal 183
Medical Protection Society (MPS) 7
Medicines and Healthcare products
    Regulation Agency (MHRA) 72
Mental Health Act Commission
    (MHAC) 178–9
Merry, A. 30, 50, 207
Milleson, M.L. 121
Ministry of Defence 15
Mitchell, Irwin 54
MMR vaccine 50–1, 100, 117, 182
Monbiot, George 92
MORI poll (2002) 38
MRSA 39, 40, 53–4, 87, 98
Mulcahy, L. 43

National Audit Office 4, 11, 37, 38, 42,
    187, 193; Report (2005) 23; Wales 6
National Care Standards Commission
    (NCSC) 6
National Clinical Assessment Authority
    41
National Clinical Assessment Service
    (NCAS) 186
National Consumer Council 64
National Health Service *see* NHS
National Health Service Litigation
    Authority (NHSLA) 4, 4, 6, 72, 168,
    195, 201–2, 209, 210–11; Annual
    Report 46; Fact Sheet 3 16, 17–19;
    'Headline Figures' 8–9, 17; statistics
    10–11, 20–1, 46
National Institute for Health and Clinical
    Excellence (NICE) 71, 72, 74, 137,
    160, 177, 179, 180; guidelines 181,
    182
National Patient Safety Agency (NPSA)
    31, 37–8, 39, 179, 184–7, 198
Naylor v Preston Area Health Authority
    195
Neuberger, Julia 100
New Labour Government; and
    compensation culture 97–102; *see
    also* Blair, Tony
New Statesman 131–2
New Zealand 207

NHS: establishment and development 59–62; staff 41
NHS and Community Care Act (1990) 60
NHS Complaints Review Committee 61
NHS Complaints System 43, 52, 76, 150, 168–70; confidence in 203; establishment 3, 49, 63; as means of obtaining information 29, 62–3; revised 168–70
NHS Confederation 147–8
NHS Indemnity 2, 4, 8, 13
NHS Redress Act (2006) 80, 187, 195, 198–204
NHS Staff Survey 36, 142
Nice Charter of Fundamental Rights 66
Nicholls, Lord 166, 167
no-fault compensation 206–8
Norwich Union 89
'No Win, No Fee, No Chance' 84
nurses 34, 91, 133–4, 142, 143, 150, 162 see also healthcare professionals
Nursing and Midwifery Council 91, 149–50

Observer 110, 131
obstetrics 12, 80
Office of Fair Trading (OFT) 7, 51, 90
Office of Health Economics 157
Office for National Statistics (ONS) 7, 39–40, 210
Ogden Tables 27
'An Organisation with a Memory' 33, 37, 185

pain and suffering and loss of amenity (PSLA) 26–7
Panting, Gerald 155
patients: autonomy 138–40; better informed 74–5; as consumers 64–7; information 69–71; involvement 176; patient-centred care 62–3, 66, 134–5; Patients Charter 49, 62; records 190–1; relationship with doctors 67–9; safety incidents 36
Patients Charter 49, 62
Pearson Commission 3, 29, 215; Report 1, 8, 65
Pennington, Hugh 116–17
Pickersgill, David 23
politicians and the media 117–18
Pollock, Allyson 40–1, 75, 174, 180

population; ageing 22, 138; increase 21–2
Porton Down 15
pre-action protocol 192–3
primary liability 212–15
Private Eye 113
private healthcare sector 6–7
Protocol for the Resolution of Clinical Negligence Disputes 44, 45, 52, 62, 66
Public Accounts Committee 130–1
Public Assistance Institutions 59
Public Confidence in British Official Statistics 210
public health reforms 191–2
Public Interest (Protection) Act (1998) 190

QED 110
quality in healthcare 71–2

R (on the application of Watts) v Bedford Primary Care Trust 175–6
Rawlins, Michael 181
Reason, J.T. 31–2
Redfern Inquiry 114
reform 136–7
Reid, John 174
Report of Media Analysis (2002) 114–15
retained organs 114–15, 116–17
Retained Organs Commission (ROC) 114–15
Rickards, Helen 114
risk management and defensive medicine 160–1
Ritchie, Jean 119
road traffic accidents 43
Robbins, Jon 59
Robertson v Nottingham Health Authority 213
Roddick, Winston 194
Royal College of Midwives (RCM) 91
Royal United Hospital (RUH) 152–3

scandals 50–1
Scarman, Lord 56, 158
Scotland: hospital acquired infections 40
Scottish Office 182
'Seven Steps to Patient Safety' 187
'Seven Steps to Patient Safety in Primary Care' 187

Shipman, Harold 50, 109, 115; Inquiry 76, 123, 146–7, 189; Report 149, 173
Sidaway 56, 158
Skidmore, P. *et al.* 56
Smith, Janet 50, 134, 173
Smith, Richard 153–4, 163, 198
Southampton General Hospital 152
Special Health Authority 179, 210
Speedy Resolution Scheme 201
'Standards for Better Health' 175
Statistics Board 210
Statistics Commission 210
statistics evidence 208–11
Statistics and Monitoring Board 210
Statistics and Registration Service Bill 7, 210
statutory intervention 194–204
Stethos 131
Steyn, Lord 86, 93, 139
stress 140–6
The Sun 109
Sunday Times 111, 112
Sweden 207

Tame, Stephen 107
targets 136, 174–6
Thalidomide 112
Thompson v James 182
The Times 107, 109, 121
Tingle, John 101
'To Err is Human: Building a Safer Health System' 35
Tomlinson v Congleton BC 93, 95, 205
Total Quality Management 71
Trades Union Congress (TUC) 82–3
trespass to the person 13, 19, 42
'Trust, Assurance and Safety – The Regulation of Health Professionals' 189

under-compensation 43–4
United States of America 34–5; compensation culture 83, 89, 104, 119–20; defensive medicine 155; insurance industry 91; legal system 48, 182–3

vaccine damage 15–16; MMR 50–1, 100, 117, 182
Veteran Affairs Medical 196
violence 143

Wales: Community Health Councils 176; Healthcare Commission 178; healthcare regulation 148, 201; hospital Registrars 216; legal procedure 194; National Audit Office 6; NHS Staff Survey 142
Walmsley, Gerald 109
Ward v Commissioner of Police for the Metropolis 52
Wells v Wells 27, 28, 76, 78
Welsh Ambulance Trust 9
Welsh Assembly 6, 137, 175
Welsh Health Legal Services 6
Welsh Risk Pool 6; statistics 14
The Western Mail 108
Whitehouse v Jordan 32
Williams, Kevin 81, 86
Willis, J.A.R. 124
Wilson Committee 61, 62
Wilson Inquiry 43
Woolf, Lord 51, 68, 94
Woolf Reforms 51
'Working for patients' 60–1, 170
'Working for patients: Medical Audit Working Paper No. 6' 170–1
Wu, A.W. 197

Zurich Financial Services 89